D0389541

How to Kill a City

HOW TO KILL A CITY

GENTRIFICATION, INEQUALITY, *and*
THE FIGHT *for* THE NEIGHBORHOOD

PETER MOSKOWITZ

NATION
BOOKS
New York

Published in the United States by Nation Books, an imprint of
Perseus Books, LLC, a subsidiary of Hachette Book Group, Inc.
116 East 16th Street, 8th Floor
New York, NY 10003

Nation Books is a co-publishing venture of the
Nation Institute and Perseus Books

Books published by Nation Books are available at special discounts
for bulk purchases in the United States by corporations, institutions,
and other organizations. For more information, please contact the
Special Markets Department at Perseus Books, 2300 Chestnut
Street, Suite 200, Philadelphia, PA 19103, or call (800) 810-4145,
ext. 5000, or e-mail special.markets@perseusbooks.com.

Designed by Jack Lenzo

Library of Congress Cataloging-in-Publication Data
Names: Moskowitz, Peter, 1988– author.
Title: How to kill a city : gentrification, inequality, and the fight for the
    neighborhood / Peter Moskowitz.
Description: New York : Nation Books, [2017] | Includes bibliographical
    references and index.
Identifiers: LCCN 2016042410 (print) | LCCN 2016048855 (ebook) | ISBN
    9781568585239 (hbk) | ISBN 9781568585246 (ebook)
Subjects: LCSH: Gentrification—United States. | Equality—United States. |
    Urban poor—United States. | Middle class—United States.
Classification: LCC HT175 .M67 2017 (print) | LCC HT175 (ebook) | DDC
    307.3/362—dc23
LC record available at https://lccn.loc.gov/2016042410

10 9 8 7 6 5 4 3 2 1

To Bubbe, who introduced me to New York

Contents

Introduction

When I returned to New York from college, I found myself belonging to two groups of people: the gentrified and the gentrifiers. I'd grown up in the West Village, just a few blocks from where journalist and activist Jane Jacobs wrote her pro-urban treatise *The Death and Life of Great American Cities* in 1961. Jacobs's book was a 400-page meditation on what made the Village great—its small, varied street-scapes; its diversity of profession, class, and race; its inherent eclecti-cism. Jacobs argued that every other city in the United States should try to emulate its success by encouraging the creation of small shops over big ones, small streets over grand avenues, and varying sizes of apartment buildings and town houses over huge complexes.

But when I came back from college, the Village looked a lot different from the egalitarian wonderland described by Jacobs. The Chinese restaurant my family would order from at least once a week had closed to make way for a Capital One bank. My favorite pizza place had become a high-end grocery store. The video store where my brother worked in high school had turned into an upscale clothier that seemed to only sell a few really expensive items at a time (that store then closed; it was followed by a store that seems to only sell a few children's toys at a time, all made out of wood). The queer scene on Christopher Street, just a few blocks from my parents' house and once one of the most famous gay streets in America, had been priced out and policed into blandness. The middle-income housing on the surrounding blocks had been converted into market-rate condos.

Bleecker Street, once filled with antique stores, had been overtaken by chains such as Marc Jacobs, Michael Kors, and Coach.

Now, in place of buildings that reminded me of my childhood, stood beacons of wealth unprecedented in the neighborhood. Three glass buildings designed by "starchitect" Richard Meier, taller than anything around them, had sprung up a block from my parents' house. And right across the street from my old house, a former artist's loft and garage had been topped with pink stucco condos and rechristened "Palazzo Chupi." When the building opened for sales in 2008, apartments sold for upward of $25 million.

My parents' building was different too. Every month, another apartment seemed to start renovation. Playwrights, artists, and mid-level professionals were moving out, replaced with bankers and businesspeople who were hostile to the old set of residents. People no longer held the front door for each other. People no longer said hi on the elevator. I no longer recognized our neighbors. I started giving stern looks to everyone I passed in my building. The sense of community that had made the West Village feel like home for me and my parents—and that had inspired Jane Jacobs over fifty years earlier—was gone.

What had happened between 1961 and now? Or even between the 1980s, when my parents first moved to the neighborhood, and now? The Village Jacobs wrote about is all but gone, and a new one that looks like a funhouse version of its former self has replaced it. A lot of the people are gone too, forced out because they could no longer afford sky-high rents. An average one-bedroom in the West Village now rents for about $4,000 a month. If you walk down the quiet, tree-lined blocks of the West Village on a weekday, you're bound to see several construction crews gutting former multifamily homes and turning them into mega-mansions. In September 2014, a Texas oil heiress sold a 12,000-square-foot "fortress-like" townhome to an unidentified buyer for $42.5 million just blocks from Jacobs's former home. Jacobs's small town house now houses a real estate office. The Village is less racially diverse today too—about 90 percent of its residents are white. The only area consistently less diverse in Manhattan is the Upper East Side.

New Yorkers tend to complain about changes in neighborhoods such as the Village by focusing on the fact that they are no longer "cool" parts of town. But to Jacobs, places like the Village weren't just cool; they proved that cities could be run with little government intervention and could foster equality without much help. According to Jacobs, the small shops, cheap rent that attracted artists and writers, varied street lengths, and mixed-use zoning policies not only made for interesting people-watching but also made a neighborhood work as a closed system. The shopkeepers weren't only business owners, they were an unpaid police force, watching out for crime and making sure kids walking alone to school got there safely; a pedestrian-friendly block not only meant a good place to walk, it meant the creation of a place where strangers could interact and come up with new ideas and new destinies for each other; a variety of types of buildings, from new luxury apartments to old tenements, meant that a diverse group of people could afford to live in one neighborhood and not be segregated by income and race.

If the neighborhood once heralded as the best example of a place that fosters diversity and equality could become one of the most expensive neighborhoods in the United States and one of the least diverse in New York, what does that say about the future of American cities? And what happened to the people who were left out of the new and rarefied West Village?

When I decided to move back to New York, I knew the West Village would be too expensive, so I began looking elsewhere. I soon realized that even studio apartments in Manhattan were unaffordable for a young journalist, so I looked in the outer boroughs. For a year I lived with my boyfriend in Astoria, Queens, then in Bedford-Stuyvesant, Brooklyn, then at the border of Williamsburg and Bushwick.

In each place I could tell something similar was going on, only now I was on the other side of it. There seemed to be two worlds living on top of each other—a set of stores, bars, and restaurants visited by me and my friends, and a set visited by the residents there before us. When I saw the scowls on my new neighbors' faces, I imagined that they felt the same way about us as my parents and I did about the new faces in the West Village.

At first this process seemed so new and so odd that I couldn't tell what was happening. Things were changing. Things were tense. But they seemed indescribable. White friends moving deeper and deeper into Brooklyn seemed to be less and less comfortable with their decisions, but still unable to prevent themselves from making them. I knew what was happening to New York was part of something immense—you could see how huge it was just by looking at any given block from year to year. Yet there wasn't really a language to describe it. And then this word started being tossed around in news articles, in Facebook rants, at bars where my old friends and I would complain about the new New York: *gentrification*.

By the early 2010s nearly everyone had heard of the term, and nearly no one had a precise definition, but it nonetheless adequately described what was happening: the displacement, the loss of culture, the influx of wealth and whiteness into New York's neighborhoods. The images I saw and stories I heard both first- and secondhand started to form a coherent picture: friends moving out of the city and heading to Austin or Philly or Los Angeles, shuttered bodegas and laundromats in every neighborhood, the new banks that replaced them, the new neighbors, and the Kickstarter campaigns by people seeking the assistance of housing lawyers and a little help with rent were all part of the phenomenon described by the word.

I was in some ways a victim of the process, priced out of the neighborhood I grew up in, but I also knew I was relatively privileged, and a walk through Bushwick or Bed-Stuy confirmed that—seeing the old, dilapidated apartment buildings under renovation, with windows boarded up and signs out front proclaiming the building's new owners, on block after block. I knew people were being kicked out. It became clear that for most poor New Yorkers, gentrification wasn't about some ethereal change in neighborhood character. It was about mass evictions, about violence, about the decimation of decades-old cultures.

But the reporting I'd seen on gentrification focused on the new things happening in these neighborhoods—the high-end pizza joints and coffee shops, the hipsters, the fashion trends. In some ways that made sense: it's hard to report on a void, on something that's now missing. It's much easier to report on the new than on the displaced. But at the end of the day, that's what gentrification is: a void in a neighborhood, in a city, in a culture. In that way, gentrification is a trauma, one caused by the influx of massive amounts of capital into a city and the consequent destruction following in its wake.

If I was going to be complicit in this process, I wanted to know what was really going on.

- - -

When you consider the scope of the problem, it becomes clear that gentrification is not a fad or a trend. Hipsters and yuppies have more buying power than the neighbors they often displace, but individual actors cannot control housing markets and remake cities on their own. The graphic designer with a penchant for organic coffee who lives in Brooklyn is not conspiring with the multimedia artist from San Francisco who loves kombucha. Gentrification cannot be fully explained by developers either: while they might have similar interests, the part-time house flipper who owns five houses in New Orleans and the condo owner in Detroit do not coordinate policy with each other. There's a losing side and a winning side in gentrification, but both sides are playing the same game, though they are not its designers. It's not a coincidence that cities with disparate economies, demographics, and geographies—Nashville and Miami, Portland and Louisville, Austin and Cleveland, Philadelphia and Los Angeles—are all simultaneously undergoing the same process.

Gentrification is not about individual acts; it's about systemic violence based on decades of racist housing policy in the United States that has denied people of color, especially black people, access to the same kinds of housing, and therefore the same levels of wealth, as white Americans. Gentrification cannot happen without this deeply rooted inequality; if we were all equal, there could be no gentrifier and no gentrified, no perpetrator or victim. Gentrification is also the inevitable result of a political system focused more on the creation and expansion of business opportunity than on the well-being of its citizens (what I refer to as neoliberalism). With little federal funding for housing, transportation, or anything else, American cities are now forced to rely completely on their tax base to pay for basic services, and the richer a city's tax base, the easier those services are to fund. That can mean attracting the wealthy to cities, actively pushing out the poor (who are a drain on taxes), or both. The latter seems to be the preferred one in most cities these days.

Different cities gentrify in different ways, but they are nonetheless taking part in the same process. And that process is so predictable that back in 1979 MIT urban studies professor Phillip Clay laid out the distinct stages of gentrification. First, a few "pioneering" gentrifiers move into a neighborhood, followed by a rush of more gentrifiers. Then corporations such as real estate companies and chain retail stores, seeing an opportunity to profit from the arrival of the pioneers, become the main actors in a neighborhood. It's not that corporations are necessarily conspiring to overpower the pioneers, but because corporate buying power is so much greater than that of individuals, gentrification inevitably leads to corporate control of neighborhoods. Finally, in Clay's stages, the process becomes completely top-down, wherein the only entities powerful enough to change and hypergentrify an already gentrified landscape are corporations and their political allies. I'd also add that there's a precursor to all of these stages in which a municipality opens itself up to gentrification through zoning, tax breaks, and branding power. This preparatory phase is rarely seen or talked about because it happens so long before most people witness gentrification in action, but this stage is crucial to understanding gentrification.

In New Orleans, Stage 0 was Hurricane Katrina. The city used the opportunity presented by the storm's destruction of poor and African American neighborhoods to attract white people and investment. Gentrification in New Orleans was happening before Katrina, but the storm kicked it into high gear. Between 2000 and 2010, the black population in the city's "hippest" neighborhood, Bywater, declined by 64 percent; it's hard to know exactly how much of this shift happened after Katrina hit the city in 2005, because there's no census data from right before the storm, but most experts agree the majority of the population shift happened after Katrina. Given that

New Orleans has had more than a decade to see the effects of that shift, it's a good place to start exploring gentrification: the disaster and its aftermath allow you to see the entire process from start to finish.

In Detroit, Stage 0 was the city's declaration of bankruptcy in 2013, which enabled it to find other ways to profit in the wake of declining industry. Detroit cut services to the poor while spending billions to attract gentrifiers. One might not think gentrification would be an issue in a city that once housed about two and a half times as many people as it does now, but in Detroit it has taken a unique form of concurrent prioritizing and deprioritizing: the city's downtown, Midtown, and Corktown neighborhoods have all experienced economic resurgence thanks to corporations pouring billions into infrastructure and real estate projects, but the rest of the city is crumbling. Rents in these three areas have increased by up to 10 percent a year, and some buildings are asking $2 a square foot for rentals, about 60 percent higher than what most apartments rented for just a few years ago.

Most people put the start of New York City's gentrification, its phase 0, in the 1970s or 1980s, when the city nearly went bankrupt thanks to a declining industrial sector and "white flight." But in fact, New York's policy makers have for nearly a hundred years been planting the seeds for a rich, real estate–focused, anti-industrial city. In a sense, this means New York's leaders were better planners: they were able to foresee the realities of a new, consumption-based US urban economy years before most, and so they made sure New York was first in line to benefit from it by making way for financial and real estate capital. They did so by gutting the city's older industries, which kept its poor and middle-class residents employed and adequately housed. Though the foresight of New York's planners presented an opportunity to design the city more equitably, that was never part of their mission. They were backed by financial institutions and real estate capital, and so their explicit goal was to inflate their backers' bank accounts. New York's decades-long gentrification history also means we can see its worst effects here: rents have risen out of reach of everyone but the wealthiest.

San Francisco is an outlier—it did not experience an economic crash that became an excuse to reorient policy to the same extent that the other three cities did, nor did it have much in the way of an industrial economy that needed to be gutted in order for it to be filled in with a bourgeois consumption-based economy. Instead, a surging tech industry pushed its way into the city (with help from its government) and rapidly transformed everything around it. Because this gold rush economy forced San Francisco to gentrify so rapidly and completely, the Bay Area is maybe the best place to peek into the future of the gentrified economy and find out what happens when the poor have literally nowhere to live in a city. The answer, as the Bay Area shows, is that they move to the suburbs, where they are underserved by jobs, transit, and community services. Across the United States, but especially in megalopolises such as the New York region and the Bay Area, the suburbs are booming with the displaced. The poverty rate in the suburbs, which for decades rose at a rate similar to poverty in cities, began quickly surpassing urban poverty after the year 2000.

Gentrification is the most transformative urban phenomenon of the last half century, yet we talk about it nearly always on the level of minutiae. Every week there's a new slew of articles about the "next Brooklyn" or the "next Williamsburg." The word *hipster* has become a kind of shorthand to describe the rapid changes many cities are experiencing. "The Hipsterfication of America," went one National Public Radio headline from 2011. "Brooklyn: The Brand" was the title of an article in the *New York Times*'s *T Magazine* detailing the "Brooklynizing" of the world. The *New York Times* came to rely so heavily on this Brooklynization-of-the-world narrative that its stylebook editor, Philip B. Corbett, chastised its newsroom for the overuse of the word *hipster* in 2010 and its overzealous comparisons of everyplace to Brooklyn in 2014.

The hipster narrative about gentrification isn't necessarily inaccurate—young people are indeed moving to cities and opening craft breweries and wearing tight clothing—but it is misleading in its myopia. Someone who learned about gentrification solely through newspaper articles might come away believing that gentrification is just the culmination of several hundred thousand people's individual wills to open coffee shops and cute boutiques, grow mustaches and buy records. But those are the signs of gentrification, not its causes.

As geographer Neil Smith wrote in his landmark book on the topic, *The New Urban Frontier: Gentrification and the Revanchist City*, "If cultural choice and consumer preference really explain gentrification, this amounts either to the hypothesis that individual preferences change in unison not only nationally but internationally—a bleak view of human nature and cultural individuality—or that the overriding constraints are strong enough to obliterate the individuality implied in consumer preference. If the latter is the case, the concept of consumer preference is at best contradictory." In other words, gentrification is not a fluke or an accident. Gentrification is a system that places the needs of capital (both in terms of city budget and in terms of real estate profits) above the needs of people.

We talk about gentrification at the interpersonal level because that's how we see it in our daily lives—rents mysteriously rise, an art gallery opens one day, then hipsters follow. But in every gentrifying city there are always events, usually hidden from public view, that precede these street-level changes. The policies that cause cities to gentrify are crafted in the offices of real estate moguls and in the halls of city government. The coffee shop is the tip of the iceberg.

If we want to have any hope of fixing this process—of ensuring that as our cities change, low-income people can stay; that the people who built our cities aren't relegated to its outskirts, pushed to communities where community is hard to come by and basic services are lacking—we have to understand what's actually going on.

I've chosen to write about the four cities in this book—New Orleans, Detroit, San Francisco, and New York—because each provides an important counterpoint to the media's narrative of gentrification as the product of cultural and consumer choice. In all four, specific policies were put in place that allowed the cities to become more favorable to the accumulation of capital and less favorable to the poor. New Orleans, Detroit, San Francisco, and New York gentrified not because of the wishes of a million gentrifiers but because of the wishes of just a few hundred public intellectuals, politicians, planners, and heads of corporations. By identifying these players, their policies, and their effects, I hope to make clear that gentrification is not inevitable, that it is perhaps even stoppable, or at the very least manageable.

When we think of gentrification as some mysterious process, we accept its consequences: the displacement of countless thousands of families, the destruction of cultures, the decreased affordability of life for everyone. I hope this book is a counterweight to hopelessness about the future of urban America that enables readers to see cities are shaped by powerful interests, and that if we identify those interests, we can begin to reshape cities in our own design.

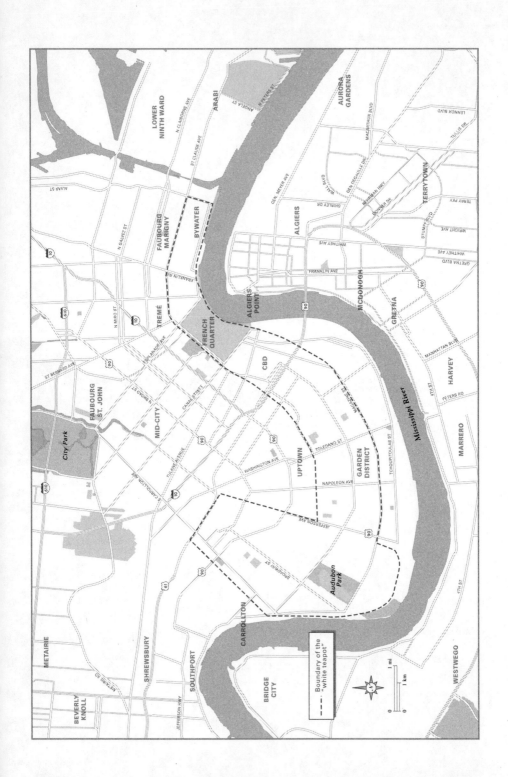

- - - Boundary of the "white teapot"

Mississippi River

METAIRIE

BEVERLY KNOLL

SHREWSBURY

SOUTHPORT

BRIDGE CITY

WESTWEGO

MARRERO

HARVEY

GRETNA

TERRYTOWN

AURORA GARDENS

MCDONOGH

ALGIERS

ALGIERS POINT

ARABI

LOWER NINTH WARD

BYWATER

FAUBOURG MARIGNY

TREMÉ

FRENCH QUARTER

CBD

FAUBOURG ST. JOHN

MID-CITY

City Park

CARROLLTON

UPTOWN

GARDEN DISTRICT

Audubon Park

0   1 mi
0   1 km

N

Part 1

New Orleans

1

Hanging On

The first thing you need to know about New Orleans is that neighborhoods in New Orleans do not work like neighborhoods everywhere else. In other cities, the rich and poor live in completely different parts of town—highways, train tracks, and other vestiges of racist urban planning ensure that the rich and poor sections of cities hardly ever mix. Here, water from the Mississippi is a constant threat, so the rich live where the land is highest, and the poor live in the valleys. That has given New Orleans a chaotic topography of inequality.

For decades, the high blocks with grand houses—St. Charles, Magazine, Esplanade—hid behind them a lowland filled with dilapidated shotguns that housed New Orleans's working class. It used to be that tourists could crawl along St. Charles Avenue on one of the city's historic-looking streetcars, gawk at 4,000-square-foot, hundred-year-old mansions sitting atop manicured lawns, and never know that if they ventured just fifty feet beyond the avenue to the north, they'd see a neighborhood that looks nothing like the New Orleans of tourist brochures and Hollywood movies. It would be easy to drive, walk, bike, or take a streetcar from the bars on Frenchmen Street through the Disneyfied French Quarter and along Magazine Street or St. Charles Avenue and never realize that just beyond these streets lie the people the city has neglected for so long.

These neighborhoods, tucked behind the ones we usually picture when we imagine New Orleans, were poor and filled with culture and community. Tremé, Bywater, Mid-City, Central City, the Upper Ninth Ward, the Lower Ninth Ward, Uptown, and Carrollton were the places where most New Orleanians lived: the musicians, the second-liners, the undervalued laborers scrubbing the banisters of hotels.

But gentrification has challenged those geographic maxims. The rich crests of the city can no longer hold the rich, who are venturing beyond their traditional redoubts. Nearly every neighborhood in the city abutting the Mississippi River gained white residents in the first decade of the twenty-first century. Those neighborhoods— the French Quarter, Central Business District, Bywater, Marigny, Garden District, Irish Channel, and parts of Uptown—have for decades created a kind of teapot shape of whiteness within the city, but between 2000 and 2010, Tulane University geographer Richard Campanella noted the teapot had both "broadened and internally whitened." The change could be seen on nearly every street, as new arbiters of hipness—coffee shops, boutiques, art galleries—bloomed on blocks with houses still devastated by Hurricane Katrina.

As the city celebrated its new life, nearly no one in power— the mayor, the governor, council people—seemed to care about the tens of thousands of black people who never returned. When I interviewed African Americans who left New Orleans after the storm, they told me they're afraid to go back because it feels like a different city, like it's no longer theirs, and in many ways they are right.

National newspapers and magazines have now taken an interest in the city, experiencing it, in the words of the *New York Times*, "with fresh eyes and ears." They've profiled ad nauseum the new, nearly all white artists, actors, musicians, and chefs who populate the city's gentrifying neighborhoods. New Orleans, according to these publications, is filled with magic hedonism and is just begging to be explored. "In New Orleans success is measured by how unhinged you can get," one musician told the *Times*. But the city isn't quite as gentrified as Los Angeles or New York. "New Orleans is not cosmopolitan," one actress said. "There's no kale here."

With its narrative rejiggered from one of poverty and death into one of resurgence, New Orleans could start anew. City officials and other supporters of the change went on a PR war in an attempt to convince the world and the city's residents that all the new people, the new restaurants, and the old streets and old neighborhoods given new names (or just rechristened with the word *new* in front of their old names, as in "the new Freret Street" and "new Marigny") mean that New Orleans, ten years after Hurricane Katrina, is back—back from the destruction that drove out half of the city's population, back from economic collapse.

To be sure, the economy is doing better, and the population is approaching pre-storm levels. But *back* is the wrong word, because the people here now are in large part not the same people who lived here before the storm. New Orleans lost more than half its entire population, an exodus of 254,000 people, thanks to the man-made failures that allowed a slow-moving but relatively weak hurricane with an eye that missed New Orleans to decimate the city. When it came back, it came back differently: New Orleans used to be 67 percent black and only a quarter white. Now white people make up 30 percent of the city, while the black population doesn't seem to be returning at the same rate, accounting for just 60 percent of the population, according to the 2010 Census. That change—67 percent to 60 percent—might seem like a modest one, but when you crunch the numbers the human toll is clear: by 2010, the city's white population had just about returned to its pre-Katrina levels, while today approximately 100,000 black people are still missing from New Orleans.

The city's priorities have been made obvious by the fact that while officials have gone on media tours celebrating the economic growth of the city ten years after the storm, the local government (along with its federal and state counterparts) has stopped tracking or even talking about its still-exiled population. From what little research there is, we know that diaspora includes tens of thousands currently living in Houston and other cities in Texas. We know others have relocated to small towns throughout Louisiana or far-flung places such as Utah and New York. But their vanishing still haunts black communities in New Orleans today.

I've heard the words *colonization, occupation,* and *genocide* used to describe what happened here after Katrina. That might seem dramatic to outsiders, but what else can you call a set of policies that in their effect, and oftentimes seemingly in their intent, kicked out a small city's worth of black people? What can you call a set of policies that encourages the white and moneyed to come in their place? The answers would seem conspiratorial if they weren't so well documented in local newspaper articles from right after the storm, which detailed politicians and businessmen railing against the old New Orleans and sounding excited to usher in a new era. "It took the storm of a lifetime to create the opportunity of a lifetime," then governor Kathleen Blanco said a few weeks after the storm. "We must not let it pass us by."

What else do you call a coordinated attempt by thought leaders, politicians, and business interests to radically change an entire city "demographically, geographically and politically," as one real estate maven put it, except a deliberate attempt to gentrify?

To many of the black people here who have stuck it out, who have been left with little since Katrina, who feel like the city did nothing to help them back or actively dissuaded them from coming home, those words—*colonization, occupation, genocide*—do not feel sensational. They feel like what happened.

- - -

The first person I talked to when I arrived in New Orleans was a woman I was subletting a house from in the St. Thomas section of the city. I made a passing remark about how nice the area seemed, and she replied, "Thank God for Katrina. That really helped clean this place up."

The block I was on, I would later find out, was located in one of the most rapidly changing sections of the city, which was made clear by the fact that no one I met in New Orleans could agree on exactly what neighborhood I was staying in. To the whites I met, it was either the Irish Channel or the Lower Garden District. To many African Americans from New Orleans, it was still St. Thomas— named after the eponymous housing projects that the city began demolishing in the early 2000s, the start of a slew of demolitions that accelerated after Katrina and left thousands of low-income African Americans displaced. Those projects have since been replaced by a private, mixed-income housing development owned by one of the biggest developers in New Orleans, Pres Kabacoff.

Soon after I arrived in New Orleans I met Ashana Bigard, who is from one of the seemingly few old-line families left in this area. She's a forty-year-old school and prison justice advocate who was able to secure a spot in the redeveloped St. Thomas. But she, like many here, is hanging on by a thread. By her own assessment, she told me, she does not fit into the new New Orleans.

"There's nothing sexy about me," she said. "I'm from here. I'm black. I'm a parent. I'm boring."

To Bigard, this area is still St. Thomas, not the Irish Channel, the Lower Garden District, or anything else. She agreed to take me on a tour to show me how much has already been lost.

I picked her up at the new St. Thomas housing complex, re-christened River Garden, where she lives with two of her children. The new development doesn't fit in with its surroundings. The old St. Thomas buildings looked like many traditional housing projects— multistory brick buildings surrounded by grass yards—but it was better kept and better constructed than most. Katrina spared most of the project, but the city of New Orleans bulldozed it anyway, and replaced it with hundreds of pastel town houses laid out on curving streets surrounding empty, unused, and heavily policed green space. The development is flanked by a suburban-style Walmart on one end. If it weren't for the concrete levee holding back the Mississippi on one side and the ritzy Magazine Street on the other, you might think you'd left New Orleans.

Bigard has struggled to make ends meet since Katrina. For the last five years she hasn't been able to find a steady job in nonprofit work, despite her wealth of knowledge—she'd worked in nonprofits with a specialty in education and criminal justice for nearly twenty years. But now, as she passes forty, she's trying to expand her horizons to scrape together cash. Sometimes she works as a waitress at one of the new fancy restaurants in the Garden District. Sometimes nonprofits ask her to "consult" for a few hundred dollars, but usually they want her to work for free. Her latest gig is showing desks for lease in a co-working space for tech companies and nonprofit workers in a newly renovated building on a newly gentrified block in a rapidly gentrifying area on Oretha Castle Haley Boulevard (often called "O.C. Haley"), named after a famed New Orleans civil rights activist who headed the city's chapter of the Congress of Racial Equality.

We drove over the potholed blocks of New Orleans, past St. Thomas and through the old Garden District, to the section of O.C. Haley in a neighborhood called Central City, which is now starting to show all the normal signs of a neighborhood in the midst of gentrification. New loft buildings, two new small museums, a coffee shop, a performing arts and screening space, a boxing gym, and an upscale Mexican restaurant have all cropped up within a five-block radius in recent years. And while the revitalization of this corridor, which was decades ago home mostly to black-owned businesses, seems like a natural progression for a city doing well economically, here, like everywhere else in the city, there was more top-down planning involved than is noticeable from the street.

In 2006, Mitch Landrieu, then Louisiana's lieutenant governor and now New Orleans's mayor, designated Oretha Castle Haley Boulevard one of four "urban Main Streets," allowing the city to funnel money to street improvements. The other urban Main Streets— St. Claude Avenue, Oak Street, and North Rampart Street—are also located in rapidly gentrifying areas. Soon after, the New Orleans Redevelopment Authority (NORA), the agency responsible for managing much of the land left vacant after Hurricane Katrina and for planning major development projects in the city, moved its headquarters to O.C. Haley and helped bring an $18.5 million mixed-use development to the area—mostly office space and condos. NORA was involved in funding no fewer than six major projects along the boulevard. It also loaned about $2 million to nonprofits and restaurants that now line the corridor. Finally, the city directed its antiblight team to prioritize demolishing abandoned buildings around O.C. Haley. "I believe in leveraging the market," Councilwoman Stacy Head said in justifying her government's spending on private business on O.C. Haley rather than, say, on affordable housing. "The government's job is to leverage the market." And so O.C. Haley became another urban success story that in reality was propped up with millions in city cash.

It's worth pointing out no one in New Orleans or anywhere else is begrudging the improvements to neighborhoods in and of themselves. But when improvements come with restaurants and rents many can't afford, then tree-lined streetscapes, bike lanes, and even pothole repair become signposts for displacement and cultural loss. They're also signs that the people who lived there before the improvements are worth less to governments than new residents. The government did not see fit to make O.C. Haley a nice neighborhood when it was poor and black and had no chance of gentrifying. Anti-blight efforts and streetscapes don't have to be linked to gentrification, but in our current system, they almost always are.

The co-working space Bigard showed me was beautiful, the crown jewel of this gentrified block. It is located in a former elementary school abandoned by the Orleans Parish School Board twelve years ago. Now reclaimed wood and gleaming tile cover every surface. Massive chandeliers hang from its center over a 23,000-square-foot "fresh-food-focused local and organic market" that occupies its bottom level.

Bigard does not know anyone who frequents these new businesses on O.C. Haley. She said none of her friends go to the new market. She earns a commission for every desk she leases in the co-working space, but at $475 a month, she said, she couldn't afford one herself. Bigard told me that while she's happy to give tours of the space, she knows she's in some way contributing to the gentrification of the area. After all, who can afford an expensive desk in an area on the border of two census tracts where over 40 percent of families live below the poverty line?

On our drive back past the new restaurants and new movie theater and new museums, Bigard told me she felt that people like her—low-income, black, not young, with kids—aren't welcome in newly redeveloped places such as this. Before Katrina there would not have been enough gentrifiers here to make a fresh-food market and co-working space feasible. Sure, the improvements are nice, but they don't feel like they're meant for her.

"Stuff like this really scares me," she said. "When they start putting in a museum in your neighborhood, you know you're not long for this world."

Bigard's life and life choices have remained largely the same since Katrina: she was an educator and activist before, and she still is. She lives in the same neighborhood and in the same city. But at one point she was able to make ends meet, and now she is not. Her life hasn't changed, but everything around her has.

- - -

In its journey from academic jargon to popular use, the term *gentrification* has been stretched and pulled. In the popular press, gentrification is most often presented as the cumulative effect of the actions of individual actors—yuppies and hipsters move from the suburbs to a previously poor neighborhood and gradually change its identity. The struggles of people like Ashana Bigard are seen as collateral damage. But gentrification is bigger than that. A proliferation of hipsters, displacement, and a worsening quality of life for people like Ashana Bigard are the effects of gentrification, not its causes. Gentrification is a purposeful act, not just a trend, and so it needs a definition that recognizes the actors and actions behind it.

Gentrification, at its deepest level, is really about reorienting the purpose of cities away from being spaces that provide for the poor and middle classes and toward being spaces that generate capital for the rich. This trend isn't limited to cities: for decades conservatives in the US government have been working to deregulate industry and defund our safety nets, to turn the United States from a welfare state based on the vision of John Maynard Keynes (the early twentieth-century economist who believed that a robust government was necessary to ameliorate the inherent instability and inequalities of capitalism) into a neoliberal, corporate-friendly oligarchy concerned only with increasing the share of wealth owned by the upper class.

Jason Hackworth, a professor of planning and geography at the University of Toronto, writes: "Gentrification is much more than the physical renovation of residential and commercial spaces. It marks the replacement of the publicly regulated Keynesian inner city—replete with physical and institutional remnants of a system designed to ameliorate the inequality of capitalism—with the privately regulated neoliberalized spaces of exclusion." In other words, gentrification is the urban form of a new kind of capitalism.

Using this definition, gentrification moves from being an unexplainable phenomenon illustrated by countless *New York Times* trend pieces to being a knowable and replicable act. And if we use that process-oriented version of the definition, it becomes clear that the effects of gentrification—the coffee shops, the hipsters (and the subsequent articles profiling them), Bigard's current financial problems—are not an accident but the predictable effects of turning cities into spaces that benefit no one but those who control capital.

In every gentrifying city—that is, in every city where there is a combination of new coffee shops and condos, hipsters, and families struggling to hang on—you can usually trace the start of that change not to a few pioneering citysteaders but to a combination of federal, local, and state policies that favor the creation of wealth over the creation of community. Usually those policies come in the form of the deregulation and privatization of urban services: transportation, education, and especially housing. By the time the hipsters arrive, the political and economic forces that paved the way for them have been at work for years.

In New Orleans, all the processes of gentrification happened at once. The chaos of Hurricane Katrina provided an opportunity to enact gentrification-friendly policies on a condensed timeline. Politicians and the developers who supported them were able to ram through laws that likely wouldn't have been passed otherwise. Local leaders, with the support of federal policies, used the storm to transform the city into one where capital could be squeezed out of every crevice. They privatized schools and housing, busted unions, and gave tax breaks and other incentives to anyone who would bring money to the city, with few strings attached to that investment. And, perhaps most importantly, they did everything they could to ensure that poor black people would not come back. Katrina was not the first time the city had tried to rid itself of its black population, but it paved the way for the city's most successful attempt.

- - -

More than half of the hurricane's human toll came from one neighborhood, the Lower Ninth Ward, which has always been a symbol and bastion of African American culture, community, and commerce, and therefore has constantly been under attack. In the 1920s a canal was built down the center of the Ninth Ward to facilitate the transportation of oil and other industrial materials. Since then the Lower Ninth Ward has felt cut off from the rest of the city— accessible only by bridge, and lacking good public transit. That has given the neighborhood its own feel, and its residents a unique sense of distrust of the city government. Before Katrina, the Lower Ninth was nearly 100 percent black, and despite its reputation as being a poor section of the city, it was actually mostly middle-income—the median area income at the 2000 census was $37,894. The area had one of the highest rates of African American homeownership in the country.

During Katrina, the concrete barriers holding water back from the Industrial Canal broke, flooding the entire neighborhood, destroying the vast majority of its homes, and killing a thousand people in the Lower Ninth alone. After the storm, residents reported hearing loud booms as the storm encroached, and rumors flew over whether the levees holding back the Industrial Canal had been deliberately blown in order to save richer areas of the city. Journalists and politicians derided the theories as paranoid, but African Americans had good reason to believe that the government would destroy one predominantly black area to save predominantly white ones.

To understand how politicians and developers tried to change New Orleans after Katrina, it's important to understand that the city has nearly always been actively hostile toward its black population.

In 1927, the Mississippi River flooded, and Louisiana flood control officials decided their best option to minimize damage was to purposely breach a levee in Jefferson Parish, a rural section of Louisiana right next to New Orleans, in order to prevent New Orleans from flooding. The area chosen to flood was predominantly black, populated by sharecroppers who were promised money for giving up their land, and sometimes forced at gunpoint out of their houses if they refused. The sharecroppers were also forced to help clean up the destruction wrought by the flood in New Orleans. They were never compensated for the land. Then in 1965, black New Orleanians experienced displacement yet again when Hurricane Betsy flooded New Orleans and adjacent St. Bernard Parish. The pattern of destruction was eerily similar to that of Katrina—poor black neighborhoods, including the Lower Ninth Ward, were inundated with water, while the rest of the city was left relatively unscathed.

Knowing that history, it's perhaps unsurprising that Katrina was taken by many in the city as a sign that New Orleans was once again trying to rid itself of black people. "The government is making moves to bring in certain kinds of people to New Orleans and get rid of everyone else," Kim Ford, a nearly lifelong resident of the Lower Ninth, told me.

The words of the city's leaders seemed to confirm her theory. The water had not yet drained out of New Orleans when real estate developers, millionaires, politicians, and conservative pundits began their campaign to convince residents and others that Katrina was a blessing in disguise. Yes, the storm was horrible, their rhetoric went, and yes, the deaths of nearly 2,000 people and the displacement of nearly half the city were tragic, but New Orleans had been poor and disorderly before the storm, and this would be a chance to do things differently. James Reiss, a businessman and descendant of a prominent Uptown New Orleans family who fled the storm in a private helicopter, gave an interview to the *Wall Street Journal* after his return that laid out how many elites viewed Katrina.

"Those who want to see this city rebuilt want to see it done in a completely different way: demographically, geographically and politically," Reiss told the paper. "I'm not just speaking for myself here.

The way we've been living is not going to happen again, or we're out." Reiss would go on to chair the city's Regional Transit Authority under Mayor Ray Nagin, taking control of New Orleans's meager public transit options.

Then governor Kathleen Blanco presented the storm as an opportunity to rebuild and do away with the city's history of poverty, especially in the school system. But most prophetic was David Brooks, the conservative *New York Times* columnist. In a column that came out just over a week after the storm—when people were still stuck in hotels or waiting for food in the Superdome—Brooks advocated for using the storm to leave the poor sections of New Orleans behind, and encourage rich people to move in in their place:

> The first rule of the rebuilding effort should be: Nothing Like Before. Most of the ambitious and organized people abandoned the inner-city areas of New Orleans long ago. . . . If we just put up new buildings and allow the same people to move back into their old neighborhoods, then urban New Orleans will become just as run-down and dysfunctional as before. . . . In the post-Katrina world, that means we ought to give people who don't want to move back to New Orleans the means to disperse into middle-class areas nationwide. . . . The key will be luring middle-class families into the rebuilt city, making it so attractive to them that they will move in, even knowing that their blocks will include a certain number of poor people.

Given how the recovery has progressed these past ten years, it's tempting to wonder if New Orleans politicians used Brooks's column as a playbook. Katrina became the perfect opportunity for politicians to institute what author and activist Naomi Klein calls "shock doctrine capitalism," using the chaos provided by the crisis to push through the reforms Brooks suggests: dismantling institutions that served the poor, and making the city more accommodating to an influx in capital. The result is a city that feels richer than before, but also unfriendly to those who do not fit into its new economy. Bigard is one of those people.

- - -

New Orleans has the highest percentage of native-born residents of any city in the United States. And Bigard, like many people here, has roots that go way back, at least to 1809. Her grandfather was a well-known Mardi Gras Indian. But despite her deep roots, Bigard said, she feels like she's losing grip on her city. Over the past decade, she's been forced to bounce between houses on Carondelet, Oretha Castle Haley Boulevard, Jackson Avenue, Louisiana Avenue, and South Lopez Street to find affordable rent. A three-bedroom house she rented on Annunciation Street, right in the heart of the Irish Channel, once cost her $550 a month; similar properties in that area now regularly rent for over $2,000. If it weren't for her spot in the mixed-income River Garden development, Bigard said, she'd likely have to move in with her mom, or leave the city completely.

Bigard's job prospects have been affected by the gentrification of New Orleans too. When Katrina struck, she'd been working at the New Orleans Parent Organizing Network (NOLAPON), which helps parents navigate the city's complex school system. But Louisiana politicians used Katrina as an opportunity to shut down nearly every public school in New Orleans and replace them with charter schools. Within months after the storm hit, 107 of the city's 128 public schools had been transferred to a new, all-charter district. When Bigard began protesting the changes, she ran afoul of NOLAPON's new, charter-friendly leadership and was fired. Since then, she's struggled to find work.

Like many in New Orleans, Bigard never received a college degree, though she tried, attending Delgado Community College and then the Southern University of New Orleans. But when her mother became sick, with medical bills reaching over $1,000 a month, Bigard had to drop out to look for full-time work. Her lack of a degree had never been a problem before Katrina, but the storm brought a slew of national nonprofits to New Orleans, and those nonprofits seemed less interested in working with people like her, instead preferring to bring down consultants and employees from Washington, New York, and elsewhere.

"I feel like we really got the train moving with gentrification by awarding so much money to these nonprofits and not setting any parameters on how that money was spent and who got that money and what they did with it," Bigard told me. "A lot of these times I'd go into these nonprofits and people would want to 'pick my brain.' If I was wearing a suit and from New York, that would be called consulting and I would be billing you $250 an hour. . . . I came from a community where you're supposed to help out your neighbors, but I'm a lot more savvy now. Now when they ask, 'Can I pick your brain? Can I pick your brain? Can I pick your brain?' I would probably say, 'What's your budget for consulting?'"

White volunteers and whites working for nonprofits have replaced much of the black middle-class labor force here. It's hard to get accurate numbers on exactly how many white non-natives came to work in nonprofits and schools after the storm, but anecdotes from residents here suggest there are quite a few. There were at least 375 Teach for America members in New Orleans schools by 2013. Hundreds of Habitat for Humanity volunteers from across the country constructed homes for free that might have otherwise been built by local laborers. As Nat Turner, a black transplant from New York who operates a farm and education center in the Lower Ninth Ward, told me, "The guys you see standing around on corners drinking beers, those used to be the guys that would repair your roof or wire your house." And white, college-educated professionals working for nonprofits, mostly people from the Northeast, seemed to take the place of people like Bigard. Geographer Richard Campanella estimates that about 5,000 new nonprofit workers showed up directly after the storm, followed by more than 20,000 young, mostly white, college-educated people working in nonprofits and other high-skilled, specialized sectors such as the booming movie industry (which was lured to New Orleans with very generous tax credits).

After struggling to find work for years, Bigard signed up for Section 8 housing vouchers in 2012. The vouchers came from a federally funded program that helps people pay for rent in privately owned, market-rate houses and apartment buildings. But the next year, thanks to a federal budget sequester, the Housing Authority of

New Orleans was forced to revoke 700 Section 8 vouchers, including Bigard's. For a few weeks, Bigard was homeless.

Eventually she found the place where she lives now—River Garden. Back when it was St. Thomas, the development provided 1,500 families with public housing. But after the city demolished St. Thomas and handed a contract to private developer Pres Kabacoff, it was built back with only 606 units, only a fraction of which are publicly financed low-income housing. There are also 62 units open to low-income families but financed privately, made affordable by tax credits that expire in 2017. Bigard lives in one of those units, and once that tax credit expires, developer Pres Kabacoff could make her unit market rate. It's not clear if he will, but given that a unit like hers rents for $1,200 to $1,500, according to the River Garden website, there's little to incentivize him to keep the rent low. If that happens, Bigard says, she isn't sure where she'll go.

"I came back after Katrina because I love my city," Bigard told me. "I feel like even with everything that's happened, people still greet you here. They talk to you. They lift you up. There's no place like that. But whether I'll be able to afford to live here, that's another story. . . . I'm going to claw, climb, do whatever I can to try to stay here. I'd like to able to purchase a house and have a good used car in my own city. Will I be able to do that? I don't know. I pray so. I hope so."

Even if Bigard stays, she said, she feels like she'll be left behind, watching on the sidelines as the new New Orleans envelops her old city. The St. Thomas projects used to be dangerous, but they also were a wellspring of activism and culture. One of the most successful tenant organizing movements in the country, the St. Thomas Residents Council, was birthed on the grounds now occupied by River Garden and Walmart. Bigard and others told me about the legendary parties and barbecues that happened nearly every weekend in St. Thomas. There was a sense of community and camaraderie. Now most residents, isolated in semi-detached single-family homes, don't talk to each other. And the rest of New Orleans, it seems to Bigard, is headed in that direction too: unfriendly, individualistic, boring.

Bigard, like many others here, understands that the arrival of new people is out of her control. Her biggest qualm with the new people in New Orleans isn't that they're here but their lack of appreciation for what makes the city unique. She said they don't seem to understand that having a city filled with music—jazz, bounce, hip-hop—sometimes involves people practicing their instruments and making a lot of noise next door to you at odd hours. They don't seem to understand that people like Bigard might have kids who sometimes make noise. The attempt at cultural control and dampening seems particularly egregious at River Garden, where residents in recent years have staged protests against management for reporting them to police for minor violations of housing bylaws: music being too loud, kitchen cabinet knobs missing, light bulbs out. "Jim Crow Can't Live Here Anymore!" read one sign at a protest in 2013.

"It used to be you'd see people sitting outside in St. Thomas, maybe playing some music, somebody barbecuing, children playing," Bigard said on a drive around the now desolate streets of River Garden. "You won't see that shit around here anymore. That's what connected us. Now you're not allowed to be a New Orleanian here. Yeah, this was high crime and high poverty. But the crime and poverty haven't gone anywhere. You've just spread it around, and you've just taken away the beauty."

How Gentrification Works

The word *gentrification* was coined by British sociologist Ruth Glass in 1964. In her book *London: Aspects of Change*, Glass described the upheaval of certain neighborhoods in London by the middle-class "gentry" from the countryside.

"One by one, many of the working class quarters have been invaded by the middle class—upper and lower," Glass wrote. "Once this process of 'gentrification' starts in a district it goes on rapidly until all or most of the working class occupiers are displaced and the whole social character of the district is changed." Even then, gentrification meant remaking a neighborhood for new incomers and to the detriment of current residents.

The first mention of gentrification stateside seems to have occurred four years later, in 1969, when a white Brooklyn man named Everett Ortner founded the Brownstone Revival Committee, a nonprofit committed to the "brownstone lifestyle." Ortner began publishing *The Brownstoner*, a magazine dedicated to convincing other middle- and upper-class white people to move to Brooklyn. One article in the magazine proclaimed, "Gentrification is not 'genocide' but 'genesis.'" Gentrification supporters such as Ortner were intent on persuading the gentry that gentrification was an organic movement made up of people who wanted to improve neighborhoods—in other words, he and others wanted to shift the focus from larger forces to individual decisions. Ortner wrote in *The Brownstoner*, "I think one should approach the acquisition of a brownstone, the way one goes into a love affair: To the non-lover it is merely a row house. To the brownstone connoisseur, it is part of an architecturally homogeneous cityscape, scaled perfectly for its function, housing many but offering each person space and privacy and a civilized style of living."

But even then, in the early days of gentrification, the process had just as much to do with a specific set of policies and corporations that benefited from them as it did with love. The first Back to the City Conference, established by Ortner in 1974, was sponsored by a real estate industry group called the Development Council of New York City as well as by the Brooklyn Union Gas company, and its purpose seemed to be less to help revitalize neighborhoods and more to revitalize the profits of Brooklyn real estate firms and the local gas company. The largely vacant neighborhoods were not good for gas sales, and gentrifiers would uplift the neighborhood's economies and the bottom line of Brooklyn Union Gas. The gas company went as far as to renovate its own four-story brownstone in Park Slope and advertised in a local paper, "The gas-lit outside appeal of the new homes is complemented by the comfort features inside: year round gas air conditioning and plenty of living space that spills over into free form backyard patios dotted with evergreen shrubbery and gas-fired barbeques."

Ortner and his fellow members of the Brownstone Revival Committee, like similar groups in cities across the country, were instrumental in crafting the narrative of good-hearted pioneers the media still cling to today. Yet Ortner's story proves that gentrification was never really about individual pioneers, but rather about a confluence of policies pushed by wealthy individuals, politicians, and the companies that stood to benefit from a gentrified neighborhood. Today gentrification has become an even more pronounced top-down process.

- - -

In 1979, MIT urban studies professor Phillip Clay outlined four distinct phases of gentrification, which remain remarkably applicable today. According to Clay, the first phase begins when individuals, unsupported by any government or large institution, decide to begin moving into a previously poor neighborhood and renovating houses. National media pay little attention, and any increase in the concentration of gentrifiers comes largely from word of mouth. There's some evidence that historically this phase of gentrification was often spearheaded by gays and lesbians in search of safe spaces outside homogenized suburbia where they could congregate. San Francisco experienced an influx of gays during World War II, thanks in part to the military's practice of dishonorably discharging gay men into the city via military bases on the Pacific Ocean. While there are no hard numbers, there is evidence that the white LGBT community, especially lesbians, also played a pioneering role in Brooklyn in the 1970s. New Orleans's largely white queer scene today also seems one step ahead of other gentrifying places. (Detroit is an outlier here, as there's not much of a queer scene.)

The second phase, according to Clay, is when those attracted to the neighborhood because of the change that's already begun start buying up real estate. Some in this second wave are hoping to take part in the neighborhood's new cultural cachet. Others are small-scale speculators, hoping they can get a house on the cheap and sell it sometime later. This is the phase when media start paying attention, and when the *New York Times* might write an article about whether said neighborhood is the next hot new thing, or even the next Williamsburg. Vacancies go down, and displacement begins.

I would argue that these first two phases are still happening in some cities—Detroit; Cleveland; Lexington, Kentucky; and others—where young people are flocking, where new restaurants are opening, and where intrepid reporters are sent to cover the surprising revitalization of once downtrodden cities. But these phases are also historical anachronisms at this point. Gentrification in places such as Detroit and Cleveland, while appearing as organic as the flocking of gay men to San Francisco, is today most often sponsored by the state and other powerful institutions.

Clark's third phase is essentially what New Orleans is experiencing right now, as middle-class gentrifiers start taking on more

prominent roles in gentrifying neighborhoods—sitting on commit-
tees and community boards, promoting neighborhoods to outsiders
as a place where the middle class can move and maintain a high
quality of life. During this phase, Clark says, you can expect banks
to begin lending more frequently in previously disinvested neighborhoods. Developers (as opposed to individuals) become the preeminent renovators and builders. Police and other security forces
increase to ensure that the new gentrified class feels safe. Tensions
between the "old" and the "new" rise.

Stage four is when a neighborhood is already gentrified and begins to become even more wealthy. Managerial-class professionals
replace the artists and punks. Properties that were held vacant by
developers are turned into high-cost condos. Displacement is rampant. And gentrification begins spilling over into other, less gentrified neighborhoods.

In 1979, these phases provided a near-complete and prescient
description of the process. But several researchers have suggested
that today we need to add a fifth phase to that list, in order to grapple with what's happened to places such as New York and San Francisco. Gentrification in these globalized cities is no longer about
individuals, and it's not even about local developers chasing cash
in cool neighborhoods. In the words of geographer Neil Smith, it's
about "the reach of global capital down to the local neighborhood
scale."

Today, many development deals are initiated by foreign investors, and many neighborhoods are affordable only to the global elite.
Buildings spring up that are meant less to house people and more
to house the wealth of millionaires and billionaires. In a stretch of
Midtown Manhattan, which has recently become filled with sky-
high multimillion-dollar condo buildings, a *New York Times* investigation found that 50 percent of apartments are vacant for the
majority of each year. In other words, the fifth and last phase of gentrification is when neighborhoods aren't just more friendly to capital
than to people but cease being places to live a normal life, with work
and home and school and community spaces, and become luxury
commodities.

These phases provide a good outline of how gentrification works, and they also rightly suggest that the process is predictable—that the pioneers and the coffee shops will likely be followed by the professionals and the condos, no matter where you are. But gentrification is also messier than that. Sometimes the phases happen simultaneously, or out of order. Detroit's gentrification, for example, seems to be largely driven by professionals, not individual "pioneers." But regardless of what order they come in, the phases all push in the same direction: gentrification heightens the worth of neighborhoods and cities until they become uninhabitable for average people.

Clay's stages of gentrification are useful to understand *how* the process happens, but they don't answer the fundamental question of *why*. Why do neighborhoods and entire cities all of a sudden become hot for reinvestment? There's a critical preparatory phase missing from the analysis, a phase zero. Cities' real estate and zoning policies are determined by local, state, and federal governments. And so for phases one through five to happen, governments have to be willing to allow for it.

There's still debate in academic circles about what forces convince lawmakers to welcome or encourage gentrification. Some view gentrification as a production-driven process: real estate developers who see profit potential in inner cities are luring in the young and moneyed, displacing those who aren't as profitable. Others argue gentrification is a consumption-driven process that is more about a million Everett Ortners converging on cities—that generations of white people raised in the suburbs have come to see the inner city as a space for personal liberation and economic possibility, and therefore create spaces within cities that conform to their needs. The negative effects of gentrification (displacement, cultural loss, etc.), in this view, are just unfortunate ancillary consequences of the compounded individual decisions of millions of former suburbanites who believe they'd be better off in the city. To be sure, consumption explanations have some merit: inner-cities are attractive cultural spaces. I know several dozen young white people who were raised in the suburbs and who believed the only place they could live a good life was in the city. They came to New York to be artists, activists, authors, and other types of creatives, and/or to liberate themselves from the familial expectations of the suburbs—to be single, gay, queer, or just different.

Others have posited that gentrification represents a more nefarious kind of individualistic expression: that of colonial power. In the same way that people of European descent colonized the Americas, some argue, gentrifiers see the inner city as a place lacking control and in need of white "civilizing" force. "As part of the experience of postwar suburbanization, the U.S. city came to be seen as an 'urban wilderness,'" Neil Smith wrote in his landmark 1996 book on gentrification, *The New Urban Frontier*. "In the language of gentrification, the appeal to frontier imagery has been exact: urban pioneers, urban homesteaders and urban cowboys became the new folk heroes of the urban frontier."

It's hard to argue that gentrifiers don't often harbor this troubling colonialist mind-set. I've heard countless times about people who think the only way to make a neighborhood better or safer is for them to move into it. And the language developers and gentrifiers use is often dripping with imperialist subtext. When a new apartment building opened on the west side of Times Square in 1983 (back then a non-gentrified area), its owners advertised in the *New York Times* with a full-page spread that celebrated the "taming of the wild, wild West" where "the trailblazers have done their work."

Often stores in gentrifying areas will hint at these semi-subconscious colonialist sympathies. In Brooklyn, there's Empire Mayonnaise and Outpost Café (outpost of what?), both of which are glaringly white businesses in predominantly black neighborhoods. In 2014, a building opened in Bushwick, a predominantly Hispanic section of Brooklyn, called Colony 1209. Its sales materials sound like gentrification-themed self-parody: "Here you'll find a group of like-minded settlers, mixing the customs of their original homeland with those of one of NYC's most historic neighborhoods to create art, community, and a new lifestyle. Let's Homestead, Bushwick-style." It's worth noting that the building received a fifteen-year tax abatement from the city worth $8 million.

But these cultural explanations don't go far enough toward explaining the *why* of gentrification, the phase zero. Yes, it's important that young white people with money find inner-city spaces attractive, but at the end of the day gentrification isn't about culture, it's about money. Gentrifiers may be seeking art, emancipation from suburban norms, and a sense of discovery, but the entire process would grind to a halt if it weren't profitable. Developers don't build condos to lose money or support the arts. They don't pressure cities to rezone entire neighborhoods because they believe in inner-city liberation. So to answer the question of why gentrification happens, we have to answer the question of how the city became profitable to gentrify.

- - -

Cities do not gentrify unless the process is profitable for real estate developers. Yes, hipsters and yuppies can move into a neighborhood and inflate local real estate values, but it is developers' profit motive that causes massive, citywide change.

The city wasn't always profitable. Up until the 1960s, developers could make much more money in the suburbs—buying land cheaply, constructing single-family houses, and taking advantage of a burgeoning mortgage industry to sell to the (mostly white) middle and upper classes. But at a certain point, profit potential in many suburbs was more or less maxed out. If you look at the inner-ring suburbs of New York, you can see why: by the 1960s, in places near commuter trains or within a reasonable driving distance of the city, nearly all of the land was developed and housing prices were high, making it hard for developers to buy on the cheap and sell at a markup. Sure, they could buy land even farther from the city and attempt to develop it, but commuters are only willing to travel so far, and New York's suburban commute times were already pushing the hour mark. The city, on the other hand, was a bargain, thanks to white flight and deindustrialization.

In 1979, geographer Neil Smith came up with what has become possibly the most influential academic theory on gentrification: the rent gap. Smith posited that the more disinvested a space becomes, the more profitable it is to gentrify. The idea behind his theory is a basic tenet of free-market economics: capital will go where the rate of potential return (i.e., the potential to make profit) is greatest. Smith realized that gentrification wasn't happening at random. It was predictable. If you wanted to find the neighborhood that would gentrify next, all you had to do was figure out where the biggest potential for profit was in a city—the place where buildings could be bought cheap and made more expensive in a short period of time.

By looking at tax data, Smith could pinpoint blocks that seemed to be gentrifiable, which usually meant buildings were in disrepair (so they could be bought cheap) and were close to other gentrified areas (so it wouldn't be too much of a stretch for gentrifiers to move in). The rent gap was the disparity between how much a property was worth in its current state and how much it would be worth gentrified. The larger the gap in a neighborhood, the higher the chance it would gentrify.

Gentrification might seem rapid when you're in a neighborhood experiencing it firsthand, but it's really a long game: real estate developers (at least the smart ones) know they can benefit from the vast, decades-long shifts that happen in metropolises. As Smith points out, developers reap profit by charging the highest rents they can to poor people and skimping on repairs, milking buildings for all they're worth, and then they benefit from kicking out those residents, making repairs, and charging much more money to new residents.

"Having produced a scarcity of capital in the name of profit they now flood the neighborhood for the same purpose, portraying themselves all along as civic-minded heroes, pioneers taking a risk where no one else would venture, builders of a new city for the worthy populace," Smith writes.

This milk-and-revitalize strategy can sound conspiratorial, and the reality often bears out that interpretation. New York's real estate and banking barons bought up cheap land in the outer boroughs before they lobbied for the deindustrialization of Manhattan, so they could profit both off the city's new condos and the industry and poor people forced into Brooklyn and Queens. But it doesn't have to be the result of clever plotting. Creating markets where profit potential is highest—that is, purchasing declining and underfunded buildings, and then quickly renovating and flipping them—is just sound economics. A rental market where the poor are adequately provided for, where there is enough space in a neighborhood to accommodate everyone, costs building owners more and is less profitable.

This constant search for the highest profit potential—what Smith calls a locational seesaw—is what created the suburbs, and it's what created the gentrified cities of today's United States. In the 1930s, most Americans were stably housed in either cities or rural areas, but the entire country was in an economic depression. By funding the construction of roads outside cities and by subsidizing and underwriting mortgages for suburban homes, the federal government created the suburban housing industry in a matter of years, and promoted billions of dollars in economic growth for developers. Later, once the suburbs were built out, developers had to search for new ways to revitalize their profit rate, and both gentrification and exurbanization were part of this search.

Using the rent gap theory, Smith was able to accurately predict the gentrification of many New York neighborhoods, including the Lower East Side, Harlem, and Park Slope. He looked at tax arrears data and found that gentrification happened right after buildings hit their highest level of tax debt—a sign landlords were milking their buildings by not doing repairs or paying their taxes in preparation for flipping them. The same sections of Park Slope that Everett Ortner was attempting to gentrify hit their highest levels of tax arrears in 1976. Sure enough, 1977 was the first year in which several buildings were converted from rentals to co-ops and condominiums. Between 1977 and 1984, there were 130 such conversions in Park Slope. The neighborhood's rapid conversions accounted for 21 percent of all such activity in the entire borough those years.

Does Smith's theory mean every gentrifier is seeking a high return on profit? Of course not. And it doesn't mean developers are even conscious of the dynamic they're playing into. But regardless of individual intent, the basic tenet holds true: gentrification works on a mass scale only because most inner cities have been purposely depressed and therefore are now profitable to reinvest in. That led Smith to conclude that "gentrification is a back-to-the-city movement all right, but a back-to-the-city movement by capital rather than people."

Most cities in the US experienced slow bleeds of capital thanks to deindustrialization and white flight, which eventually made their inner cities ripe for gentrification. But New Orleans's economic devalorization was instant, thanks to Katrina. The city's real estate was already relatively inexpensive before the storm, but Katrina pushed values low enough that even hobby investors could afford to snatch up a few damaged properties. And the storm made the potential value of the place higher: before Katrina, many New Orleans neighborhoods were not exactly welcoming of (white) outsiders. Crime was high. Most neighborhoods were majority black. The storm changed that, allowing developers to envision entire neighborhoods as majority white or at least more mixed, more upscale, and therefore more profitable. With real estate prices low and the potential for remaking the city high, the rent gap was bigger than ever, and so it made economic sense to gentrify New Orleans.

Private profit only partially explains gentrification, though. Gentrification may not happen without the confluence of shifting cultural desires and newly focused real estate capital, but its pervasiveness—its existence not only in major cultural and economic capitals but also in rural towns and midsized postindustrial middle American cities—can be explained only by the active promotion of gentrification by a third party, a party large enough to influence policy: the government.

For the past half century, as the federal government has repeatedly slashed funds for everything from public housing to neighborhood development, anti-poverty programs to public transit, cities have been left to fend for themselves. And that's pushed many into "entrepreneurial" and neoliberal forms of government—encouraging the growth of businesses and industries that in turn encourage the attraction of high-income and upper-middle-income families into cities. Through their taxes, those families help pay for the basic necessities of cities that used to be funded by the federal government.

At the same time, cities have been forced into slashing the budgets of necessary but expensive parts of any good city: parks, transit, programs for the poor. In other words, cities are looking for the rich and the upper middle class to use their tax dollars and spending power to fund what used to be paid for by America's semi-robust federal welfare state.

Detroit, New Orleans, and countless other cities are hoping the spending power of millennials who can afford to live consumption-oriented lifestyles will provide the tax dollars that everyone relies on. In richer cities with more infrastructure, such as San Francisco and New York, governments are relying on those millennials, along with big companies, millionaires, and billionaires, to provide the bulk of their tax revenue. In 1960, economist Friedrich Hayek, one of the fathers of neoliberalism, laid out this gentrification strategy: "Though the majority of residents may never contemplate a change of residence, there will usually be enough people, especially among the young and more enterprising, to make it necessary for the local authorities to provide as good services at as reasonable costs as their competitors." Hayek, who also advocated for a near-zero-spending federal government, was saying cities needed to fight for the young and moneyed in order to survive.

Nearly sixty years later, you can see that strategy playing out in most American cities: in New Orleans's all-out attempt to attract companies, especially the movie industry, to move into the city; in Detroit's various incentives for young people to move to the city; in San Francisco's policy of giving Twitter and other tech companies millions in tax breaks to stay in the city and build offices in its poorest neighborhoods; in New York's policy of subsidizing housing for the richest with the idea that they'll help fund the rest of the city.

"They are the ones that pay a lot of the taxes," New York's billionaire former mayor Michael Bloomberg said. "They're the ones that spend a lot of money in the stores and restaurants and create a big chunk of our economy. . . . [I]f we could get every billionaire around the world to move here, it would be a godsend."

Federal spending on cities has been declining for decades, but it was President Ronald Reagan, elected in 1980 with a mandate to slash budgets, who really sealed the fate of many urban centers. Reagan cut all nonmilitary spending by the US government by 9.7 percent in his first term, and in his second term cut the Department of Housing and Urban Development's budget by an astonishing 40 percent, hobbling cities' abilities to pay for public housing. The Department of Transportation also had its funding cut by about 10.5 percent during Reagan's first term and 7.5 percent in his second. Those cuts forced cities to turn to alternative sources of funding, in particular bonds, to finance things such as public transit and road repair. But not just anyone can issue a bond—governments first had to prove they'd be able to pay that bond back. And there are only two entities that decide if a government or company is capable of paying back a bond: Standard & Poor's and Moody's, ratings agencies that until relatively recently mostly concerned themselves with rating companies' investment-worthiness. But now, with cities looking to take out loans to fund their operations, the agencies rated cities in the same way. They'd downgrade the rating of any government with high spending (i.e., a basic social safety net) and not enough income (i.e., too many poor people). That's exactly what happened to Detroit: its costs were too high and its income too low, and so its credit rating was downgraded again and again until it was nearly impossible for the city to get a loan.

The result, to paraphrase planning and geography professor Jason Hackworth, was that cities were forced into becoming more entrepreneurial in a short period of time. They hired city managers and PR teams in a quest to turn themselves into profitable entities, as if cities were corporations. It's not uncommon these days for smaller cities to launch campaigns in larger ones, attempting to lure monied twenty- and thirtysomethings away. At one point ads promoting "Life in Cbus" (Columbus, Ohio) with slogans such as "Where Standing Out Never Means Standing Alone" littered Metro stations in Washington, DC. Philadelphia also paid for promotional billboards in Washington, DC, as well as in Chicago, and started an organization called Campus Philly, which runs incentives to get people who come to the city for college to stay once they graduate.

New Orleans has been less direct, but no less committed to wooing rich people to the city. Through its tax credit programs, the city has incentivized tech companies and movie and TV studios to set up shop in the city. It sold off properties (many abandoned since Katrina) in poor areas to luxury developers. It began marketing residential neighborhoods beyond the French Quarter in its tourism ads, especially rapidly gentrifying ones such as the Marigny and Bywater (this inspired a pretty great parody video in which a black New Orleanian makes fun of all the new white tourists in the Bywater getting their bikes stolen).

That's all left New Orleans a radically different place than it was pre-Katrina: it's richer, whiter, and slightly less populous. And this newer, richer, whiter city was built on the forced removal of tens of thousands of poor black people, which sounds terrible—unless you're a member of a city government that is only concerned with its bottom line. If that's the case, things are going great.

"Hurricane Katrina was an awful event," Ryan Berni, a senior aide to Mayor Mitch Landrieu, told *Politico* in 2015. "But it presented the opportunity for New Orleans to become this country's laboratory and hub for innovation and change."

3

Destroy to Rebuild

When African Americans in the city say it's hard to live in New Orleans, many of them are not just talking about a lack of jobs, inadequate housing, or racism. They mean it is literally hard to stay here without being displaced, that it was hard to have returned here after Katrina, and that they feel they are constantly at risk of being pushed out. Between the rhetoric of politicians who said they saw Katrina as an opportunity to revamp the city, the unavailability of money for repairs and housing for people left homeless by the storm, and the one-way tickets to places far away from New Orleans that were handed out to the storm's victims by the Federal Emergency Management Agency (FEMA), the message seemed clear: *The city is better off without you.*

There did seem to be a concerted, if unstated, effort to prevent many from returning after Katrina. Ruth Idakula, a former city worker and current activist with the Center for Ethical Living and Social Justice Renewal, is from Nigeria and has lived in the United States for twenty-four years. She settled in New Orleans because it felt like, in her words, "Africa in the Western Hemisphere." She now lives in an apartment in the Bywater, the neighborhood perhaps most synonymous with gentrification here. But it wasn't easy getting back. After being forced out of her Garden District home by Katrina, Idakula had to essentially lie her way back into New Orleans. After the storm she lived in Shreveport, a city in northwestern Louisiana, for four months, and then Atlanta for four months. Itching to come back, she called FEMA week after week, seeing if she could get money to help her resettle in New Orleans. On her fourth or fifth call, Ida- kula said, a FEMA official told her, "The reason you're not getting any money is because you keep saying you're going back to New Orleans."

There was no official policy to displace people, but FEMA seems to have preferred to send people anywhere but back. New Orleans residents who couldn't afford to settle somewhere else or return on their own were placed in all fifty states—anywhere but the city they'd left behind. It's unclear exactly how many people stayed out of New Orleans after the storm, but of the 1.36 million applications for assistance filed with FEMA after the storm, 84,749 came from Houston, 4,186 came from New York, 29,252 came from Atlanta, and 966 came from Minneapolis and St. Paul. A year later, there were at least 111,000 Katrina evacuees living in Houston, any- where between 50,000 and 100,000 living in Baton Rouge, and 70,000 living in Atlanta.

"FEMA was scrambling to get people anywhere they could," one professor who studied the diaspora told me. "If they had a church in Alaska saying they'd take a few people, FEMA would put them on a plane."

There's no federal mandate that suggests the government should attempt to return people home after a disaster. So Katrina's victims were given housing anywhere it was available. Nearly 600 New Or- leanians were housed in Utah, of all places, after the storm. Tens of thousands more were scattered between southern states such as Georgia and Texas. Many never came back, either because they couldn't afford to or because they didn't want to—their homes and communities had been destroyed, and they'd already begun making new lives and building new communities where they'd settled.

But Idakula was determined to go home. Needing the money and running out of options, she changed her application to claim she planned to settle in Atlanta, and when she checked her bank account a few days later, she found a direct deposit from FEMA.

Living in New Orleans now isn't easy for Idakula. Home prices in Bywater, where she lives, doubled post-Katrina. That mirrored the jump in rent across the city: in New Orleans the average amount spent on rent citywide rose from 14 percent of income before the storm to 35 percent. Idakula is able to afford her two-bedroom home only because her landlord, a retired activist who wanted to make sure someone black and involved in social justice could still live in Bywater, charges Idakula $500 a month.

She told me she has no problem with white people moving to the area, but she wishes they had an understanding of the power they carry. When white people, followed by white businesses, show up in a place like Bywater, they seem not to integrate into the fabric of a neighborhood, but take it over. Many black-owned businesses on St. Claude Avenue, the fast-gentrifying strip at Bywater's northern edge, simply never reopened after Katrina. And while the ones that took their place don't have "Whites Only" signs in the window, their clientele suggests there's a clear dividing line between the old and new New Orleans. On St. Claude, there's the Healing Center (also owned and developed by Pres Kabacoff), which includes an upscale food co-op and art spaces; there are also new queer punk bars, organic juice joints, and expensive coffee shops and brunch spots. It's not that there's anything wrong with these places in theory, Idakula said; it's just that it feels like they've replaced what was before them without acknowledgment. The new people, according to Idakula, are not commingling with longtime residents in a melting pot, but instead are reaping benefit from the physical removal of 100,000 black people.

"It's not sharing the table," Ruth told me. "It's coming here and shoving our shit off the table and then demanding we eat your shit."

Wayne Glapion has a similar feeling. He grew up in Tremé, a neighborhood famous for its concentration of free people of color— African Americans who were not enslaved in the eighteenth and nineteenth centuries and usually had some European ancestors— and more recently for its concentration of jazz musicians and other cultural icons in the city. Glapion, a New Orleans–born music manager, has been battling ever since the storm to hold on to his piece of Tremé, a traditional double shotgun house that his parents bought in 1945.

For Glapion, every step back was a difficult one. After Katrina struck, he was forced to paddle in a small boat from that house to dry land. He then walked to the Convention Center, one of the city's rescue operations centers notorious for the disarray and lack of services. A bus eventually took him to an army base near Fort Smith, Arkansas. He'd been separated from his extended family by the storm and heard some had been taken to Fort Worth, Texas. Glapion wanted to get back to them, so he left the base on foot, hoping to walk the nearly twenty miles to town to find a car, plane, or anything else that would get him to Fort Worth. A few miles into his walk, a white couple stopped him and asked, "Are you a refugee from New Orleans?"

"I didn't think of myself as a refugee," Glapion told me. "But I guess I was."

The couple offered to pay for a rental car for Glapion, and so he drove to Fort Worth. He left two weeks later to return to New Orleans and rebuild his grandparents' house.

"The grass was still gray, there were no birds, no insects," he said.

Glapion would work at gutting the house every day, sleep in his van most nights, and every Wednesday and Sunday drive three and a half hours to Lake Charles, where his cousin lived, to shower. Nearly every day in New Orleans he'd be approached by National Guard troops or private military contractors who told him he couldn't be there. He often feared for his life as he gutted his house, and for good reason: racist violence was rampant in New Orleans after Katrina. In the aftermath of the storm, one black New Orleanian named Henry Glover was found shot and burned nearly beyond recognition in the back of a police car. Five police officers were found to be involved in the shooting and apparent attempted cover-up of Glover's death. One, David Warren, who shot the unarmed Glover, was sentenced to twenty-five years in prison, but was acquitted after an appeal in 2013. It wasn't until 2015 that Glover's death was ruled a homicide. Police also shot and killed two unarmed people who were attempting to get to a hotel on higher ground via a bridge.

"These are some of the 40,000 extra troops that I have demanded," then governor Kathleen Blanco said. "They have M-16s, and they're locked and loaded. . . . I have one message for these hoodlums: These troops know how to shoot and kill, and they are more than willing to do so if necessary, and I expect they will."

Glapion didn't see himself as a "hoodlum," but he knew the cops might view him as one. But he risked arrest, or worse, and continued to rebuild.

"They threatened to send me to Angola [the Louisiana State Penitentiary]," he said. "But they didn't understand the importance of this city. I was trying to get it back to what it was."

Glapion spent years keeping the house up, slowly making the repairs it required, but despite his best efforts, he wasn't able to hold on to it. Neither FEMA nor Louisiana's Road Home program ever provided enough money to fully repair the house, so it was left partially dilapidated, and eventually he ran out of funds. Recently he sold the home to an investor who plans to convert the two-family shotgun into a single-family home. Glapion still lives in New Orleans, but now in another neighborhood, further north than Tremé.

"It's not the same city anymore," Wayne told me over coffee at a café near a club he promotes downtown. "It's still vibrant. And it's gonna come back. But I'm not going to say better than it was, because I know too many people who couldn't come back. The city's going to have a somewhat new face."

- - -

Gentrifying New Orleans took more than keeping black people out. Institutions needed to be dismantled. First came the public schools. Before Katrina, the New Orleans public school system was like many others in poor US cities: underfunded, overcrowded, and underperforming. Less than two years later it looked nothing like any other school system in the country. It was still underperforming, overcrowded, and underfunded, but it was now, with the exception of only four schools, the nation's first all-charter school district.

Nearly every conservative pundit and institution, from the American Enterprise Institute to one of the biggest backers of neoliberalism, economist Milton Friedman, called on Louisiana to use Katrina as an opportunity to transform the city's school system.

"This is a tragedy," Friedman wrote in a *Wall Street Journal* op-ed. "It is also an opportunity to radically reform the educational system."

Just weeks after the storm, Governor Blanco signed Legislative Act 35 into law. The bill empowered the state to take over any "failing" school districts across the state, though its timing made it obvious that the law's intent was to take over the New Orleans school system. Louisiana already had a law on the books allowing it to take over schools that achieved an average of 45 points or less on the state's standardized School Performance Score for four years in a row. But by July 2004, the state had only exercised its power to take over one Orleans Parish School Board school. Three months before the storm, the state had taken over only four OPSB schools, as the vast majority of New Orleans's schools did not fall below a score of 45 for four consecutive years. But Blanco's new LA 35, passed in the wake of Katrina, drastically changed the state's standards: after Katrina, any school that fell below the state average of 87.5 could be transferred to state control. The vast majority of New Orleans schools failed to meet this threshold, and the state was able to move nearly every New Orleans school to a new Recovery School District (RSD) within two years of the storm. Research from Tulane University found that many New Orleans schools fell just under that 87.5-point score but were transferred to the new district anyway, while no other schools in Louisiana that scored above a 60 were taken over by the state. Activists called the takeover an educational land grab.

Fast-forward ten years, and conservatives and other pro-charter reformers are now using New Orleans as a model for cities struggling to educate their kids. Some data suggest the RSD is indeed successful: its high school graduation rate is now almost 80 percent, up from 54 percent in 2004. But it's unclear if that's as good a sign as it seems, as only about 6 percent of high school seniors in the RSD are graduating with ACT test scores high enough to get them into a college in Louisiana. That's still 2 percent better than before the storm, but by no means a success story.

There's also evidence that black students aren't getting the same benefits from the new school system as everyone else. A 2013 survey found that while 53 percent of white and Hispanic parents thought the school system was better after Katrina, only 29 percent of black parents felt the same way.

And New Orleans's system of school choice requires parents to apply for schools at the beginning of each school year. The process involves mountains of paperwork and can be confusing. That means it favors parents with extra time and money, and it often means that the students struggling most end up in New Orleans's worst schools. School choice also translates into longer travel times for parents and their kids, especially since many of the city's new schools do not have extracurricular activities such as music and arts programs. To attend those, students have to be picked up by parents and driven to other schools, as no public transportation for extracurriculars is provided.

The takeover of New Orleans's school district also enabled the state to dismantle a bastion of the city's black middle class: the teachers' union. The United Teachers of New Orleans represented 7,500 teachers before the storm. Ninety percent of teachers in the Orleans Parish School Board were black. But when the state took over New Orleans's schools, all 7,500 were fired and had to reapply in the new state-run district.

"It is about breaking unions," the head of the United Teachers of New Orleans, Brenda Mitchell, said at the time. "It is about breaking the spirit of working-class people. It is about denying them their rights."

Those who were hired back were stripped of their collective bargaining rights, in many cases were threatened with dismissal if they discussed their salaries, and were given "at-will" contracts, meaning their employment could be terminated at any time. And it's unclear how many of those 7,500 teachers were in fact hired in the new district. One clue as to how many weren't rehired comes from a Tulane study that looked at the years of experience teachers in New Orleans had pre- and post-Katrina. During the 2004–2005 school year, only 9.7 percent of New Orleans teachers had less than one year of teaching experience. Nearly 30 percent had twenty-five or more years of experience. But in the 2007–2008 school year, 36.7

percent of teachers had one year or less of experience, and only 11.6 percent had more than twenty-five.

The other bastion of black New Orleans was the city's public housing, which came in the form of traditional brick projects: C. J. Peete, Melpomene, B. W. Cooper, St. Thomas, St. Bernard, Desire, Florida, Lafitte, Iberville, and Press Park. Today, nearly all are gone. Some have been replaced by mixed-income, privately run, for-profit housing such as River Garden. Some are still empty lots awaiting private development.

In nearly every city in the United States, the public housing stock has been decimated by a federal program called Hope VI, which was instituted under President Bill Clinton. The program rewards local housing authorities for demolishing traditional public housing (usually those big brick buildings that people often call "the projects") and rebuilding with suburban-style, low-density, mixed-income housing instead. Frequently those new units are built not by housing authorities but by private developers and nonprofits. The idea behind Hope VI was to alleviate the symptoms associated with concentrated poverty—in particular, high crime. But what Hope VI has done in practice is encourage the demolition of tens of thousands of units of affordable housing and then come up short in terms of funding their replacements.

Between 1990 and 2008, 220,000 units of public housing were demolished, and at least 110,000 of those can be directly traced to the Hope VI program. But Hope VI has provided funding for only 60,000 units of mixed-income housing as a replacement. Some cities were hit particularly hard by Hope VI. Chicago lost nearly 16,500 units of housing. Philadelphia lost 7,800. New Orleans started out with less public housing than those cities, but the destruction of 5,628 units of housing has nonetheless been a burden to the poor here.

Plans to demolish several New Orleans housing projects, including St. Thomas, were under way years before Katrina, but with tens of thousands still evacuated from the city, and the city's politics shaken up by the storm, the demolitions were able to proceed at a much faster pace. The rhetorical attacks on public housing began just days after the storm.

"The storm destroyed a great deal," Finis Shelnutt, a real estate developer, told the German newspaper *Der Spiegel* in September, "and there's plenty of space to build houses and sell them for a lot of money. . . . Most importantly, the hurricane drove poor people and criminals out of the city, and we hope they don't come back. . . . The party's finally over for these people and now they're going to have to find someplace else to live in the US."

Local politicians used the storm as an excuse to ramp up attacks on public housing as well. "There's just been a lot of pampering, and at some point you have to say, 'no, no, no, no, no,'" said Oliver Thomas, a city councilman at the time. "We don't need soap opera watchers right now."

One state representative went as far as to say that public housing residents should be sterilized. And former US representative Richard Baker, who'd represented Baton Rouge for ten terms, said: "We finally cleaned up public housing in New Orleans. . . . We couldn't do it, but God did."

Soon after Katrina, the demolition of St. Thomas was fast-tracked, and the City Council began debating what to do with the city's remaining four projects. Thanks to a well-organized protest movement and infighting in the City Council, the removal of the city's remaining 4,500 units of public housing was delayed. But in 2007, with its first white majority in more than two decades, the City Council finally voted to knock down the remaining public housing stock. Assuming an average household size of 2.2 people (the US government standard), that means 12,381 people, 99 percent of whom were African American, were removed from stable public housing in New Orleans in the last two decades, most right after Katrina.

The projects in New Orleans were also home to a well-organized tenants' rights movement, and displacing thousands of black New Orleanians by demolishing public housing quelled a stronghold of black activism. In St. Thomas in the 1990s, activists such as Robert Horton, who goes by the name Kool Black, helped form first-of-their-kind networks for community policing and after-school activities for kids. And St. Thomas was one of the first public housing projects to establish a board of residents that worked with nonprofits in the area to ensure that government-funded services in public housing were actually benefiting residents.

In the city's new housing developments, there are no tenants' rights groups, and residents told me there's no sense of community either. Instead, management groups run by nonprofits and private companies monitor the mixed-income developments with a close eye and a penchant for unnecessary discipline.

"What is activism going to look like in these places? What is speaking truth to power going to look like? What is social services going to look like in these new places?" Kool Black asked me when we met near his apartment, about ten miles away from St. Thomas in a sprawling, suburban-ish section of the city called New Orleans East, where he's lived since the demolition of the projects. "This is what they destroyed with Hope VI."

The storm also decimated the city's market-rate housing stock, and the programs put in place to help those living in single-family dwellings come back to the city were deeply flawed and racially biased as well. Road Home, Louisiana's main program meant to help homeowners rebuild their houses, was meant to distribute billions of dollars from the federal government. But by 2008, two-thirds of the funds hadn't yet been doled out. And in 2011, a court found that Road Home distributed grants in a racially biased way, awarding homeowners in majority-white neighborhoods more money to rebuild than those with similar homes in majority-black neighborhoods.

Those who couldn't make it home, or who could only afford to partially fix up their Katrina-damaged homes thanks to lackluster government grants, often found their properties seized and auctioned off by the city. If the city considers a home blighted (which could just mean, for example, it needs a paint job or its grass is overgrown), the city cites it and imposes steep fines often adding up to thousands of dollars a month. If the owner doesn't fix the property within a month or can't pay off the fines, the city imposes a lien on the property and then waits another thirty days. If the owner is unable to bring the property up to code by then, the city claims the property as its own and puts it up for sale in an online auction. Since

2010 the city has sold off or demolished at least 13,000 properties, most of which were abandoned after Katrina and many of which are in rapidly gentrifying areas.

With far fewer public housing projects and a thinned housing stock, New Orleans is now more expensive than ever. In 2016, one nonprofit found New Orleans was the second-least-affordable housing market in the country based on how many people devoted 50 percent or more of their income to rent. The increased unaffordability represents another factor in the city's mass displacement. I talked to several former New Orleans residents living in Houston and other parts of the South who did not experience direct discrimination via FEMA or other governmental agencies. But they'd found relatively affordable housing elsewhere—in Houston or Dallas, Atlanta or Shreveport—and so they decided to stay. They wanted to return, but they were simply priced out.

- - -

This is what gentrifiers and gentrification boosters often fail to grasp about gentrification: it's not that most poor people or people of color hate the idea of anyone moving to the city, but that gentrification almost always takes place on top of someone else's loss. Gentrifiers see cities through fresh eyes, unencumbered by mental maps that might suggest something more nefarious than revitalization had happened before their arrival. Gentrifiers might even have noble intent—to become a part of a community, to help better a community, to fight for political change. Or they might just be there for the cheaper rent. Either way, it is rare to see gentrifiers take a full reckoning of history and recognize that their presence is often predicated upon the lessened quality of life of someone else, the displacement of someone else, or, in the case of New Orleans, the death of someone else. A gentrifier's intent isn't meaningless. A new neighbor concerned with his or her new neighborhood can make strides toward healing the wounds brought by gentrification. A neighbor concerned with preserving the culture of a neighborhood or joining in political action can make a real difference. Intent helps, but intent cannot stop gentrification. As New Orleans's history shows, being white and having more money than most people in a given neighborhood gives you more buying power, more privilege, and more autonomy than those who have been systematically held back from achieving the same levels of wealth. I believe this is why gentrifiers do not like to acknowledge that they are gentrifiers: they do not want to feel like perpetrators of violence and inequality.

The irony is that in remaining ignorant of their class positions, gentrifiers often become victims of the process. If you look toward San Francisco and New York, cities that have a few decades of gentrification under their belts, you'll see that the gentrifiers—punks, artists, LGBT communities—are inevitably replaced by a flood of hipsters with more money, and those hipsters with more money are then pushed out by yuppies with even more money. Small, independent businesses give way to Starbucks and bank branches. Rising housing costs put a strain on everyone, even the white middle class. And the rejiggering of a city to squeeze out profits hurts nearly every citizen, regardless of socioeconomic background: budget cuts means public transit gets worse, museums and other cultural institutions suffer, public schools have to do more with less. There are few winners in gentrification. As Ruth Idakula put it, if the city is a ladder, gentrification pushes everyone down one rung: the most disenfranchised get pushed off completely, the middle class ends up on the bottom rung, and even the rich feel pressure from the top.

Only those who can afford to do without the government institutions most of us rely on every day—those with private transportation, money for private schools, and enough funds to either buy real estate or withstand rent fluctuations—can float above the effects of gentrification. And while it's hard to sympathize with the wealthy, even they are affected in less tangible ways. A completely gentrified neighborhood is a boring neighborhood, and a completely gentrified city (a good example being New York) is a boring city, one that can't provide the social life, diversity, and sense of authenticity that gentrifiers seek. As Jane Jacobs wrote, "We must understand that self-destruction of diversity is caused by success, not failure."

Gentrification brings money, new people, and renovated real estate to cities, but it also kills them. It takes away the affordability and diversity that are required for unique and challenging culture. It sanitizes. And because it is obvious to most that this is happening (even hypergentrifiers in New York and New Orleans mourn the loss of culture in those cities), no one wants to be seen as a gentrifier. Who would want to be held accountable for helping kill a city?

- - -

John and Alicia Winter moved to New Orleans for the same reasons most people move to New Orleans: it's cheap compared to other major cities and, as John put it, it "feels European."

"This is like the closest to a European city in America," he told me. "It reminds me of Brussels."

John is from London, Alicia's from Texas, and both lived in Houston before deciding to move here. John programs software for banks and energy companies and works from home, so he can work anywhere. Alicia works in education. Now that they've moved, she's hoping to open her own day care center. The thirtysomething couple said they were ready to start new lives in a truly urban setting, and both decided that Houston represented everything wrong with American cities—it was sprawling, it lacked a sense of community and diversity, and they needed a car to get anywhere.

"In Houston they're not passionate about the city," John told me.

Alicia agreed. Plus, she said, Houston was missing New Orleans's diversity.

"It's nice to be in a place with a range of incomes," she said.

I met John and Alicia Winter at a street fair on Freret Street, a previously nearly abandoned strip of land in the northeast of the city. Freret is not far from some very fancy neighborhoods. It's just north of St. Charles, which is lined by stately houses on both sides and has a famous streetcar line down its middle, and just east of Tulane and Loyola Universities, where professors and administrators inhabit some swanky digs. The area right around Freret Street has

for decades housed a sizable middle-class black population. But the
commercial strip of Freret Street for decades housed mostly vacant
storefronts. Now the area is rapidly gentrifying. The proportion of
vacant buildings in the Freret neighborhood dropped from 28 to 16
percent between 2008 and 2010, a sure sign that people who can
afford to renovate things are moving in. Home values have more
than doubled, from a median of $81,000 in 2000 to $184,000 in 2013.
And white people have multiplied too: between 2000 and 2013, in
Freret's most gentrified census tract, the African American population dropped from 82 to 72 percent, while the white population
climbed from 13 to 22 percent.

Freret feels like so many gentrifying neighborhoods in US cities. If you spun around a couple of times, you might think you were
in Williamsburg, Brooklyn, or San Francisco's Mission District.
The Mojo Coffee on one of Freret's corners could be in Brooklyn
or Portland, or really anywhere with enough twentysomethings with
MacBooks to sustain a business that makes most of its money from
$4 cups of coffee. The tattoo place could come from Austin, Texas.
The burger joint could be in Uptown Minneapolis. In the same way
the outskirts of every city host a confluence of chain stores—Target,
Bed Bath and Beyond, OfficeMax—every city now seems to contain
a Freret Street.

The fair where I met John and Alicia Winter, called the Freret
Street Festival, takes place every year in March and is essentially
an advertisement for the "new" neighborhood. Those generic coffee shops, restaurants, bars, and galleries splay their wares on the
sidewalk, and the fair's attendees (nearly all of them white) stroll
through, consuming $6 sliders, parmesan fries, cold-pressed juices,
and other hipster-approved items below banners reading "Welcome
to the New Freret."

John and Alicia were there checking out their new neighborhood. A few months prior, the couple had purchased a home on Up-
perline Street for $370,000, a price they acknowledged was much
steeper than it would've been a few years ago. They fell in love with
the neighborhood as soon as they moved, but they wanted to feel
like they were part of its fabric. So they stopped into the Freret

Neighborhood Center, a nonprofit that helps low-income people in the area, to see if any volunteer opportunities were available. John wondered if he could maybe teach a computer class. Alicia wondered about the area's child care needs. They took the business card of one of the center's staffers and left.

Both had heard of the term *gentrification*. John said he hated what the process had done to a neighborhood in London called Dalston. He has a lot of friends there and said the place had changed around them, going from edgy and hip to bland and filled with yuppies.

When I asked if John and Alicia saw themselves—two young white transplants making enough money to buy a $370,000 house— as gentrifiers, both said they'd never thought about it, but that perhaps they were.

"I don't know if we're doing the same thing as in Dalston," John said. "But maybe we're the pricks changing the neighborhood. Sometimes I feel guilty and wonder if the neighbors think, 'There goes the neighborhood' when they see me."

But both John and Alicia said they felt like they were working hard at integrating themselves. In addition to checking out volunteer opportunities, John said he made sure to hire a local to help run his software development company, even though that local had less experience than other candidates. And Alicia said she planned to make sure her new day care center was affordable, or she'd at least set up a scholarship program. Yet despite all their good intent, it seems that people like John and Alicia Winter can't stop a changing neighborhood's more deleterious effects.

Down the street from the Freret Neighborhood Center is Dennis' Barber Shop, which Dennis Sigur has run in the same location for forty-three years. He's seen the neighborhood go from bustling and mostly black before the city's economic crash and white flight in the 1970s to gentrified now. His shop is not meant for gentrifiers— nothing prevents them from coming in, but Dennis makes no effort to attract them. His employees are black, and from what I could tell, so are all of his customers. The shop is busy, Dennis said, but less busy than it used to be. Yet he sees new businesses catering to white people opening constantly.

"Our customers are getting further and further away," he said. "We're struggling. But the welcome mat is rolled out for the newcomers."

Freret's newcomers have gotten a bit of red carpet treatment: After Hurricane Katrina, the state designated Freret a cultural district, allowing businesses opening along this strip to receive tax incentives—exemptions from income taxes for artists, tax credits for rehabbing storefronts, and the like. Only new businesses were eligible, not long-running ones like Dennis' Barber Shop. The city also passed a zoning overlay that allowed bars and restaurants to concentrate in the area like almost nowhere else in the city. In a city that already has an abundance of liquor options, the City Council is hesitant to issue new liquor licenses, but not on Freret Street. Thanks to that zoning overlay, any new restaurant on Freret can apply for a liquor license without seeking the City Council's approval. That allowed several new restaurants to open in rapid succession and attract a young, white, liquor-swigging crowd in a matter of months. That might not seem like a big deal, but imagine an alternative scenario in which restaurants on Freret were required to go through the same permitting process as everywhere else in the city. Imagine that many of the stores weren't allowed to exist tax free for a number of years. There's a chance Freret would've developed very differently.

Most New Orleanians I spoke with seemed to have no problem with the incentives used to lure people to forlorn parts of the city. But some took issue with the way they were used. If incentivizing businesses is often synonymous with bringing all-white, upscale businesses to an area, it seems obvious that the process isn't working for everyone. In the spring of 2013, a hundred Freret-area residents crowded the cafeteria of a charter school to discuss a proposal to raise property taxes in the neighborhood and use the revenue to hire private security to patrol the area. At the meeting, two white people sat at the table representing those for the idea. Two black residents represented those who were opposed. There was so much opposition to the proposal—mostly black residents who feared security guards would add to the already rampant police harassment of black people in the neighborhood—that the proposal was shelved. But it nonetheless highlighted that in New Orleans, the revitalization of an area nearly always comes with tension between those benefiting from the new city and those who feel they've been left behind.

"It's going to come to the point where if you don't have a good income you can't stay," Dennis Sigur told me. "There's a growing divide between the new and the old."

- - -

This middle phase of gentrification—after the "pioneers" have settled in and capital goes on autopilot, seeking out any neighborhood that seems potentially profitable—tends to divide everyone in a city, not only into black and white, rich and poor, but also into groups within those groups. Gentrifiers begin filtering into self-defined niches in order to differentiate themselves from those they feel are ruining the city. No one wants to be labeled a gentrifier, and a new class emerges: the white, relatively well-off who also hate gentrification.

Leslie Heindel fits into this category. I met Leslie through her mother, Lisa, a real estate agent whom I'd visited to talk about New Orleans real estate values. But while I was interviewing Lisa in her office in the upscale Garden District, her daughter kept stopping her work and audibly sighing. Eventually Lisa suggested she chime in. It turns out gentrification is something Leslie and her friends talk about on a near-daily basis.

Leslie said she sees gentrification as an ever-present threat to her way of life. To stay afloat in New Orleans, she works at least two bartending jobs at a time in addition to the administrative work she does at her mom's office. She, like a growing number of twenty- and thirtysomethings, rents an apartment as opposed to owning one. She doesn't have the money to afford a down payment on one, especially now that real estate values are skyrocketing in her city.

Over cigarettes and draft beers at a bar in the Irish Channel, just a few blocks from where Ashana Bigard lives, Leslie and her friends told me about everything wrong with New Orleans today— the movie industry coming in and taking up space and houses and jobs; Airbnb, which allows people to rent their houses for short periods of time and has been shown to cause rent inflation; the increased touristification and Disneyfication of every neighborhood near the French Quarter; and the lack of community that comes with all those things.

"I've worked at this bar for ten years," Leslie told me through a cloud of Marlboro Lights smoke. "There are nights I know nobody here."

Leslie and her friends have the luxury of being middle class, so their fear of gentrification has less to do with outright displacement and more to do with a sense of being squeezed into different neighborhoods and smaller apartments and having to take on more work in order to stay in their city. They see themselves being pushed down Ruth Idakula's metaphorical ladder.

"Everyone who grew up here has experienced a different New Orleans," Leslie admitted. But, she and her friends said, the changes since Katrina have been different, faster, and more tumultuous.

"If you had talked to me six years ago, I would have said we were moving in the right direction," Leslie's friend Crista Rock, a video producer, said. "I would've said the movie industry is great, and all the entrepreneurial stuff is great. I don't think anyone could've foreseen this. I had real big hopes for us."

The industries Leslie and Crista complained of had been wooed here with taxpayer money. Like every state in the country, Louisiana uses tax breaks and other incentives to lure and keep companies, but Louisiana uses more of them than most places. The state gives away 21 cents per dollar of the government's budget to companies—a higher percentage than any other state besides Texas and Michigan. In Louisiana, there's a ten-year tax exemption for buying materials used in manufacturing, a 40 percent tax break for companies using technology developed in the state, a 25 percent tax break for companies that record sound in Louisiana, a 100 percent five-year tax break for restoring old commercial structures, and the list goes on.

In 2011, the state gave $214 million to make sure shipbuilder Huntington Ingalls stayed within New Orleans. The same year, it approved tax incentives worth $1.5 billion for Cheniere Energy, a natural gas and oil company that paid its CEO $142 million in 2013.

But no industry in Louisiana gets tax credits more often than film and television production, which is centered in New Orleans. Cheniere might've been the biggest single deal, but Louisiana gives away hundreds of millions for TV and movies every year. In 2013 alone, the state gave away $251 million in tax credits to the industry. Every time the A&E reality show *Duck Dynasty* filmed an episode in Louisiana, the show received incentives worth $300,000.

Those incentives bring to New Orleans thousands of high-paying jobs, which usually come with salaries higher than New Orleans's median income of $36,964. This essentially creates two economies—one filled with low-paid natives, and one filled with people who make higher salaries, subsidized by Louisiana taxpayers. That second category views Louisiana's real estate as a relative bargain. Leslie told me most of her clients now come from out of town, especially New York and Los Angeles. And so, in her own small way, Leslie is helping push herself down the ladder.

- - -

But how's the view from the top of the ladder? If not even many gentrifiers think gentrification is good, why does it keep happening? Pres Kabacoff is one of the city's biggest developers—he's the one who turned the St. Thomas housing projects into for-profit mixed-use housing. And he's intimately tied in with city decision making. He chairs the city's Housing Task Force Committee and is a member of the Urban Land Institute, a powerful national urban planning group. When Kabacoff talks, city officials listen.

Kabacoff is a genial guy with some surprising views for a multimillionaire who makes money off private development. For example, he believes the federal government should spend way more on housing poor people, and he thinks the United States spends too much on war and not enough on things such as education. But when it comes to gentrification, Kabacoff has some troubling views for someone who wields so much power in a majority-poor, majority-black city.

"If you're not growing, you're dying," he told me from his dark-wood-filled office, located in a building he owns downtown.

"It's certainly not a good solution to stop development to protect neighborhoods."

In Kabacoff's view, the best way for New Orleans to grow is to start looking more like New York and San Francisco: "We lost our middle income dramatically and it becomes a vicious cycle. The middle class don't require a lot of services, but they pay for services that are provided. When your middle class leaves and your poor get more concentrated, your service needs go up—the tax base is gone and you go into a vicious downward spiral. And you get what happened here, and in Detroit, and Newark, and Gary, Indiana."

But what about the Ashana Bigards and even the Leslie Heindels—the people who feel they're being pushed further and further down the ladder by his attempt to bring a sizable middle and upper-middle class to the city? His answer, essentially, was that this is an inevitable consequence of progress.

"It's true when a neighborhood comes back many people who found it to be an affordable place are priced out," he said. "But the cold truth is, if you're going to revitalize a neighborhood that's in bad shape or where market rate won't go—because the amount of crime, the amount of poverty or the amount of minorities, or whatever keeps market rate uncomfortable moving there—one of the realities is that when the market rate come in, those people move to another neighborhood. It's a pain in the ass, but they move."

Given the city's apparent willingness to incentivize, unchecked, the kind of revitalization Kabacoff and other major developers promote, I asked Kabacoff if he thought New Orleans was on its way to becoming like New York or San Francisco, where people are marching in the streets over gentrification, and where even those in the middle class feel like they're hanging on to their cities by a thread.

"You might argue New Orleans could use a little gentrification," he told me. "In San Francisco and New York, you reach that saturation point and once you reach that, people start to march. Am I worried about people marching in New Orleans? Not yet. We've got a ways to go."

It'd be easy to paint Kabacoff as a villain, a 1 percenter toying with his city without regard to the people who live in it, but his ideas aren't so different from Leslie Heindel's, or the policies of most members of the New Orleans City Council, or the ideas of academics and planners and pundits who see gentrification and revitalization as near-synonyms. Most people who aren't directly displaced by gentrification seem to want just enough of it to improve their lives, but not too much—they don't want it to overwhelm their own bank accounts. Hipsters are fine with coffee but eye boutiques and banks with suspicion, yuppies are fine with the boutiques and banks but see landscapes radically altered by development as cultural losses, and developers such as Pres Kabacoff are fine with those landscapes as long as they don't inspire protest. The problem is that these steps are all part of the same process, and once you start turning the city into a capital-accumulation machine, it's kind of hard to turn back.

- - -

It's hard to say what New Orleans will look like in ten or twenty years, but it's become obvious that the city is almost solely focused on economic growth, not on repairing or moving beyond the trauma of Katrina. The press today in New Orleans rarely mentions gentrification or displacement. The politicians of New Orleans have all but given up trying to get any of the 100,000 displaced residents back to the city. Those former New Orleanians have disappeared, and the city has opened a new chapter, one that seems to contain no mention of race or class, just "progress."

In an essay analyzing political rhetoric after Katrina, Colorado State University ethnic studies professor Eric Ishiwata writes that the storm shed light on the fact that many Americans still don't accept the existence of extreme racism and extreme poverty in this county. The idea that there's a group of people who on a daily basis are having their rights violated and their lives threatened occurs to many Americans only in moments of national trauma. Katrina was one of those moments. Weeks after the storm, the lead story in the September 19 issue of *Newsweek* would deem these "forgotten" people the "Other America." And four days after Hurricane Katrina, Michael Brown, then director of FEMA, explained the disastrous

FEMA response by saying: "The American people don't understand how fascinating and unusual this is—is that we're seeing people that we didn't know exist that suddenly are showing up on bridges or parts of the interstate that aren't inundated."

According to Ishiwata, phrases like these—"people we didn't know exist," "the other America"—show that "a large segment of Katrina's victims had, to the point of the disaster, been cast as personae non grata—citizen-subjects rendered invisible by the reigning neoliberal ideology of a 'colorblind America.'"

In other words, until they were abandoned by their governments and forced onto bridges where CNN cameras delivered images of them into the homes of millions of Americans, poor black people's lives in New Orleans rarely weighed on the conscience of Americans, even the Americans meant to protect them, such as FEMA director Michael Brown.

Katrina opened a window that allowed us to peer into the real America, but as soon as the disruptive event was over, that window closed, and the country's consciousness went back to its usual state of ignoring the fact that black people, especially low-income black people, are daily denied democracy and equality in this country. As Ishiwata points out, we didn't just go back to forgetting that issues of inequality and racism exist; we went back to forgetting that an entire group of disenfranchised people exists.

Closing that window explains why it took only days before people seemed to stop caring about the rebuilding of New Orleans, to stop caring that nearly 100,000 African Americans were not able to return after the storm. To many politicians and thought leaders such as David Brooks, the idea that we'd need to get a majority-black, majority-poor city back to its former self seemed unnecessary, even irresponsible. After taking a tour of the Houston Astrodome, where thousands had been bused after Katrina, former first lady Barbara Bush told a radio show that people seemed better off there than in New Orleans.

"So many of the people in the arena here, you know, were underprivileged anyway," she said. "So this is working very well for them."

Less than a week after the storm, when asked if he thought billions should be spent rebuilding New Orleans, House Speaker Dennis Hastert said: "I don't know. That doesn't make sense to me. . . . It looks like a lot of that place should be bulldozed."

The country's collective ignoring of black New Orleanians' lives also explains why there was no federal effort undertaken to figure out where exactly all the evacuees from Katrina had ended up. Ten years later, not one federal agency is studying the diaspora caused by Katrina. The biggest study of their whereabouts was performed by the nonprofit RAND Corporation, and that tracking program ended five years ago.

A decade after the man-made failures that preceded and followed Katrina tore New Orleans apart, the "other America" narrative has been completely forgotten. The chasm has closed. And a new narrative—one of rebirth and growth—has overtaken the country's popular media. The city has been "resurrected," according to the *Daily Beast*. Its growth is an "economic miracle," according to the *National Journal*. The city is indeed growing at a rapid clip, making its way up the lists featured in business magazines and newspaper travel sections of the top ten places to live or work or fall in love. New Orleans, despite the tens of thousands still missing from it, is "back." And now, with the benefit of hindsight, despite all that went wrong, and all those the recovery failed, its leaders are confirming that, yes, just like David Brooks said, Katrina was truly a blessing in disguise.

This ignorance of the lives of others is what allows gentrification to happen. Sharifa Rhodes-Pitts points out in her book *Harlem Is Nowhere* that whenever a neighborhood gentrifies, you hear white people and the media using phrases such as "People are starting to move to that neighborhood," or "No one used to go there, but that's changing." The implication is that before these places gentrified, no one lived there, or at least no one of importance. This is what is happening in New Orleans and every other gentrifying city. If you ignore the destruction of the lives of the people who've always mattered the least, things are going great. If you acknowledge that their lives exist and that they matter, then it becomes immediately obvious something is terribly wrong. So what does it mean that we are not only ignoring these people but increasingly erasing their narratives in the name of progress?

Here's the image we've created of the gentrifying city: People are experiencing New Orleans through fresh eyes and ears. People are moving to Detroit to change it and make it better. They're spotting areas of Brooklyn that have yet to be discovered. They're finding San Francisco's next hot markets. They're discovering renewal in the ruins of abandoned sections of town. Neighborhoods are being revitalized. Entire economies are being turned around.

But we know that from the perspective of the gentrified, revitalization looks like displacement, new business opportunities often look like racial preference, and hot neighborhoods mean a loss of community.

I think both these perspectives are true: some people are discovering neighborhoods they think are hot, others are discovering they can no longer afford to live in those neighborhoods. Some people really are finding hope in the new New Orleans and the new Detroit; others are not. Whether or not gentrifiers, policy makers, and others with power and money can grapple with both narratives—the one about discovery and betterment, and the more complicated, uncomfortable one about loss, about economics and race—will determine the future of our cities.

As Jane Jacobs wrote in *The Death and Life of Great American Cities*, "Private investment shapes cities, but social ideas (and laws) shape private investment. First comes the image of what we want, then the machinery is adapted to turn out that image."

So what image of our cities do we hold in our hearts?

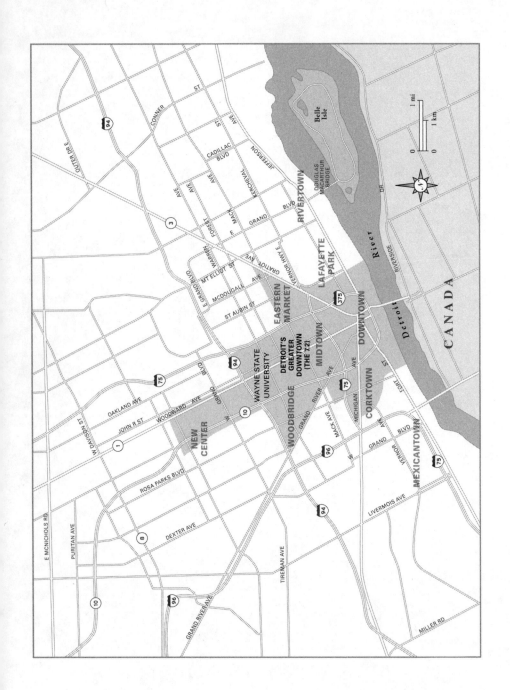

Part 2

Detroit

4

The New Detroit

On an early summer day in 2015, Detroit Bikes, one of at least four high-end bicycle manufacturers in Detroit, opened its first retail shop downtown. The shop had recently signed a lease on the ground floor of the Albert, one of Detroit's premier new loft conversions, which sits across from Capitol Park, a newly renovated park in an up-and-coming section of the city's until recently barren business district. Outside, the storefront employees passed out stickers with the company's logo and chatted up the few pedestrians passing by— some walking their dogs, others biking or walking to work. In most other cities this would be unremarkable. And today, in Detroit, it's becoming commonplace. But even five years ago, this scene—people walking downtown, shopping, buying hundred-dollar bike saddles— would strike many Detroiters as ridiculous.

Inside the shop, Detroit Bikes founder Zak Pashak served up locally made tamales as potential customers milled about the store and surveyed the company's offerings: two models of bikes, each priced at $700; $100 leather Brooks bike seats; $65 Bern helmets; some high-end messenger bags; other standard bike gear.

"I love downtowns, and this is the middle of a historic city," Pashak told me after we took a seat on a bench in Capitol Park. "You just have to be aware of what you're moving into and be as good a guest as possible."

Not long ago, Capitol Park was crumbling. But in 2009, the city undertook a renovation of the park and sold several city-owned buildings surrounding it to private developers. Since then, at least fifteen development projects, mostly conversions of historic office buildings and run-down apartments into high-end condos, have been completed. Capitol Park is now one of the most expensive addresses in Detroit. You can still see parts of the old neighborhood poking through—homeless people still hang out in the park, a couple of cheap cafés and delis take up a few corners—but for the most part, the neighborhood now caters to the newly arrived aspirational-class youngsters: there are expensive and hip restaurants, ironically dive-y bars with pricey cocktails, even a John Varvatos store where shoes start at about $400. Gentrification in much of Detroit seems to have skipped the beginning phase with the artsy folks, the laid-back coffee shops, and the activists and instead jumped straight from broke dystopian metropolis to yuppified playground.

Max Gordon, twenty-four, whom I found wandering Detroit Bikes, moved from one of the city's wealthier suburbs a few months ago. He's now the property manager of the apartment building that Detroit Bikes rents ground-floor space in, and he is wholeheartedly in favor of the transition the new buildings have helped bring about.

"Down here is the place to be," he told me outside the store. "We're on the cutting edge of everything going on."

The Albert is jointly managed by two of Detroit's biggest development companies, Bedrock and Broder & Sachse. Bedrock, the largest in the city, is owned by Dan Gilbert, the head of Quicken Loans, one of the largest mortgage companies in the United States. And Dan Gilbert is a kind of cheerleader for the new Detroit. In 2010, he moved Quicken's headquarters and its thousands of employees from the suburbs to downtown Detroit. Since then he's been on a skyscraper-buying spree: he now owns at least eighty buildings downtown. He's known for curating the feeling of the streets here, recommending park designs to the city, throwing events to draw in tourists, and picking shops that fit in with his high-end yet independent aesthetic. He personally chose Detroit Bikes as a tenant in the Albert.

Gilbert's mission, he says, is not only to make hundreds of millions of dollars on Detroit's cheap real estate but also to transform Detroit's downtown into a world-class destination for tourists, businesses, and especially young people. As his favorite motto goes: "Do well by doing good." That mission has made him a lightning rod in the city. He's hailed by business leaders, city officials, and the local and national media (one article even called him a superhero). He's also criticized by activists for turning Detroit into somewhat of an oligarchy in which he and a few other powerful people control its redevelopment, especially downtown, which locals now often refer to as "Gilbertville."

Part of Gilbert's strategy has been not only to buy up Detroit but also to rebrand it. His development team has plastered hundreds of posters across the city's downtown with "Opportunity Detroit" in a white faux-graffiti font on a black background. Buses carrying his workers also carry the logo. Some of the Opportunity Detroit posters come with inspirational quotes. "Finding opportunity is a matter of believing it's there," reads one.

Max Gordon, sleekly dressed in a green polo, tight jeans, and a watch made in Detroit by Shinola (another new high-end manufacturer in town; their bikes start at $1,000, their watches at $500), is one of new Detroit's and Gilbert's true believers. He told me that the thousands of young people moving to Detroit's downtown were not simply a trend but a movement.

"To be involved with the young people coming downtown and the Bedrock family of companies is great," he said. "Living here is like college when you were in freshman year. Everybody's looking for friends. I think it's great."

When asked about gentrification, Max dismissed the word as divisive.

"We have to turn everything upside down to turn it right-side up," he said, quoting verbatim from one of the Opportunity Detroit posters that surround Capitol Park. "It's an area that requires a lot of work."

Zak Pashak, while a little more toned down in his rhetoric, nonetheless agreed that Gilbert's critics, and critics of Detroit's redevelopment in general, ought to ease up. After all, development, even if it comes with "suspend[ed] democracy," as Dan Gilbert once put it, is better than no development.

"I think Gilbert is fantastic," Pashak said. "You couldn't ask for a more benevolent billionaire. But a lot of the people are just against change. That's why I don't like the word *gentrification*. Detroit needed change."

Zak said he believed he was part of that change, but I pressed him on the gentrification question. I asked if he ever felt as if two Detroits might be emerging—the new Detroit, in which people can afford $1,200-a-month studio apartments and $700 bicycles, and the other Detroit, where the per capita income is about $15,000 a year.

"We've got to make sure the people here are being lifted up from the rising tide," Pashak said in response.

The reality, though, is that the rest of Detroit is still struggling economically. And for those who lived around Capitol Park before this latest wave of redevelopment, the new Detroit has been anything but a boon.

Broder & Sachse bought the building at 1214 Griswold Street in 2013 and rechristened it the Albert, after one of Detroit's most famous Art Deco architects, Albert Kahn. Before 2013, the building housed about a hundred low-income seniors who were able to afford to live there thanks to Section 8 housing vouchers. All were evicted by Broder & Sachse, given vouchers to move elsewhere, and scattered throughout the rest of the city. Now the building houses mostly white millennials. Apartments at the Albert now start at $1,200 a month. Broder & Sachse received a ten-year tax abatement from the city when they began their conversion.

Across the park sits another luxury rental building. That one, owned by Dan Gilbert's Bedrock, once housed artists. They too were evicted a few years ago. Both evictions caused protest in Detroit. But the evictions, according to Pashak and Gordon, are the price of progress.

"This is the way the market was going," Pashak said. "Everyone here had the best of intentions."

Todd Sachse, vice president of the development company behind the Albert's progress, seemed to hold a similar view: "I would bet you that of the 100 people who moved out of here, 95 of them are happier today," he told the *Detroit Free Press*.

That's not exactly true: every one of the former residents I spoke with from the Albert seemed at best ambivalent about their departure. Sure, 1214 Griswold was falling apart, they told me, but it was convenient—downtown and near everything. Some had planned on living there until their deaths. Now many have been forced to move to Detroit neighborhoods surrounded by nothing but freeways and gas stations.

Jerome Robinson, seventy-two, used to work the assembly line for Ford and Chrysler. He grew up in what is now called Midtown. When a spot opened up in 1214 Griswold in 2007, he was ecstatic— Robinson's eyes are bad, he can't drive anymore, and his pharmacy, bank, library, and pretty much everything else he needed were within walking distance. Five years later he was told to leave. He now lives in a small apartment not too far from where he grew up, but cut off from the rest of the city by a freeway. There's little transit around him, no pharmacy, no bank.

"It bothers me," he told me in his new living room. "We had a riot in '67. And the Caucasians, I mean they ran. And then in the 1970s, we got a black mayor, and they ran some more. And then these guys come in and start buying up stuff and tearing down and rebuilding stuff, and they're coming back.

"People can say whatever they want about these rich people coming in and doing this that and the other, but I was comfortable down there," Robinson continued. "I wanted to stay there. And they kicked me out."

The rent-gap theory—that capital flows to the rate of highest return, and return is highest after a city has been economically drained and primed for gentrification—explains the economic rationale behind the new Detroit. Detroit has been in decline for decades, but its bankruptcy in 2013 put it in position for a rent-gap rebound: not only was the city broke, but it was now run by an emergency manager named Kevyn Orr, who was intent on slashing city services and making the city more palatable for investment. And that explains why people such as Zak Pashak are now courted by powerful players like Dan Gilbert to fill Detroit's core, while people such as Jerome Robinson are ignored (and patronizingly told that they should enjoy what is happening). Detroit did not gentrify because of the whims of people like Pashak. Pashak and his friends are the pawns of a much larger strategy of redevelopment.

- - -

In 2008, Richard Florida, perhaps the most famous urbanist in the United States, came to Detroit to keynote the Creative Cities Summit 2.0. The topic of his talk was "the re-imagining of Detroit." In 2013, Florida came back again, this time to keynote the Detroit Policy Conference, where he was joined by Matt Cullen, the CEO of Dan Gilbert's investment group, Rock Ventures, along with other leaders from around the city to talk about "designing Detroit's brand."

"Already you can see the renewal, revitalization, not from the government, but from the bootstraps, from creative people," Florida said in a five-part video series released before the conference. "Every single person is creative and what's key to rebuilding Detroit is harnessing the creativity of everyone."

And in 2015, Florida was back in the city once more, this time leading Create: Detroit, a conference focused on "building a more creative and inclusive city." That conference was sponsored by, among others, Gilbert's Rock Ventures and the luxury goods company Shinola.

"We don't have to create Detroit," Florida said at that conference. "Detroit is creating itself."

In each speech, and in the video series that preceded his second appearance, Florida focused on the downtown and Midtown core of the city—praising its gritty urban fabric and its historic architecture, highlighting that college-educated graduates seemed to be moving there and that new companies were opening doors there. Left unmentioned by Florida at each of those three conferences was the fact that the city was still shrinking rapidly each year, even as Florida spoke of its rebirth. Detroit, despite its continuous release of creative energies, lost 25 percent of its population between 2000 and 2010. It was still declining in 2015, when its population reached its lowest level since 1850. But Florida did not focus on that part of Detroit's story. He did not mention that most people in the city, especially those not involved in its creative rebirth, still think it's a hard place to live: a full third of Detroiters say they plan on leaving within the next five years. But that's Richard Florida's business: convincing cities that gentrification is their only choice for an economic reboot.

Ever since his landmark book *The Rise of the Creative Class* was published in 2002, Florida, who is also the director of cities at the Martin Prosperity Institute at the University of Toronto and a senior editor at *The Atlantic*, has been urging broke cities to attract the "creative class" in order to revive themselves. And since there's quite literally almost no US city more broke than Detroit, maybe it's no surprise that, as one activist told me, "they love some Richard Florida here."

Florida's 2002 book provided a beacon of hope to cities struggling to rebuild their economies in the wake of a national shift away from industrialized urban centers. Globalization meant factories were closing and relocating, first to nonunion states and then overseas. And it signaled the start of the crumbling of a middle-class aspirational dream of stability and material success. Cities, in their decrepit postindustrial states, became symbols of the end of that dream. Florida provided an antidote.

Florida proposed that cities revitalize themselves by attracting the "creative class," an amorphous category of workers Florida created to describe essentially any profession in which someone relies on a modicum of creativity to do his or her job—doctors, lawyers, artists, movie producers, accountants, hair salon owners, "high end sales" people (a category including cashiers, managers, door-to-door salespeople, real estate brokers, and models), and so on.

According to Florida, this class of people accounted for 24 percent of the American workforce in 1980 and increased to 32.6 percent of the workforce by 2010. Florida takes this as a sign that the creative class is strong, not that, say, there are inevitably more independent entrepreneurs and creative freelancers when there are fewer full-time jobs. (In this same style of historical forgetting, Florida attributes the decline in unions to the decline in the need to push for better working conditions, not the purposeful and directed attack on organized labor during the last half century.)

The solution to the massive loss of manufacturing jobs across the United States, according to Florida, is to turn every worker into a "creative worker." How exactly this would be done remains a mystery that Florida doesn't really elucidate in his book. How does the Starbucks barista serving the creative-class lawyer become a creative barista? How do you turn an entire economy that's built on low-wage labor into a creative economy? How do you account for the fact that the rise in the creative class seems to be coupled with the decline in the middle class?

While Florida acknowledges the limitations of the creative class—it won't solve economic inequality, it won't magically revitalize entire cities—he nonetheless devotes most of his book to laying out a strategy of how to structure entire cities to cater to its preferences, with the idea explicit throughout that if they come, your city will become rich, or at least richer than it is now. Florida's book is essentially a blueprint for gentrification. He tells cities to attract artists and other "bohemians" by catering to the whims of millennials, who, according to Florida, love things like running and living an active lifestyle (but not team sports), art galleries, buying antiques and other unique items, and fun dining experiences (not white-tablecloth restaurants). Millennials, Florida says, are on a never-ending "quest for experience," and it's a city's job to provide a road map for that quest if it expects to take in enough money to govern.

It's not enough for cities to just hope for these things to happen, Florida writes. Cities must plant the seeds of creative growth by investing in the three areas that attract creative people: technology, talent, and tolerance. In other words, cities need to invest in the high-tech sector, in education, and in ensuring that their cities are tolerant of creative people (especially gays and lesbians, who Florida says are often the creative class's canary in the coal mine) if they expect to become bastions of bohemia.

Cities seem to gobble up Florida's ideas not only because they're delivered with the excitement and verve of a Baptist preacher but also because they promise a relatively easy and business-friendly solution for postindustrial American cities. No taxes need to be raised, no new roads need to be built, no new laws have to be passed—just a few tax cuts here, a few incentives there, a sprinkle of advertising and branding, and bam, your city's a boomtown.

That's part of the reason Florida's book has become required reading in many urban planning and economic development departments. The original edition sold 300,000 copies, an unheard-of number for an urban planning book. And while there are no official surveys to back this up, I'd bet that every single head of every economic development team in nearly every midsize city in America is familiar with the book.

Downtown and Midtown Detroit are the crown jewels of Florida-led new-age urban revitalization models. There are new restaurants and galleries and lofts on every block. Average incomes are up. The anchor institutions of the city—Quicken, Rock Ventures, Detroit Institute of the Arts, the Kresge Foundation, the Kellogg Foundation—are all bringing new jobs to the city. If you stand on the corner of Woodward Avenue and Selden Street, it'd be impossible to deny that a lot of new stuff is happening here after years of no growth. Detroit, at least this narrow part of it, is a Florida-inspired success story, and so Detroit, at least this narrow part of it, is the new place urban planners point to as a success. The Congress for New Urbanism held its 2016 conference in Detroit. In addition to the usual hotel-based workshops, attendees could sign up for tours of Detroit's revitalized neighborhoods. The year prior, UNESCO dubbed Detroit a "City of Design," and launched a campaign with local branding firms and business groups to showcase Detroit's "commitment to the creative sector around the globe."

Urban planners and other Florida followers seem to believe Detroit proves that attracting the creative class works. All you have to do is ignore the rest of the city and its (mostly black) residents, who keep slipping further and further off the grid.

To his credit, Florida essentially admits this problem in his book: "One problematic consequence [of the rise of the creative class] is the accelerated sorting of people and cities into an economic hierarchy. Our society is not just becoming more unequal, its inequities are being etched into our economic geography. . . . The new geography of class might be giving rise to a new form of segregation—different from racial segregation or the old schism between central city and suburb, and perhaps even more threatening to national unity."

And Florida has said in a series of articles for *The Atlantic* that some cities, including Detroit, are beyond salvation by the creative class: "We need to be clear that ultimately, we can't stop the decline of some places, and that we would be foolish to try." Detroit was one of the places Florida mentioned.

But believing that hipsters can reverse the consequences of late-stage capitalism is a more attractive thought for city planners in cash-strapped cities than realizing that many American cities are, for now, screwed thanks to postindustrial decline and growing inequality. Gentrification may provide a new tax base, but it also reshapes what cities are, turning them into explicit supporters of inequality, reliant on it to self-fund, yet still unable to meet the needs of their poor. A real solution to the economics of American cities would require more work—more taxes, more laws, more intervention from the federal government. Those things are hard. Gentrification is easy.

So with little money in municipal coffers and little hope for a better future, it seems that politicians and planners (and in the case of Detroit, the corporations and nonprofits that have replaced them) have managed to turn a blind eye to the warnings of the profession's foundational texts. Cities have pursued whole-hog Richard Florida's strategies for wooing millennials without considering the serious limitations of those strategies and the profound effects they may have on everyone else. They ignore that Richard Florida has admitted that the creative class is not a silver bullet, and they forget that Jane Jacobs, the other most famous urbanist in America, talked not only about what makes city blocks cute and community-oriented but also about all the ways in which governments encourage the destruction of places for the middle class. It seems that in their desperation to find something, anything, that will get their cities going again, city leaders have deemphasized all the risks and potentially lackluster results inherent in the gentrification-as-renewal strategy and instead embraced a strategy of "please just come." Like Detroit's former economic development czar said: "Bring on more gentrification. I'm sorry, but I mean, bring it on."

- - -

In the years preceding Detroit's official bankruptcy, a confluence of neoliberal policy doctrine passed down from the leaders of successfully gentrified cities such as New York and prophets like Richard Florida, along with capital from people such as Dan Gilbert who were finally willing to take a risk on Detroit (and take advantage of its rock-bottom real estate prices), set the city up for a radical refocusing.

No longer would Detroit present itself as a poor city in massive need of help. Instead, it would become a boot-strapping, millennial-attracting juggernaut, and anyone not on board would be left behind. That meant redirecting the energy and resources of the city's government from adequately governing an entire city to remaking a relatively small, gentrifiable area. In 2010, the city's mayor, Dave Bing, proposed shrinking the municipal boundaries of Detroit, cutting off the money-losing sections of the city in favor of the downtown core. The proposal drew immediate protest from the people who live in those outer sections (the majority of Detroit's population), but the idea behind it stuck.

Since then, planners, creatives, and the corporations they work hand in hand with have focused nearly all their energy on downtown, Midtown, and a few other select areas, while ignoring the rest of the city, denying it media coverage and equal political representation, allowing its houses to crumble, and starving it of transportation networks. The new Detroit is now a nearly closed loop. It is possible to live in this new Detroit and essentially never set foot in the old one.

When a new (usually white-owned, hipster- or yuppie-oriented) store opens, it's often profiled by Model D Media, a news outlet funded by nonprofits and corporations to cover what's happening in Detroit in a positive light. Big Detroit-centric foundations such as the Knight Foundation or the Kresge Foundation might issue press releases about the new businesses to drum up support. They might give out small grants to help with renovations. Urban Innovation Exchange, which is partially funded by Knight, might help that business connect with the plethora of other nonprofits in the area dedicated to helping "innovative" new businesses thrive—Hatch Detroit, Detroit Creative Corridor Center (DC3), and TechTown, to name a few. The city, through its Detroit Economic Growth Corporation, might get involved—issuing more grants, paying for historical renovation costs, promoting the business on social media. Then bigger media outlets such as *Curbed* or the *Detroit Free Press* might do a little profile on this new business that seems to be making it in a down-and-out neighborhood despite supposedly long odds. Eventually, the *New York Times* might come to town and declare that the business is, for example, "a gleam of renewal in struggling Detroit."

In that article, the *Times* profiled five businesses, all owned by white Detroiters. Detroit is 83 percent black, but the new Detroit—the one that gets all the attention and press—is overwhelmingly white. Research by Wayne State University grad student Alex B. Hill found that 69.2 percent of the grantees of nonprofits, fellows at various nonprofits committed to revitalization, and those chosen to take part in tech and business incubators were white.

Given this echo chamber, maybe it shouldn't be surprising that the young leaders of this new Detroit are somewhat crass defenders of their cause, seemingly impervious to criticism that their newly revitalized city is also an exclusionary one. The new Detroit is unable to account for the fact that while the tide of particular sections of Detroit does indeed seem to be rising, the rest of the city continues to fall to pieces.

"So many people walk in and say, 'Oh, I guess they couldn't find a black entrepreneur,'" said Angela Foster, a white former suburbanite and the owner of a coffee shop called Coffee and (___), located in a predominantly black neighborhood. Coffee and (___) received grants from the city to open. "It's not a black and white thing. It's whatever neighborhood people want to do something in. That's it. That's absolutely it. . . . I don't see how a city this big with so much property and so much opportunity, I don't see how anyone could be left out. . . . I guess I'm not buying into this conspiracy theory. You have to know where to look. Some people aren't social creatures. So maybe those are the people being left out."

One business association made up of young white entrepreneurs even called themselves the Conquistadors. The group busied itself with ensuring that the food pantry run by a church in Corktown, one of the city's newly hip areas, did not detract from its surrounding hipness by providing a safe space for homeless people to stand outside while they awaited food.

"I mean, I wouldn't starve people by any means," Phil Cooley, the owner of Slows Bar B Q, perhaps Detroit's most famous new business, and a member of the group (which no longer calls itself the Conquistadors), told me. "But just continually giving them food, giving them food, giving them food, without having anything surrounding them about how you could get a job or get out of this vicious cycle—it's frustrating."

Despite his somewhat uncaring attitude toward the less fortunate, when the *New York Times* profiled Slows in 2010, the paper opened with this line: "How much good can a restaurant do?"

Cooley has embraced his role as a kind of poster child for the new Detroit. Quotes from him have been included in seemingly every story about the city's revival, from the *New York Times* profiles to Model D Media's feature on how Slows helped transform the neighborhood of Corktown and the *Crain's* profile of him done as part of the newspaper's "20 Detroit Power Brokers in Their 20s" series.

"I guess I chose to live here because I'm young and dumb," Phil told me from the second-floor offices of Ponyride, the co-working and artist studio space he started in Corktown. Ponyride has received funding from the city and various nonprofits, and attention from Martha Stewart and American Express. "I wanted to feel like I was doing something. And Detroit felt like a place where I could

have a voice. Detroit is a democratic city. . . . We never wanted Detroit to be an island."

But the new Detroit is in many ways being built as if it were an
island, or perhaps more accurately a city-state within the city, in no
way related to or governed by what exists outside it. Soon you'll be
able to travel within its gentrified core by foot, bike, and light rail
without ever leaving. It is quite literally becoming a closed loop.

The Detroit Riverfront Conservancy, a nonprofit funded by
some of the city's biggest corporations, including General Motors,
has built a path along the city's riverfront that connects the downtown to its east and west. From its east side along the river, you can
take the Dequindre Cut, a former railway turned bike and pedes-
trian path, to Eastern Market, a 150-year-old farmers market that
recently was upgraded with more artisanal offerings. If you're trying
to get from downtown to Midtown (the other hip section of Detroit,
which was called Cass Corridor until recently, when real estate interests rebranded it), you can walk, bike, or now take the brand-new
M-1 Rail, a 3.2-mile-long trolley that was marketed as public transit
but funded mostly with private dollars from the likes of GM, Dan
Gilbert's Rock Ventures, and a slew of nonprofits.

Anti-gentrification activists are quick to point out that more and
better transit options aren't in and of themselves bad for a city sorely
lacking them. Transportation advocates have for years been trying
to get Detroit to take public transit seriously. But when you consider
that Detroit is 142 square miles—bigger than Boston, San Francisco,
and Manhattan combined—and that all its new transit is located
within the 7.2 square miles that make up the city's gentrifying core,
the question must be asked: who exactly is this transportation for?

The M-1 Rail is perhaps the best example of Detroit's gentry-
focused new infrastructure. It was originally envisioned as a real
public transit system that would connect Detroit's northern suburbs,
where many commute from, to its downtown, where many work.
Now, however, the M-1 will be about a fifth its original length and
will only connect the business-heavy downtown with the residential, art, and education district of Midtown. Speculators have already begun snapping up real estate to turn into high-end apartment

buildings along its route. The M-1, its supporters freely admit, is no longer public transit, but a real estate development tool.

"It's a circulator to get people in Midtown and people in downtown circulating in a bigger marketplace," Sue Mosey, the head of Midtown Detroit Inc., the city's most powerful neighborhood economic development organization, told me in her glass-walled offices one afternoon. "It isn't the responsibility of M-1 to do the public sector job to get transit for the region or the rest of the city. That isn't M-1's job. That's the city's job. That's the regional government's job, the federal government's job, the state's job. Our jobs are not to solve everybody else's problems in the city."

M-1 is also a good example of the modus operandi of Detroit's development these days—touted as good for the public, planned by a confluence of powerful nonprofits that have little accountability to Detroiters, and funded by, and largely for the benefit of, the city's most powerful companies.

But the flowery rhetoric employed by Detroit's redevelopers often masks that fact. In the parlance of new Detroit, Zak Pashak isn't just creating expensive bikes, he's making sure people here are being lifted up by the rising tide of bicycle manufacturing. Phil Cooley isn't just a profiteer, he's participating in the burgeoning democracy of Detroit. Dan Gilbert's favorite business phrase—"Do well by doing good"—seems to be the official slogan of the new Detroit, embraced by hundreds of young white entrepreneurs who believe they're not only making money but helping rescue an entire city. That's why speaking with Midtown Inc.'s Sue Mosey was refreshing. She can talk about the profit motive of the new Detroit without resorting to euphemisms for trickle-down economics.

The biggest problem, Mosey told me, is that there is practically no city government left in Detroit. Midtown Inc., which has no accountability to anyone except those who fund it (developers and nonprofits such as the Kresge Foundation), has become the de facto department of planning for its section of the city. The real city government, which went through bankruptcy in 2013—the largest bankruptcy in municipal history—does not have enough money, expertise, or manpower to plan its own streetscape.

"We're rezoning everything right now," Mosey said. "We pay for all the planning, all the specialists, we hold all the meetings. Then we work with the city to meet all their requirements."

Mosey admits that leaving basic city services such as transportation and planning up to people like her privileges the sections of the city that can afford to get those things done. Midtown, thanks to its proximity to downtown, is a profit-producing locale—major companies and many of Detroit's big foundations are located there. That provides Mosey and Midtown Inc. with a budget of about $10 million a year to govern their own little micro-city. Midtown Inc. can hire planners. Nearly every other neighborhood in Detroit cannot.

"I do agree that a broken public system does not help challenged neighborhoods, and that needs to be fixed," Mosey told me. "It's not right. And it shouldn't be like that. But that's not my fault. I'm doing my job. I'm paid to do my job, and my organization does it, and we do it well."

Hardly anyone is saying there's anything wrong with new restaurants and new stores, new buildings and better security. Most Detroit residents I interviewed were not begrudging toward the newly arrived white hipsters from the suburbs and the coasts. After all, those who came had reasonable reasons: cheap housing, the ability to start a new business, new jobs. And most native and longtime Detroiters have complex and conflicted views about downtown's redevelopment—some even praise Gilbert for stepping in and investing in the core of the city when no one else would.

It's not the investments and new people themselves that are necessarily harmful; it's the attention, in press and money, that's paid to those investments and people. While Dan Gilbert is lavished with praise by the city government and newspapers, and while he and others receive hundreds of millions of dollars in tax breaks and other incentives, a new rail line, and bike lanes, the rest of Detroit has learned to live without streetlights and regular trash collection, without a consistent or helpful police presence, with hundreds of thousands of foreclosures on bad mortgages (some made by Gilbert's Quicken Loans), with the persistent threat of water shutoffs from a broke water utility, with blight and bad schools and high poverty.

Sure, it's great that Detroit is to some extent being revitalized, but Detroit has been in need of revitalization for decades. Its population has been shrinking since the 1950s. Black people in the city have been working that entire time to try to keep Detroit from falling apart. Why, some have asked, is it that the country seems to pay attention only when the white people show up?

- - -

On a side street downtown, surrounded by dozens of Gilbert-owned buildings, sits Café D'Mongo's Speakeasy, a thirty-year-old bar that looks much older than that. The spot had been a gathering place for Detroit's black elite—it wasn't uncommon to see council members and mayors at D'Mongo's back in the day. But in 1993, Larry Mongo, its owner, shut it down. The area had become too run-down, the crime too high to justify staying open.

"The white people left," Mongo told me, sitting on one of the diner-style stools at his bar. "Then it got so bad the homeless left, then it got so bad the pigeons left. Then it was only me."

The place remained locked up for fifteen years, until 2008, when a drunk driver smashed his car through the front glass of the bar. Mongo was out of the city, and by the time he showed up, a group of white kids—new gentrifiers in the city's downtown—had gathered to protect the café from potential vandals and thieves. Mongo saw these new kids, who were apparently willing to live in Detroit's bombed-out downtown, and decided to reopen his bar. It's been open since then, and it's nearly always packed.

On a recent Saturday, Mongo, who is black, held a special event for the people who'd convinced him to reopen. That night, a jazz band played in one cramped corner as a standing-room-only crowd, almost all of whom were white and dressed in the kind of clothing sold by Detroit's hippest new retail shops, chatted and sipped classic cocktails. Mongo sat at a table outside. He told me he was calling the celebration "Pollinator Night." To Mongo, the term *pollinator* describes what gentrification has become in Detroit: the white kids move into a neighborhood, and investment and attention follow.

Mongo said all the kids from Quicken, Rock Ventures, and the rest of the companies moving downtown are great for D'Mongo's Speakeasy, but he can't help but think it's troubling that the city seems on its way back up only now that they've arrived.

"The city doesn't really see black life as life," he told me. "When the pollinators come, that's when the civilization comes. . . . It makes me angry, but you know something? That's the way it is."

5

The 7.2

Detroit's gentrification isn't so much about the displacement of one group by another, as it is in New York or San Francisco. In the 1950s, the city was home to nearly 2 million people. Today, fewer than 700,000 people live here. There's plenty of room for the city to grow, plenty of abandoned structures and vacant land that can be reinhabited.

Instead, gentrification here operates in two separate, concurrent processes: the rich, mostly white newcomers to the city and their allies in business get accolades from the press, the government's attention, and the financial backing of Detroit's nonprofit sector, while the rest of the city—the remaining 134.8 square miles outside the 7.2—slowly falls off the map, bled out by foreclosures, blight, and a lack of city services. For those who stay but cannot afford to be within the 7.2, the city is literally going to seed around them.

Cheryl West is one of the ones outside the 7.2. When I met West, she was standing in her front yard, surrounded by sixty cardboard boxes containing her life. A few volunteers from Detroit Eviction Defense—the city's preeminent anti-eviction group—guarded her boxes and helped tape them up. Two gave an interview to a documentary filmmaker from Ecuador. Other men who were being paid a low hourly rate by Wayne County—the county that encompasses Detroit—lugged everything else from West's former house and tossed it into a dumpster parked curbside. A sheriff's deputy let

West take one last look inside her house and give me a quick tour. She showed me the pink-carpeted living room; the kitchen, which had already been partially gutted by the house's new owners; the spot where her father's piano used to sit. West, sixty-eight, had lived here for sixty years. She'd seen her neighborhood go from majority white to black, through riot and police violence, through relative wealth and struggle. She'd seen it become what it is now—beautiful but severely decayed, its large four- and five-bedroom homes either boarded up or already gutted by people seeking scrap metal to sell, the storefronts on its main avenues shuttered, their windows broken, their roofs collapsed. We exited the house, and the deputy told the dozen or so neighbors, activists, and passersby assembled on West's lawn that from that moment on, only those employed by Wayne County could enter.

Cheryl West's family was in many ways an exception to the rules that governed Detroit and much of the United States at the time. When West's family moved in, every house in the neighborhood, along with many other neighborhoods in the city, had deed restrictions barring African Americans from buying them. However, despite those restrictions, West's parents were able to buy the house from a Jewish couple looking to leave the city. They were the first black homeowners on the block. Her father was also the first African American music teacher in the Detroit Public Schools, and her sister was one of the only African American journalists to cover Detroit's 1967 uprising for a national publication.

"We witnessed that riot and lived through it," she told me from her lawn. "And I feel like there's another one coming."

West lost her house in the same way tens of thousands of Detroiters have lost their homes in the last few years: she couldn't afford its astronomically high taxes. As more and more residents leave Detroit, the burden of paying for the city's services falls on fewer and fewer households. Most residents of Detroit are poor, but they are nonetheless expected to fund roads, water lines, and everything else in the city through their property taxes, which can be thousands of dollars a year on houses that currently aren't worth much more than $10,000 on the market.

For years, the city and the county encompassing it had allowed West's taxes, along with the taxes of tens of thousands of others, to build up without taking action. When what she owed was too much to even qualify for a payment plan, they seized the house. West told me she'd tried to gain admission to a tax program started by the state of Michigan for those struggling to stay in their homes, but because of a technicality (she didn't live in the house for about a year while she helped take care of one of her last living family members in California) she was denied four times. In fact, one-half of all people who attempted to enter that program were denied. So Cheryl's house was sold at tax auction by Wayne County for $20,000 in 2015 to a young African American woman who owns several in the neighborhood. Cheryl is currently staying on the top floor of a friend's house up the block. Her things are in storage. And now another house sits empty, though only temporarily, on a block that already has plenty of gutted houses in a neighborhood with more empty lots than full ones.

Meanwhile, the 7.2 is booming, at least compared to the rest of Detroit. Detroit has 53,000 vacant homes, but within the 7.2 square miles that make up downtown (Gilbertville), Midtown (where Sue Mosey works), Corktown (where Phil Cooley owns property), and three other centrally located neighborhoods, more than 90 percent of homes are occupied. Detroit lost 25 percent of its population between 2000 and 2010, but the 7.2's loss was only half that. Its boosters say the area is also getting more diverse. In reality, it lost 5 percent of its black population in those years and gained 3 percent more white people. While everywhere else in Detroit the housing stock continued to disintegrate, the 7.2 added 1,300 new units of housing, a 5 percent increase. Between 2010 and 2012 there were sixty-five new building projects completed within the 7.2, and another sixty-five are under construction or in the planning phases. If you look only at the 7.2, it seems as though Detroit is doing pretty well. It looks like the wooing of the creative class is really paying off.

But incentives and investments large and small predestined this area of Detroit to come back while the rest of the city falls off the map. As early as the 1990s, business leaders and the heads of foundations encouraged the city to focus its investments solely within the 7.2, which is both more densely populated and has a denser stock of buildings than most of the rest of the city, and closer to the skyscrapers where the city's elite work. That investment has picked up steam in recent years, with Dan Gilbert buying at least eighty buildings downtown. When he moved Quicken to Detroit's downtown, the state gave Gilbert a $50 million tax break, the largest incentive in the state that year. Then, when Gilbert bought an iconic Art Deco building downtown in March 2015, Detroit's mayor, Mike Duggan, cooed, "I'm excited that somebody successful is acquiring all these properties. . . . I couldn't be more pleased with what Dan has done and his contributions to the community."

Gilbert's investment hasn't ended with buildings—he's built an entire security force that patrols downtown and monitors more than 500 security cameras attached to buildings Rock Ventures owns. From a command center in a Rock-owned building, Gilbert's force watches nearly every corner of Detroit's downtown. His agents coordinate closely with Detroit's police. Gilbert's security, along with a police force privately funded by Wayne State University in Midtown, have become a kind of shadow police agency, ensuring that low-level offenses in Detroit's gentrified core remain at a minimum. Wayne State, Detroit's main university, has taken security one step further by certifying its sixty officers with the state so that they can perform the same functions as real police. Now 60 percent of calls within Midtown are answered by Wayne State's patrol. The average response time in Midtown is ninety seconds. In the rest of Detroit, it can be up to an hour, even for deadly crimes.

Gilbert has also chipped in for other projects that would usually be funded by cities—the M-1's $179.4 million cost will be paid mostly by corporations and nonprofits, including Quicken. The biggest funder was the Kresge Foundation (mission statement: "Creating opportunity for low-income people"), which contributed more than a quarter of the total. Gilbert has also funded the revitalization of parks and plazas downtown.

And there are other, less visible ways Gilbert has spread his vision of a bustling, millennial-filled core city. Employees of Compuware (owned by Quicken), Quicken Loans, DTE Energy (Detroit's main energy company), and a few other companies can get $20,000 of forgivable loans to purchase a home or apartment within the downtown area, or $3,500 in rental subsidies. Midtown Detroit Inc. has a similar program that has raised $10 million from employers in the area to incentivize 2,000 people to live in Midtown, according to Sue Mosey. Occupancy in Midtown is now at 98 percent.

The people who are benefiting from all these subsidies—the gentrifiers of the 7.2—do not seem to realize the work that has gone into bringing and keeping them there. They consider themselves cunning pioneers who've figured out how to make the economics of a rough city work, ignoring the fact that hundreds of millions of dollars that could be used to keep people like Cheryl West in their homes are propping up their lifestyles of conspicuous consumption. And they do not seem to realize that they are benefiting directly from the past oppression of those whom they hope to lift with their rising tide.

Detroit was made cheap and therefore attractive to gentrify because, beginning in the 1930s, its black residents were systematically denied jobs in the booming auto industry and, later, mortgages in the suburbs as the housing industry took off. Detroit's black residents were hired last and fired first when the auto industry collapsed; they were foreclosed upon and denied basic city services. The racism of Detroit's geography means that the city's population decline has been incredibly uneven: between 2000 and 2010, the white population of the city decreased by 35 percent, while the black population decreased by 24 percent. Detroit's rebirth has been built on the backs of people who were too poor to leave. And the 7.2 can exist only as a heavily subsidized state, perpetuating the historical constriction of subsidy and wealth to the rest of Detroit.

Of course, private companies and foundations can do what they wish with their money. As Sue Mosey told me, they're not required to do the public sector's job of ensuring that the poorest of Detroit's citizens have good parks, fair policing, transit, jobs, and housing. And activists here aren't even suggesting that they do that job. The problem in Detroit isn't necessarily the money being poured into

Midtown and downtown but the fact that it's happening in a vac-
uum. The private and nonprofit sectors have virtually replaced the
public sector in the city's most gentrified areas. And with the ab-
sence of a public good, there's no guarantee that Midtown, downtown, or any of Detroit's other gentrifying tracts will be amenable to
anyone but those who make Quicken Loans–level salaries.

If the early stages of gentrification in the city are any clue,
that's exactly what's happening. John Varvatos shoes, bars with $15
cocktails and coffee shops with $4 coffee, Shinola watches, Detroit
Bikes—these are meant for people with large disposable incomes.
And while there's no sign on these businesses' doors specifically pro-
hibiting the old, largely African American Detroit from entering,
their gentrified aesthetic and high prices may have the same effect.

"Nobody wants to inject race into the marvelous story of downtown's rebound, driven largely by young creatives who grew up in the
suburbs and are now fiercely Detroiters. I don't either. It's a downer,"
Detroit News columnist Nolan Finley wrote in 2014. "[But] it's a clear
red flag when you can sit in a hot new downtown restaurant and
nine out of 10 tables are filled with white diners, a proportion almost
exactly opposite of the city's racial make-up."

As Tonya Phillips, a black Detroiter and the executive director
of Southwest Detroit Community Justice Center, put it to me, the
new Detroit is nice; it's just not built for her.

- - -

While nonprofits and corporations are the main funders of Detroit's
new economic segregation, the government at all levels has placed
its thumb on the 7.2's side of the scale. Just weeks after Detroit filed
for bankruptcy—a process that would see city workers' pensions cut
and a variety of city services reduced—Dan Gilbert traveled to the
White House and convinced President Barack Obama to spend $300
million on Detroit, including $35 million for the M-1, and $150 million on blight removal, knocking down unoccupied houses throughout the city. It's unclear exactly how that $150 million was and will
be spent, but a good chunk will go toward demolishing homes that

Gilbert's Quicken Loans were partially responsible for making blighted in the first place. Quicken has for years insisted it did not engage in the same practices that led millions of Americans into foreclosure after the 2008 financial crisis. But an investigation by the *Detroit News* found that Quicken had the fifth-highest number of mortgages ending in foreclosures in the city. Half of those foreclosed properties are now blighted.

Maybe the most egregious example of government funding going toward the 7.2 was the 2013 deal made by the Detroit City Council to pay for 60 percent of a new hockey arena for Red Wings owner Mike Ilitch. Ilitch, a Detroit billionaire pizza magnate (he owns Little Caesars), already has an arena: Joe Louis Arena, located on Detroit's waterfront. The new facility will come with housing, office space, and upscale retail, all located on Midtown's most gentrified strip. The project will cost the city of Detroit $261.5 million. Ilitch will get to keep all of the revenues from the arena. The money the city spends on the deal would have otherwise gone to fund Michigan public schools. The state says it will make up the difference, so Detroit students won't be affected. It's unclear exactly where the state will get the money from instead.

While the Red Wings arena deal is a particularly large example of government waste in Detroit, it's not unique. The city also awarded Marathon Petroleum $175 million in tax breaks to expand its oil refinery in the city. In return, the city got fifteen new jobs. And in 2012, the mayor's office sold 140 acres of public land in the center of the city to another Detroit multimillionaire, financial services executive John Hantz, for $520,000. Hantz had promised to develop the land into a tree farm, though many in the city believe his urban agriculture idea was a ploy to get cheap land in the center of Detroit that can eventually be converted into profitable housing.

Outlandish subsidies for multimillionaires isn't a phenomenon seen only in Detroit. Michigan gives away 30 cents of every government dollar to private companies. And in other cities, stadiums and ballparks are routinely paid for by governments, all with the hope that they'll help stimulate revitalization, even though economists nearly unanimously agree that spending public funds on private stadiums is one of the least efficient ways for governments to spend money. But the strategy is perhaps particularly troubling in a city where garbage collection, street repair, and streetlights are considered privileges.

"Our history is this scattergun approach," said Eric Larson, one of Detroit's biggest developers and the CEO of the Downtown Detroit Partnership, which helps coordinate investments in the city's core and which was involved in the Red Wings arena deal. "That doesn't work. Finally we're starting to focus and concentrate investment. . . . Whether we like it or not, if we don't have the large entities that are taxed the way they're taxed, the city doesn't have anything to operate on."

Mark Wallace, another longtime developer and the head of the Detroit Riverfront Conservancy, put it another way: "As we make Detroit better for one person, we make it better for everybody."

Yet when community activists have tried to ensure that this trickle-down development strategy does indeed result in trickle-down benefits, developers have fought them tooth and nail. For years city activists have sought to pass an ordinance that would require the developers of Detroit's biggest projects (including the Red Wings arena), as well as developers of projects seeking $300,000 or more in public funds (also including the Red Wings arena), to enter into contracts with the public that would provide guarantees of local jobs and other quality-of-life measures. The entire development community lined up against it. A bill introduced in the state's legislature would ban community-benefits ordinances altogether in the state of Michigan, even though Detroit is the only city in the state considering one.

I asked every developer and pro–new Detroit figure I spoke with what they'd say to all those who feel like they've been left out of the recovery—those who see hundreds of millions of dollars in public funds, and billions in private funds, go toward just about 3 percent of the city's landmass while they get left out. And all said something similar: eventually everyone else will be helped too.

"Nothing happens overnight," Sean Jackson, a Rock Ventures employee who is close with Dan Gilbert, told me one night. "I would say wait and hope."

- - -

Detroit did not need a hurricane to rid itself of the poor. There may not have been a natural disaster or a military occupation in the Detroit outside of the 7.2, but I've nonetheless heard it compared to apartheid South Africa and called "a Katrina without water." While the 7.2 gets hundreds of millions of dollars, the rest of Detroit, the unprofitable Detroit, is being bled out.

These phrases might sound like rhetoric, but the numbers involved in Detroit's destruction lend themselves to dramatic terminology. Beyond the newly built-up downtown and Midtown, Detroit is in crisis. Detroit's median income is about $25,000, roughly half that of the United States as a whole. It has a poverty rate three times higher than the rest of the country.

Its unemployment rate is nearly 25 percent, double or triple the rate of most other big cities. And because Detroit charges some of the highest household water rates in the country (about $70 a month on average, compared to the national average of $40), nearly a quarter of the population is behind on their water bill. In 2014, the city began shutting off water to those residents, leaving thousands without access to fresh water. Experts from the United Nations called the move a violation of human rights.

Detroit, like everywhere else in America, was also hit by the subprime mortgage crisis in the 2000s, only much, much harder. Sixty-eight percent of all mortgages to Detroiters in 2005 were subprime, compared with 24 percent nationwide. Gilbert's Quicken Loans made some of those loans; others were made by the same banks that demanded Detroit pay them back by slashing city employee pensions during the city's bankruptcy. Now more than half of those homes are abandoned and blighted, nearly all of them in the outer parts of the city. The county has also been directly involved in the mass exodus: while it's easy to snap up a house for $5,000 or $10,000 in many Detroit neighborhoods, houses are often assessed as if Detroit is still a hot, or at least non-apocalyptic, real estate market. It's not unheard of for residents to be paying $3,000 or $4,000 a year on a house with a market value of just twice that.

Many here felt they shouldn't have to pay those outrageous property taxes, considering that most Detroit neighborhoods didn't have the normal amenities taxes buy—for example, streetlights and regular garbage pickup—until recently. That apathy and the high tax rates, combined with the city's down-and-out economy (Detroit's per capita income is less than $15,000), made a tax foreclosure crisis inevitable. Yet Wayne County sat on those back taxes for years, allowing them to pile up until they became unpayable for many. It was only in 2015 that the county began cracking down, when many families' tax bills had reached more than $10,000. The county seized and sold 30,000 homes at auction that year. At least 10,000 of the homes were occupied. The years ahead promise to be equally punishing.

"We deferred, and waiting clearly made it more difficult," Wayne County deputy treasurer Dave Szymanski told me at a county-sponsored event for tax relief. "Is that fair? It's the reality of the situation. There were just too many properties."

It's hard to comprehend the scale of what's happening to Detroit's outer neighborhoods. The city is sprawling enough that you might not notice a couple of houses becoming abandoned, a block in one corner of the city going to seed. But there are a few places where the misery is concentrated enough that you can comprehend its strength. The Cobo Center on a January day in 2015 was one of them.

The Cobo Center is the city-funded convention center on Detroit's waterfront. It's already one of the largest convention centers in the country, but Detroit is currently overseeing a taxpayer-funded $300 million expansion of the place. It hosts the usual expos and gatherings, as well as the Detroit Auto Show each year. But in 2015, over the course of one week in January, it held no fewer than 10,000 Detroiters who'd shown up in a last-ditch effort to save their homes. Most were there to enter into tax payment plans with the county; others had come to seek help from a slew of nonprofits providing guidance (though no financial help) for how to deal with landlords, the county, and banks.

The convention center's name was sadly apt for the devastation its temporary inhabitants represented. Cobo is named for Albert Cobo, mayor of Detroit from 1950 through 1957 and a notorious

racist in both rhetoric and policy. Cobo ran on a campaign oppos-
ing "Negro invasions." Many have blamed Detroit's decline on white
flight, but few have pinpointed the people responsible for it, including Albert Cobo, who did everything in his power to encourage it.
Cobo forced the concentration of public housing in the center of the
city, refused to build integrated public housing, and supported the
construction of highways out to the suburbs. Cobo was a one-man
concentrator of urban African American poverty and disperser of
white wealth.

Inside the center named after him that January, the culmination of decades of bad and racist housing policy could be seen on
the faces of thousands of Detroit residents who waited patiently in
folding chairs in one of the convention center's immense halls. Each
took a number from a red ticket machine as if they were approaching a deli counter. One by one, they were called up to sit at a plastic
folding table with representatives from Wayne County's Treasurer's
Office and work out a payment plan. Nearly every person in the hall
was African American.

"Everybody's black," one activist remarked to me as she helped
foreclosure victims find their way around the building. "Who is the
criminal mastermind who put this together? This doesn't just happen. Something at this scale doesn't just happen."

To be sure, there were positive stories that came out of Cobo.
Gabriel McNeil, a fifty-two-year-old chef, worked out a plan with
Wayne County to lower his back taxes from $10,000 to $6,000. He
had to pay $653 upfront, and will now make monthly payments of
$66 a month, down from $250.

"I could pick up soda cans and pay that," McNeil said. "I'm real
comfortable."

But the overall mood at Cobo was one of desperation. There was
Krystal Malone, a forty-four-year-old part-time substitute teacher.
She bought a house for $10,000 last year without realizing its taxes
would come out to about $5,000, and so she fell into $9,000 of debt.

"Why was the property valued so high?" she asked. "Across the
street is all abandoned properties. Five thousand dollars a year on a
$10,000 house. What sense does that make?"

There was Lula Smith, who had lived in Detroit since 1956, and who began falling behind on her taxes after her husband died and she was diagnosed with thyroid cancer in 2011. She was at Cobo as a last-ditch effort after having attempted to enter into a payment plan several times over the last few years. At Cobo, the county offered to lower her payments to $300 a month.

"At least it shows they care," she said. "I think they're really trying to help. I'll believe them until they prove me wrong."

For many Detroiters, the county's assistance was too little too late. Detroit lost 237,000 people between 2000 and 2010. It'd be easy to blame that on the region's economy, but most of those people moved right across Detroit's borders into suburbs with less blight, lower taxes, better roads, better lights, and a better police force. Macomb County, right next door to Wayne, saw its black population triple between 2000 and 2010. Those left in Detroit's outer neighborhoods are people who either can't afford to live anywhere else or are fighting for their right to stay.

Disa Bryant, forty-eight, fits into both of those categories. She inherited a house from her aunt in 2004 in the desirable Russell Woods section of the city. At the time, she worked for the state of Michigan in its medical records department. But the financial crash of 2008 forced Michigan to cut its budget, and Bryant was let go. After she fell behind on payments for a few years, in 2014 the county put her house on the auction block. Bryant offered $5,000 to buy it back, but an investor outbid her at $8,000. That investor is now attempting to evict Disa if she can't pay $1,000 a month in rent.

"They sell you off to the highest bidder and that just sucks," she said. "The house has been in my family for forty years. Why can't they buy a vacant home instead of putting someone out on the street?"

There's a perverse answer to Bryant's question, an activist from Detroit Eviction Defense explained to me one day: Detroit may have tens of thousands of vacant homes, but the ones that have been lived in have usually been maintained lovingly by the people living in them. The roof repairs, flooring, lighting, and yard upkeep have already been paid for by the existing tenants. Kicking people out is a better investment. And there's no way to know exactly to whom properties such as Bryant's are going. Some undoubtedly are sold to individuals, but most, it seems, are sold to small limited-liability companies, or LLCs. One eviction expert named Joe McGuire told me that over the past couple of years, countless small investment groups have descended on Detroit, snapping up properties by the dozen. Their business mailing addresses will often be the home of someone in a far-flung locale with an Internet connection and the expertise to sort through Detroit's eviction listings.

"It was actually easier dealing with the big banks," McGuire told me. "There's a certain kind of rationality at play with them. They just care about money. But now it's just small-time crazy people. When you're dealing with them, you're even further away from effecting real change. And if you win, you win against some guy who owns seven houses, not Bank of America."

That's the situation Kenny Brinkley and Sandi Combs are in. Brinkley, a well-known Motown saxophone player, couldn't find work after heart surgery in 2002. By 2010, the house he and Combs owned had gone to tax foreclosure. The company that bought the home, Detroit Property Exchange (which advertises its phone number as 1-888-FLIP-DETROIT), said the couple could pay rent toward repurchasing their home. But after four years, the couple found out that their payments hadn't gone toward anything, including property taxes. The property was sold again at tax auction, and this time it was picked up by a California company called Sussex Immobilier. Since purchasing the property, Sussex has been attempting to evict the elderly couple. Detroit Eviction Defense has so far managed to keep them in their home by delaying court dates and finding problems with Sussex's eviction paperwork.

When I visited Brinkley and Combs in their modest home, Brinkley told me he couldn't talk too much about the pending eviction out of fear it would cause his heart problems to flare up. So I sat on their plush, faded couch at the front of their living area and spoke with Combs.

The house is well lived-in. Knickknacks—photos, plants, memorabilia from Brinkley's sax-playing days—took up nearly every surface. Just hiring movers for all this stuff would be an expense Brinkley and Combs could not afford.

"It could be any day now," Combs told me. "They could come with a dumpster and throw everything into the trash."

As I spoke with Combs, Brinkley seemed to be keeping his mind occupied by pacing the house, scrubbing the kitchen, and watering their dozens of plants. But after a while, despite his earlier statement that he would not talk, he cautiously approached the couch where Combs and I were sitting.

"I'm trying to stay busy to keep it off my mind," he said. "But I just have to face it. It's there."

This is the state of the outer sections of Detroit: threats of evictions, water shutoffs, crushing poverty, reduced government services. Study after study document the stress and depression that come with being poor. You can feel that acutely here. People are on edge, afraid, upset, and resigned—and this is in not just one neighborhood but the entire city, minus the 7.2 square miles at its core. People here feel abandoned, pushed to their limits, and unsure of what to do.

Several months after I left Detroit, I heard that Sandi Combs and Kenny Brinkley had been forced to leave their house after a new set of owners came with chainsaws to cut down the massive trees the couple had planted in the front yard forty years earlier. That same day, Brinkley had a heart attack. A few days later, a nonprofit announced that it had purchased a new home for the couple farther out in Detroit, and held a little celebration in a carpeted conference room downtown. The local media reported it as a happy ending.

6

How the Slate Got Blank

At the back of Alfonso Wells Memorial Playground, a small neighborhood park in northwest Detroit, sits a concrete wall covered in colorful murals. Today the wall seems somewhat randomly placed—it's not separating much of anything except some grass from a street. But it's there for a reason: in the late 1930s a developer tried to secure a mortgage, backed with mortgage insurance from the federal government, to build a housing development in the then largely white neighborhood. The Federal Housing Administration determined that the proposed houses would sit too close to those of an "inharmonious" racial group to qualify for mortgage insurance. In order to meet federal requirements, the developer built the wall—six feet tall, a foot thick, and a half mile long—to separate a black neighborhood from a white one. The federal government approved the project a few weeks later.

How do you solve a problem as old as the United States? Gentrification may be a relatively recent phenomenon, but as geographer Neil Smith notes, it's really just the continuation of the "locational seesaw"—capital moves to one place seeking high profits, then, when that place becomes less profitable, it moves to another place. The real estate industry is always looking for new markets in which it can revitalize its profit rate. Fifty years ago that place was suburbs. Today it's cities. But that's only half the explanation for gentrification. In order to understand why cities are so attractive to invest in, it's important to understand what made them bargains for real estate speculators in the first place. It may sound obvious, but gentrification could not happen without something to gentrify. Truly equitable geographies would be largely un-gentrifiable ones. So first, geographies have to be made unequal.

One 2014 study from the University of Chicago Booth School of Business found that poorer neighborhoods near already gentrified areas gentrified much faster than adjacent middle-class areas. As Smith's rent gap theory suggests, this makes economic sense: gentrification is more profitable if the area being gentrified is initially cheaper. So the question is, how did those areas become cheaper?

The United States has a long history of dispossessing the poor of adequate housing through explicitly racist planning and housing policy. If gentrification requires cheap real estate, before areas can be gentrified they must be divested from, and the history of American housing is largely the history of a purposive concentration of African Americans and a subsequent disinvestment in their lives.

Few would argue that American housing is equitably distributed. It's obvious to anyone who drives around an American city that there are areas of wealth and areas of poverty, that train tracks and highways often separate Hispanic neighborhoods from white ones, black ones from Asian ones. Most know without much thinking that "the projects" are in the "bad neighborhoods," that big houses filled with wealthy people tend to be located not in city centers but on their outskirts. Because these features are universal to every city in the United States, we've internalized this geographic inequality as natural and normal. But a closer look reveals that larger, top-down forces are at play in the distribution of people and wealth in American cities.

Cities may appear chaotic, but the location, design, and makeup of their neighborhoods are the result of careful planning. In their book *American Apartheid*, sociologists Douglas Massey and Nancy Denton provide clear evidence that American cities maintained or expanded housing segregation even as people of color gained civil rights and wealth and moved into northern cities in greater numbers from rural areas in the South.

Massey and Denton measure the racial dissimilarity of US cities' neighborhoods through an "index of dissimilarity," calculating the percentage of black Americans who would have to move within a given city for every neighborhood to accurately mirror the overall demographics of the entire city. The higher the percentage, the more segregated a city is. The researchers found that before the 1900s, American cities were relatively integrated. In 1860 in the biggest cities outside the South—Boston, New York, Philadelphia, San Francisco, and a couple of others—the average dissimilarity index was 45.7, meaning about 46 percent of African Americans would have to move into different neighborhoods in order for each city to be well integrated. The biggest southern cities were actually more integrated in 1860—their average index was 29. But by 1910, northern cities had an average dissimilarity index of nearly 60, and southern cities had one of nearly 40. Cities were becoming more segregated. By 1940, dissimilarity in southern cities had reached 81; in northern cities it had reached 89.2. In other words, by 1940, 89.2 percent of black people in northern cities would have had to move in order to achieve a truly integrated city. By 1970, the dissimilarity index in the United States as a whole had reached an all-time high at 79 percent. It's worth pointing out the increase in segregation in the North came as black Americans were moving by the millions from the South to find industrial jobs in northern cities. In other words, the more black people who came to a city, the more segregated it became.

In the last fifty years, segregation's gotten better, but not by much: by 2010 the index had dropped just below 60, still nowhere near true integration. In Detroit, the index still stands at nearly 80, making Detroit the most segregated city in America. Massey and Denton conclude there's only one possible explanation for why, even as people of color gained rights in other areas of life, the United States became more and more segregated: white America has deliberately created segregated ghettos.

Detroit is not an outlier—every city in the United States has been impacted by segregation—but the effects of racist housing policy were well documented here, and so the city provides a good example of how deleterious segregation has been in the United States.

The economic boom created by World War II drew tens of thousands of African Americans to Detroit, where they sought employment in the factories making military ships and vehicles. They were met with violence every step of their journey. Threats of violence when blacks moved into majority-white neighborhoods were so common that in 1942 *Life* magazine ran a story with the headline "Detroit Is Dynamite." "It can either blow up Hitler," the magazine wrote, "or blow up the U.S."

The next year, racial tensions over housing, policing, and job discrimination boiled over into one of the worst riots in Detroit's history. Black and white Detroiters were killed, but whites had the advantage of the police on their side. By the end of the riots, 1,893 people had been arrested, 700 injured, and 34 killed. Twenty-five of those killed were black, and seventeen of those people were shot dead by police. No whites were killed by police.

The riot grabbed headlines, but it was far from the only example of racial tension in the city. Nearly every facet of life in Detroit for African Americans was plagued by racist violence and discrimination during and following World War II. Detroit's economy was booming, but unions still tried to bar black workers from joining their ranks and auto factories only hired African Americans for dangerous, low-paying work.

While unions and corporations did their best to keep Detroit's black residents economically disadvantaged, politicians and white residents did their best to ensure they stayed trapped in the most economically disadvantaged neighborhoods. In the 1940s, it wasn't uncommon for white neighborhoods to post large billboards on their streets warning black Detroiters to leave. Most of the signs simply read "Whites Only," though one on the West Side read, "Negroes moving here will be burned, signed Neighbors."

Housing-based violence continued and even increased through the 1960s. When black Detroiters moved into new neighborhoods, often their lawns would be torched; sometimes their houses would be burned down. New black residents in white neighborhoods frequently would have stones thrown at them. In 1963, the city documented sixty-five incidents of housing-based violence, but because many cases were never reported, that's likely an undercount.

There were subtler but still effective ways of keeping black Detroiters out of white neighborhoods. In the 1940s, neighborhood associations often included restrictive covenants in their bylaws that essentially barred black people. These covenants would sometimes be explicit; other times they'd list requirements that were nearly impossible for nonwhites to meet—for example, to move into some Detroit neighborhoods, a person's boss would have to sign off on housing applications; in some neighborhoods only relatives of current residents could move in. One neighborhood on the city's northwest side mandated that property "shall not be used or occupied by any person or persons except those of the Caucasian race." More than 80 percent of the city outside its downtown core had these kinds of restrictions in the years after World War II. Neighborhood improvement associations, now considered benign bodies concerned with the beautification of neighborhoods, were most often established in Detroit and elsewhere to help keep black people out of rich white areas.

• Detroit real estate agents helped segregate the city too. As in other places, they followed the code of ethics specified by the National Association of Real Estate Boards, and until 1950 that code stated that realtors should "never be instrumental in introducing into a neighborhood a character of property or occupancy, members of any race or nationality, or any industry whose presence will be clearly detrimental to real estate values." The surrounding suburbs were also active in keeping Detroit's poor black population stuck in place. Dearborn, a city just a few minutes' drive west of Detroit, elected Orville Hubbard mayor in 1941 (and fourteen times after that) after he promised to keep the city "lily white." "Housing Negroes is Detroit's problem," he said. Grosse Pointe, just to Detroit's east, assigned a point system to people looking to purchase homes. Potential residents had points deducted based on their "degree of swarthiness," and Jews were able to move in only if they were personally vouched for by people already living in the neighborhood; African Americans weren't able to move in at all.

Mayor Albert Cobo, the man the Cobo Center is named after, lent the city's approval to the countless acts of racism perpetrated throughout its neighborhoods. Elected in 1949 largely on a promise to keep low-income housing out of white neighborhoods, Cobo quickly got to work promoting segregation. He gave the same neighborhood association heads who established restrictive race-based covenants in their neighborhoods prominent roles in his government, including on the city planning commission. The Mayor's Interracial Committee, a quasi-governmental body that was established before Cobo took office and was meant to help quell racial tension in the city, denounced Cobo's policies, especially his refusal to integrate low-income public housing, as having "the sole purpose of rebuilding and perpetuating the Negro ghetto." So Cobo disbanded the committee.

As racist as Cobo and some of his predecessors were, local governments were limited in just how much segregation they could perpetuate. Only the federal government had the power to promote and enforce true apartheid conditions across the country. The federal government, unlike Cobo, rarely explicitly stated racism as its end goal. Instead, it cloaked its racism in the language of economic prosperity and individual consumer choice.

In 1931, in the midst of the Great Depression, President Herbert Hoover assembled more than 400 housing experts for the President's National Conference on Home Building and Home Ownership. The idea was to restart the American economy through housing. "I am confident that the sentiment for home ownership is so embedded in the American heart that millions of people who dwell in tenements, apartments and rented rooms . . . have the aspiration for wider opportunity in ownership of their own homes," Hoover said.

His assembled horde of housing experts agreed that the encouragement of home ownership was the best thing a government could do to grow America's economy. To that end, the experts advised Hoover to create what we've come to take for granted as run-of-the-mill mortgages. Before Hoover's housing assembly, mortgages with payback periods of more than ten or fifteen years and low down payments were virtually unheard of. Banks feared the risk of lending to someone who could not afford to pay back the loan within a relatively short time frame. By extending the payback period and lowering down payment requirements, the new type of mortgage would allow families previously too poor to buy housing to purchase a home.

Two years later, with the economy even further into the throes of the Great Depression, Hoover's successor, Franklin Delano Roosevelt, pounced on Hoover's mortgage idea and created the Home Owners' Loan Corporation (HOLC) to refinance the mortgages of families at risk of losing their homes with the kind of low-interest, low-down-payment mortgages pushed by Hoover. This made economic sense: without the ability to refinance, many Americans could have gone into foreclosure, worsening the country's economic depression. So between July 1933 and June 1935, HOLC made more than a million mortgage deals for a total of over $3 billion. But because of the massive risk inherent in the federal government getting involved in normal people's mortgages, HOLC could not lend to just anyone. So the agency devised a comprehensive system for predicting the ability of people to pay back their mortgages. That system was blatantly racist.

Each neighborhood of every major American city was coded A, B, C, or D and assigned a corresponding color of green, blue, yellow, or red. "Homogenous" areas—identified by HOLC as areas with lots of new construction and filled with "American business and professional men"—were given A labels and colored green on maps. An "infiltration of Jews" or any other minority in a neighborhood would bar it from being given an A and the color green. So would old, semi-dilapidated housing. Blue neighborhoods were slightly less good investments in the eyes of the feds—perhaps they had a few Jews, or housing units that were too densely packed and crumbling. Yellow C neighborhoods were ones that were considered "definitely declining"—these were most often racially mixed areas in city centers. And neighborhoods labeled "D" and colored red were defined by the feds as neighborhoods "in which the things taking place in C have already happened"—in other words, where there was a combination of racial integration and poverty. Almost every majority-black neighborhood in the country was given a D and "redlined" on the federal government's maps, barred from receiving federal funding for mortgages. The effect of these redlining maps was compounded as nearly every major bank adopted the federal government's system. Within a few years of the HOLC system's start, it was almost impossible to get a mortgage in much of the United States if you were black.

In 1934, FDR created the Federal Housing Administration (FHA), which ten years later would be joined by another home-owner program created through the newly established Veterans Administration (VA). Both programs were established with the intent of not only moving more Americans into homes but also funneling billions of dollars into the construction industry in order to boost the lackluster American economy.

"The building trades in America represent by all odds the largest single unit of our unemployment," one housing official told Congress in 1934. "A fundamental purpose of this bill is an effort to get the people back to work."

Unlike HOLC, the FHA and VA programs did not give out mortgages. Instead, for the first time in US history, they created a government mechanism to insure bank mortgages. Any home that met FHA construction standards would be backed by government funding if the private mortgage went under, which enabled banks to start making riskier bets and making loans in numbers never seen before. The modern mortgage industry was essentially created by the two bills.

The Home Owners' Loan Corporation had already started to make mortgages with lower down payments the norm, but the FHA helped solidify the idea that Americans could buy a home with very little cash up front. After the creation of the FHA, mortgages with 20 percent or sometimes even 10 percent down were common—spurring not only the construction of new housing but also the development of a new class of Americans who could all of a sudden move into private, detached housing and grow their nest egg as that house appreciated in value. In 1933, construction began on 93,000 new homes. By 1937, just three years after the FHA was created, housing starts had risen to 332,000. In 1941, 641,000 homes began construction. After World War II, construction really boomed: the United States added 13 million homes between 1945 and 1954. And VA mortgages accounted for 40 percent of these homes in 1946 and 1947.

The FHA, VA, and HOLC all explicitly used race in determining where they would approve mortgages. FHA established a set of rules for identifying neighborhoods where fewer mortgages might fail. Its 1939 underwriting manual stated, "Crowded neighborhoods lessen desirability" and "Older properties in a neighborhood have a tendency to accelerate the transition to lower class occupancy." The manual also set standards for setbacks from curbs and minimum widths for houses. And it discouraged mixed-use planning—buildings with storefronts, it said, were less than ideal. Instead, blocks should be purely residential, commercial, or industrial, following the urban planning orthodoxies of the time, which held that space and calm were always good, while crowdedness and chaos were undesirable. It's hard to parse out whether the FHA's aesthetic requirements were just about aesthetics or whether they were another, subtle way of encouraging racial division. In St. Louis, Missouri, for example, zoning laws from the 1910s and 1920s were proposed with the explicit intent of keeping white residents in high-value, residential-only neighborhoods and pushing poor black people into the mixed-use central city. Regardless of the FHA's intent, its zoning preferences meant that multiuse, multiracial sections of cities such as St. Louis were ineligible for most home loans.

The manual also contained the same blatant racism as HOLC's rules. "If a neighborhood is to retain stability," the FHA manual stated, "it is necessary that properties shall continue to be occupied by the same social and racial classes." The manual recommended that neighborhoods that wanted to be eligible for mortgages enact restrictive covenants like those used in Detroit to bar blacks and others from new neighborhoods.

The FHA manual was perhaps the single most detrimental document in the history of urbanism in the United States. With a few lines of anti-density, racist planning policy, the federal government essentially forced the creation of the suburbs and the near-complete disinvestment of the inner city. Not only were builders discouraged from building in cities; if they wanted insured mortgage funding, they couldn't build in cities at all. Cities were dense, mixed-use, and diverse, all qualities the FHA thought undesirable for new-home construction.

It would be easy to dismiss the guidelines as clumsy or a product of less enlightened times, but the FHA knew exactly what consequences its practices would have. In a 1939 memo about Washington, DC, FHA officials admitted the guidelines would end up concentrating poor African Americans in city centers and moving richer whites out to the suburbs: "The 'filtering up' process [white people moving to the suburbs], and the tendency of Negroes to congregate in the District, taken together, logically point to a situation where eventually the District will be populated by Negroes and the surrounding areas in Maryland and Virginia by white families."

Yet the FHA did not change its policies for years, and banks followed the agency's lead. Historical data on FHA loans nationwide are slim, but surveys from individual cities show how vast the influence of the FHA was. In the city of St. Louis, for example, only 12,116 mortgages were backed by FHA insurance between 1934 and 1960, while St. Louis County (the suburbs of St. Louis) received nearly 63,000 FHA-backed mortgages. Nassau County, which encompasses many New York City suburbs on Long Island, received 87,000 mortgages; the Bronx received 1,641.

The FHA's racist policies continued for decades. As late as 1966, for example, there had not been one mortgage backed by the FHA issued in the urban centers of Camden or Paterson, New Jersey, yet nearly half of all suburban housing in the 1950s and 1960s was backed by the FHA or the VA.

The FHA's preference for suburban-style construction and its redlining of nearly every black neighborhood in America had the effect of trapping poverty in urban centers and trapping African Americans in poverty. In postwar boomtowns such as Detroit, black people were already at a disadvantage in finding jobs and getting paid fairly for those jobs—leaving them with lower incomes and nest eggs than whites. That disadvantage was further compounded when the FHA's loans enabled white flight to the suburbs and forced black people into cities. And that plight was then further compounded when suburbs subsequently banned blacks from living in them, and when factory work (specifically car manufacturing in Detroit) followed white people to the suburbs. Between 1946 and 1956, GM, Chrysler, and Ford spent nearly $8 billion on new factories, nearly all in the suburbs of Detroit. The decentralization was so quick that by the time orders came in for military gear during the Korean War in the 1950s, only 7.5 percent of military purchases came from within the Motor City's city limits. African Americans were essentially prevented from reaching these jobs by design: they were barred from living in suburbs and often too poor to afford transportation via car out to the factories.

Black people in Detroit and all across the country not only were pushed into city centers and held there by racist suburban policy but were repeatedly internally displaced by the forces of "urban renewal." Federally funded highways began cutting through Detroit after World War II. The highways weren't just ways to subsidize white flight to the suburbs; local politicians considered them a "handy device for razing the slums." Detroit displaced nearly 2,000 black families from one area along Gratiot Avenue in 1947 for the sole purpose of getting rid of a section of the city that used more tax dollars than it gave back. Mayor Albert Cobo called urban renewal the "price of progress."

- - -

The effect of decades of segregation is that black Americans are poorer and less likely to achieve success than whites. In *Stuck in Place*, a study of the apartheid-like conditions of black America, New York University sociologist Patrick Sharkey found that over the last half century there has been virtually no improvement in the income of African Americans. While white children today who come from middle-class families can expect to earn on average $74,000, $20,000 more than their parents, black children can expect to earn $45,000 a year—not only significantly less than white kids, but $9,000 less than the average earned by black people in the middle class a generation ago. Half of middle-income black kids fall *down* the economic ladder compared with the previous generation, while only 14 percent of white kids do.

Sharkey argues that there's only one possible reason: "When white families advance in economic status, they are able to translate this economic advantage into spatial advantage by buying into communities that provide quality schools and healthy environments for children." This simply is not possible for most black families.

The United States' racist housing legacy may seem only tangentially related to gentrification today, but the two processes are part and parcel of the same historical trajectory. If black Americans had been able to achieve the same kind of success through housing that whites had, gentrification would not be such a race-based phenomenon. Instead, the intentional destruction of black urban life has become the canvas on which gentrifiers now paint.

Over and over again, media organizations, hipsters, and artists refer to Detroit as a "blank slate." That ignores not only the 700,000 other people who still live there but also the historical reality that the "blank slate" was created through decades of brutal racism. The fact that gentrifiers are often taking advantage of the cheap rent caused by racially restrictive housing policy also complicates the narrative gentrifiers and the mainstream media like to perpetuate about being saviors to decimated urban areas. When Jamie Dimon, the head of JPMorgan Chase, announced the bank would invest $100 million in the city's downtown in 2014, the press hailed him as a risk taker. And, as we have seen, Dan Gilbert has been called a superhero. This of course belies the fact that the same kinds of institutions—and often the very same institutions, as is the case with old banks such as JPMorgan Chase—were instrumental in destroying Detroit and keeping its poor black residents poor. Gentrifiers may see racial inequality in Detroit, but few acknowledge where that inequality comes from. These gentrifiers are often the kids of the same white families that were able to leave Detroit thanks to subsidies from the federal government in the form of highways and low-interest loans on houses—loans that were denied to black families because of redlining.

Now, just like generations before, though with the geography reversed, the same dynamic is playing out: white people are being subsidized by the local, state, and federal governments to reinhabit cities, while black Detroiters are ignored or even forcibly pushed out. Fifty years ago subsidies came in the form of billions spent on highways and suburban housing. This time they come in the form of billions used on tax breaks for stadiums and condos, for renovations of storefronts and homes, for streetcars and bike lanes.

Gentrification is often presented as a sort of corrective to the suburbs: instead of white flight and unsustainable cookie-cutter planning, we get dense, urban, and diverse cityscapes. But gentrification is simply a new form of the same process that created the suburbs; it's the same age-old, racist process of subsidizing and privileging the lives and preferred locales of the wealthy and white over those of poor people of color. The seesaw has just tipped in the other direction. Gentrification does not mean that the suburbs are over, or that cities are becoming more diverse. All it means is that our geography of inequality is being redrawn. Gentrification is not integration but a new form of segregation. The borders around the ghettos have simply been rebuilt.

- - -

Lauren Hood grew up in Detroit. She's black and navigates the two worlds of the old and new Detroit. Until recently, Hood was the community engagement manager at Loveland Technologies, one of the hottest tech companies in the city. Loveland has developed software that allows the city of Detroit, along with anyone else with an Internet connection, to view detailed information about any piece of land in the city—its owner, its blight status (is it in need of being demolished? Is it occupied?), and often a photo. Loveland's technology is used by the city and funded by some of its major players, including Dan Gilbert.

Hood told me her work there left her feeling unfulfilled, and recently she quit. Still, she occupies a space few others do: she's black, she's part of the professional class in the city, and she lives in the 7.2. But she's also part of that other Detroit, the people being pushed out of the city both by the government's current focus on the 7.2 and by a legacy of racism. Hood is a fourth-generation native Detroiter. Her parents were part of the black middle class that built Detroit. Her mom was an administrator for the state government; her father worked for GM. And Hood has seen their Detroit nearly disappear as the new Detroit she's part of now takes shape seemingly overnight.

"I made up this character named Ms. Jenkins," Hood told me on a recent drive up Detroit's main street—Woodward Avenue, which goes from downtown through Midtown and out toward the deteriorating residential sections of the city and eventually to the suburbs. "When people are like, 'Oh, all this development, it's good for Detroiters,' I'm like, 'It's good for Detroiters like you, but is it good for Ms. Jenkins? The woman who has been here for decade after decade, who owns a home on the East Side? All these things that are good for Detroit, which Detroit are they good for?'"

On the way down Woodward out of Midtown, Hood pointed to her loft-style apartment, located a block away from where the new taxpayer-funded hockey arena and entertainment complex will be built. She pointed to the tracks being laid for the M-1, to buildings that are being converted from abandoned shells to luxury condos. Then, as we got farther and farther away from the city's center, she pointed to different kinds of things—closed stores, homes burned to the ground, improbable signs of life such as a well-kept lawn on an otherwise desolate block or a clothing shop still in business on a street with little else.

"When I was growing up, all these places were occupied," she said. "All of the people here had good, solid jobs. What happened?"

We continued driving north, and Woodward turned more and more desolate until it was dark. There was virtually nothing open on either side of the road. The drivers around us seemed concerned only with speeding further north to Detroit's suburbs.

Eventually Hood turned left off Woodward into a neighborhood near Seven Mile (which is, as the name implies, seven miles from Detroit's downtown) into an area filled with grand but dilapidated houses. She then made another turn down a small tree-lined residential street where plywood, chains, and padlocks had replaced front doors—an attempt to prevent scavengers from stealing copper wiring. The houses without the plywood were already scavenged, turned into unusable shells one piece of cheap metal at a time. They had no windowpanes, no lights. Hood stopped in front of a house on the corner. It was two stories, simple but nice. It wouldn't be out of place in the tonier neighborhoods of most industrial American cities. The house showed signs of decay at its fringes—paint chipping, a cracked window. At least, she said, it was occupied. And then she told me, "This is where I grew up."

Lauren comes to check on the house every couple of weeks as a kind of ritual to remind herself whom she's fighting for. She feels as if it's her responsibility to make sure her childhood home doesn't fall apart like most of the houses surrounding it did.

"I think about how fast this all happened," Hood said. "What were we paying attention to that we didn't notice that people were leaving, that properties were deteriorating? It seems like it happened overnight."

If Hood is looking for a Ms. Jenkins, it could be her own mother. Detroit was never very friendly to Ida Hood or her husband, Lawrence, but they stuck it out year after year, through multiple break-ins and car thefts, as their favorite stores and restaurants closed during the period of white flight, and as many of their friends left for the safer suburbs. But on a cold January day in 2013, a group of teenagers ran up to Ida and Lawrence as they carried groceries from their car to their house. One teen pointed a gun at Lawrence's head. They robbed the Hoods of everything. The cops took half an hour to show up. And that was what finally convinced them to get out.

"I think I have PTSD," Ida told me, speaking from her new home in Farmington Hills, a suburb twenty miles northwest of Detroit. "The level of anxiety just increased day by day. We couldn't sleep, we couldn't eat. We had to get out of there. . . . The first good night's sleep I had was once we moved here."

Lauren isn't a conspiracy theorist, but she struggles to figure out the underlying logic in the redevelopment of a city in which people like Ida and Lawrence Hood are forgotten while money and praise are lavished on the new, largely white Detroit.

"Maybe that was the idea all along," Lauren told me. "To get rid of them."

After pausing for a minute at her former home, Lauren began the journey back toward her loft in the city center with me in the passenger seat. If the drive out made it feel like the city was slowly disintegrating into nothing, the drive back made it feel as if we were seeing a city being constructed in real time—burned husks of buildings turning into fully formed ones, sidewalks becoming bright with the yellow of streetlights and the white-blue hue of shopping centers and gas stations. There was a brief lull as we drove through Highland Park, the municipality within Detroit's borders that's so poor its fire department's alarm system involves a fax machine pushing an empty soda can onto the floor. But rather quickly after that, things looked more lush again. You could see the locational seesaw of capital in real time. When we crossed back into the 7.2, it was as if we had entered a dome of luxury tightly sealed at its borders. This is where capital has decided investment is important, and so this is where the people who can afford it live the good life.

"The 7.2 is turning into the Hunger Games," Lauren said as she pulled up to her house. "They might as well put a barbed-wire fence around it, and everyone else can fight for scraps."

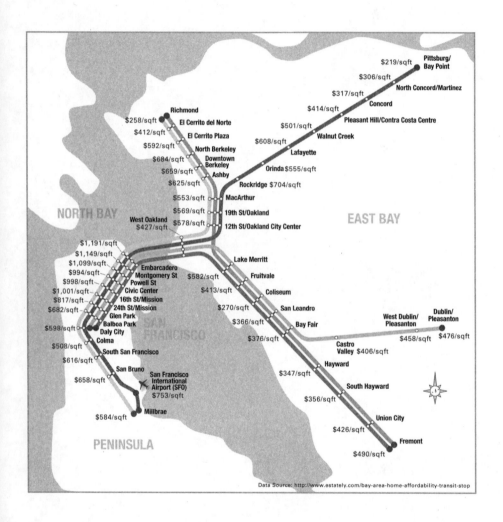

Pittsburg/Bay Point $219/sqft
North Concord/Martinez $306/sqft
Concord $317/sqft
Pleasant Hill/Contra Costa Centre $414/sqft
Walnut Creek $501/sqft
Lafayette $608/sqft
Orinda $555/sqft
Rockridge $704/sqft

Richmond $258/sqft
El Cerrito del Norte $412/sqft
El Cerrito Plaza $592/sqft
North Berkeley $684/sqft
Downtown Berkeley $659/sqft
Ashby $625/sqft
MacArthur $553/sqft
19th St/Oakland $569/sqft
12th St/Oakland City Center $578/sqft
West Oakland $427/sqft

NORTH BAY

EAST BAY

Lake Merritt
Embarcadero $1,191/sqft
Montgomery St $1,149/sqft
Powell St $1,099/sqft
Civic Center $994/sqft
16th St/Mission $998/sqft
24th St/Mission $1,001/sqft
Glen Park $817/sqft
Balboa Park $682/sqft
Daly City $598/sqft
Colma $508/sqft
South San Francisco $616/sqft
San Bruno $658/sqft
San Francisco International Airport (SFO) $753/sqft
Millbrae $584/sqft

Fruitvale $582/sqft
Coliseum $413/sqft
San Leandro $270/sqft
Bay Fair $366/sqft
$376/sqft

West Dublin/Pleasanton
Dublin/Pleasanton $476/sqft
$458/sqft
Castro Valley $406/sqft
Hayward $347/sqft
South Hayward $356/sqft
Union City $426/sqft
Fremont $490/sqft

SAN FRANCISCO

PENINSULA

Part 3

San Francisco

The Gentrified City

Jimmie Fails feels like San Francisco: breezy, welcoming, a little weird. He's a beanie-wearing, skateboarding twentysomething who grew up here and who basically only knows here (he left once for about a year, living in New York, but hated the sense of isolation and competitiveness). And he's known around here because of it—he gets pounds and high-fives and hears "hey, what's up" all around town.

So as San Francisco has changed, Jimmie's life and his identity have changed too. He's lost friends to different, cheaper cities and lost patience with the newcomers who view him, the native, as foreign. He feels less and less like San Francisco is a part of him, and more and more like an anomaly within it, like a relic.

One day Jimmie decided the best way for him to proceed was by dramatizing his life story—by becoming the star of his friend's movie, *The Last Black Man in San Francisco*. The movie is a semibiographical film about a black twentysomething San Franciscan, played by Jimmie, who loses his family's big Victorian house to foreclosure and tries every trick in the book to get it back. When the film is released, you'll be able to see him skating around his hometown on the big screen, reminiscing about what's changed. It's a kind of elegy to San Francisco.

When I met Jimmie he was in the middle of production. His best friend from high school, Joe Talbot, was behind the camera, directing. The movie was being shot in desaturated color with sweeping vistas, long takes, and backing tracks that sound straight out of *Casablanca*. So while *The Last Black Man* is about the new San Francisco, it's shot as if it were very old—a kind of aesthetic middle finger to the sleek, tech-obsessed veneer currently overtaking the city. Jimmie and Joe are young, but they seem more at home in this old aesthetic than they do in the new San Francisco. They are too disheveled and carry too much swagger to fit into the new city. Seeing them walk around San Francisco is like seeing one of the city's row houses still standing among a sea of glass condos. As the city speeds into the tech future and cultural irrelevance, they're like living signposts proclaiming to others that maybe it's not too late. In that way, *The Last Black Man in San Francisco* is an act of protest. It's also Jimmie and Joe's last shot: if it doesn't work, if it doesn't make money on the festival circuit, they, like so many other broke artists in need of a cheap place to produce work, will leave.

Calling Jimmie "the last black man" is obviously an exaggeration, but given the demographics of San Francisco, it's pretty tame hyperbole: the black population of San Francisco is down to 5.8 percent of the city, less than half of what it was in 1970. The majority of that change took place in the last twenty years. There are still big Hispanic and Asian populations in the city, but their numbers are dwindling too. The Hispanic population of the Mission, San Francisco's historically Latino neighborhood, for example, has dropped from 60 percent to 48 percent since 2000. If the trend continues, Latinos could make up less than a third of the neighborhood by 2025. San Francisco once was the most diverse county in the region, but now it is the only county that is losing diversity, while every other surrounding county (the suburbs) is making gains. The city will be majority white by 2040. The exodus is a constant topic of conversation here. Everyone in the city who does not make tech-industry-level money seems to have one foot out the door, ready to leave. The old San Francisco looks woozy, battered, waiting for one last wave of capital to finish it off.

Jimmie is able to stay in San Francisco only because Joe's parents, two creative types with a stable income, were lucky enough to buy a big house on the border of the Mission several decades ago. Joe and Jimmie live in the basement. But they can't stay there forever, and being an artist doesn't pay enough to afford an apartment in a city where the median rent for a two-bedroom apartment is over $5,000.

When I first met the duo they were shooting promo photos in Golden Gate Park to send out to people to raise money for production. They'd convinced five women from a just-concluded outdoor yoga class to hold their poses while Jimmie stood behind them and Joe took pictures.

"This is the closest I'll ever get to doing yoga," Jimmie said.

After a quick shot, we hopped in one of the production cars and drove around the city for a bit. Joe, who is a little older than Jimmie, pointed out the changes: the new Starbucks locations (several dozen), the glass condos jutting out between all the colorful old Victorians, the shuttered bars, and, most jarring to them, the new people—the ones working at Apple and Google and Facebook and the myriad other tech companies. They seemed so oblivious to everything around them. In polos and button-downs, they seemed too straight for San Francisco. Joe and Jimmie had observed that the newcomers tended to see the city as a series of commodity choices (tacos? beer? ramen? a condo in the Mission?) and saw none of the gritty weirdness underneath their noses. But you could tell, neighborhood by neighborhood, that they were taking over, now ubiquitous enough to become the norm, compared to which everything else becomes a deviation.

"It's an identity thing. You start to wonder if you belong here," Jimmie said. "They don't even see me when they walk by me."

Although some of them do. A few months back, a white woman accused Jimmie of breaking into Joe's parents' house (he was entering at night with his key). A few months before that, Jimmie was walking behind a white man near Dolores Park, a gentrification hotspot a few blocks from Joe's parents' house, when the man turned to look at Jimmie and, presumably fearing a robbery, ran through the park and right through an active set of sprinklers, soaking himself.

Jimmie's view of these kinds of people is surprisingly sympathetic: he said that if he had as much money as they do, he'd probably be doing the same thing, living in condos and running from black

people. One activist told me he actually feels bad for the tech workers who've descended on the city: they pay previously unheard-of
sums for small apartments, get shuttled in buses to Palo Alto at 7:00
a.m. and back home at 6:00 p.m. (and often work through the night),
take an Uber to whatever restaurant they might be eating at that
evening, and then repeat the process the next weekday. Sure, they're
living lives of privilege, but it's a particularly banal, almost robotic
privilege that feels unenviable. Which makes it all the more frustrating that their presence is destroying the rest of the city.

For an outsider, it's hard to get what's at stake in a place like
San Francisco. As a gay guy from New York, I can look at the gay
bars in the Castro, an area of the city historically home to a large gay
population, and think, "This is an okay gayborhood." But if you've
lived here for thirty years, your first thought might be, "This used to
be a hotbed of political radicalism, and now it's gay Disney World." If
you're me, you might walk through the Mission, eat some tacos, and
think it's a cute neighborhood. You might not know that right above
the taco shop is an apartment building where families are paying
$1,000 a month for a room that's ten feet by ten feet. You might not
know that activist artist collectives such as Las Mujeres Muralis-
tas painted vibrant portraits of working-class struggles and working-
class beauty in the 1970s and that many of those artists have now
left. But I think I got a taste of the stakes when I was spending time
with Jimmie and Joe. I related to them, especially to Joe, who, like
me, is white and relatively privileged, but still feels a duty to represent a dying part of his city.

We were in an alley close to downtown, a few blocks from Twitter's headquarters—the same headquarters that got tax breaks from
the city totaling up to $56 million just for locating in a less built-up
part of downtown when I really understood the future San Francisco faces. The alley felt like another leftover piece of the city: it
was dirty, there were syringes, it smelled like piss. As Joe set up
the shot with his small crew—a quick take of Jimmie skateboarding
down the alley—Jimmie told me about his childhood: how he grew
up in this huge house shared by about a dozen family members, how
his parents lost it because they got into some trouble with drugs,

how he bounced among different apartments and housing projects around the city for most of his life, and how he feels extremely conflicted about the state of his city today.

"I never want to try to make someone feel bad for me, because everyone struggles," Jimmie said. "But I feel some type of way about it. Just because they're fucking up the culture."

During one of the takes, a window in one of the buildings lining the alley opened. Someone leaned out and shouted, "Are you the *Last Black Man* people?" This happens all the time, Joe told me. The movie, even though it was years away from release, had struck a chord in the city. People here knew about it. We were invited up by the man in the window to what turned out to be a large loft split into about a dozen different artists' studios. Two young black artists, Erlin Geffrard and Tim Aristil, took me on a tour. Geffrard's paintings stylistically resembled ancient Egyptian art but with the iconography updated with things like McDonald's signs and handguns. Things looked a mess in the studio, and Geffrard explained the building had been bought and would soon be turned into office space for tech companies. Both he and Aristil were likely leaving the city within the next couple of weeks.

"It's not rewarding anymore," Aristil told me. "You used to walk around and be inspired by hearing interesting conversations. Now you just hear people talk about business and about how much the city sucks."

Beyond the intangibles, studio space is simply too expensive. Geffrard said he was looking at places in the East Bay, maybe Oakland. Aristil said he was probably moving to L.A. It's cheaper there. It seems like all his friends are moving there, or to Philly or to Detroit. The *Last Black Man* crew chatted with the two artists for a bit longer and then said some cordial but intense good-byes. As I followed the crew out of the building I couldn't help but hope that *Last Black Man* succeeded, critically and financially. We'd just seen two artists' lives uprooted by San Francisco's economy. If the movie didn't work, another two artists would likely be leaving the city too.

- - -

San Francisco has gone through economic ups and downs, but it never experienced the same slow bleed of residents and money as Detroit, nor the same kind of crash New York had in the 1970s. There was a bad earthquake in 1989, but San Francisco rebounded relatively quickly—it was not analogous to Hurricane Katrina's effect on New Orleans. Like most cities, San Francisco did have its own FHA-spurred white flight. But, as San Francisco–based writer and activist Rebecca Solnit points out, because there was never a large industrial sector as in cities in the East, when the city emptied out half a century ago it was filled in not solely by working-class people but also by hippies, artists, and various other outcasts. That long and unique history of progressivism has also given San Francisco one of the strongest tenant activism movements in the country. After years of pressure, in 1979 the city's Board of Supervisors approved a rent control bill that pegged rent increases in any apartment built before 1979 to yearly inflation. The bill also made it relatively hard to evict tenants in the city. There are some exceptions: if you live in a single-family home, which many San Franciscans do, you're not protected, and if you live in a place built after 1979, you're not eligible for rent control. Still, the city's rent control ordinance is more stringent than probably anywhere else in the country. The fact that evictions are at record highs despite those laws shows just how valuable the land is.

A report from Board of Supervisors member David Campos found there were 2,120 notices of evictions filed between February 2014 and February 2015—55 percent more than five years prior. That number counts only the landlords who followed the letter of the law and filed notice with the city. It doesn't count those who illegally pressured tenants out of their homes. Buyouts, where a landlord offers money for families to leave their apartments, are becoming common here too. People are being offered anywhere from $5,000 to $100,000 to leave their homes, according to activists. One of the only legal ways to evict someone who's a good tenant is an Ellis Act eviction, in which the landlord "goes out of business"—that is, completely removes all the apartments in a building from the rental market. Those apartments can then come back on the market as condos. There were nearly 450 Ellis Act evictions in 2013 (a subset of the more than 2,000 total evictions). Ellis Act evictions can also be used as threats—a landlord tells a tenant to take a buyout offer or face an Ellis Act eviction. The nonprofit San Francisco Tenants Union estimates that for every Ellis Act eviction there are about three buyout offers. If you conservatively estimate there are 200 Ellis Act evictions a year, add in the 600 or so buyouts that might represent, plus another 1,900 or so regular evictions, and multiply that total by the average San Francisco family size of about 2.2 (according to the San Francisco Association of Realtors), you're left with 5,500 people evicted from their homes each year. With rental prices sky-high, it's likely many of those evicted from rent-protected apartments leave the city completely or become homeless.

Some areas, such as the Mission, are particularly vulnerable. The Mission is San Francisco's main Latino neighborhood. Its relatively affordable housing stock, the fact that it's serviced by both of San Francisco's train systems (Muni and BART), and its proximity to downtown made it a perfect target of gentrification. There's little neighborhood-level data on evictions, but between 1990 and 2011, the number of Latino households fell by 1,400, while white households increased by 2,900. There's less data on Chinatown, but Joyce Lam, an organizer for a progressive organization in Chinatown, told me that evictions are increasing. "Recent immigrants, they end up on the streets, or moving out to the suburbs," she said. "Or mostly they just don't come to San Francisco anymore." Pressure on people of color has spread to other parts of the Bay Area too: in Oakland, the black population fell from 43 to 26 percent between 1990 and 2011.

It's also hard to know how many people are leaving for reasons that don't fall under any official rubric. Here's an example: I was walking around the Mission with a friend named Anabelle Bolaños when we bumped into a family sitting in their small concrete yard outside their three-story row house, just a block off the Mission's main strip. Leticia Guzman, sixty-six, told me she and her family had lived there since they bought the place in 1971. Many of her friends have already left, for Oakland, Richmond, Daly City, or South San Francisco (a separate city from San Francisco). Over the past few months, several men in suits had been coming to Guzman's

door. Some offered to buy her house. One said he was from the insurance company and wanted to check inside, but when she called
her insurance company a representative said they hadn't sent anyone. She assumed he was a real estate agent trying to get a look at
the inside of the house. If Leticia leaves San Francisco, either because a buyout offer is attractive enough to consider or because she's
gotten tired of dealing with the increasing harassment, she won't
be counted on any official reports. Her sister Carmen, fifty-four,
who has already left, doesn't show up on those reports either. There
wasn't enough space for Carmen plus her husband and kids in the
family row house, so she looked everywhere in the city. Finally she
found a place, but it was across the border in South San Francisco.
She's not officially displaced, but she grew up in San Francisco and
now cannot afford to live here.

It's not just San Francisco—the working class is being pushed
out of the Bay Area too. Leticia Rios, a nanny for a couple who both
work in tech, lives in Mountain View, about forty-five minutes south
of San Francisco, where Google's main campus is located. She's been
there for fourteen years, but her rent was recently raised by $1,000 a
month. Even though she and her husband have full-time jobs, they
can no longer afford Mountain View. They began looking farther and
farther afield until they realized it might not be worth it: between
their jobs at opposite ends of Silicon Valley and the housing prices,
moving out of the area entirely began to seem more appealing. Rios
told me she's planning on moving her kids to Nevada or Chicago. Her
husband will stay behind until they settle into a new life, and then
he will come to look for work. Because Mountain View does not have
rent control laws, Rios's eviction-by-rent increase will not be recorded
on any official forms. It will not register in any future statistics about
the Bay Area. Without such data, it's hard to paint an accurate picture of the extent of the crisis. Most of what we know comes from
census data and anecdotal stories. And that makes it harder to fight
back against gentrification.

With rents so high, housing has become precarious not only
for low-wage workers but also for police officers, lawyers, and those
in other middle-class professions that once bought you a relatively

stable life. I talked to several public school teachers in the Mission. They make good middle-class salaries, starting at about $50,000. That's not enough for one teacher I spoke to, Jake Harris, to afford an apartment with his partner in the city. So he lives an hour away on the Oakland/Berkeley border.

"There are a lot of kids who come to school who need extra support," he told me. "I don't think it's healthy for me. I don't get enough sleep. It's hard on my patience and I need a lot of patience to deal with these kids. From an emotional standpoint, it's not sustainable."

What happens to a city when artists, teachers, lawyers, and anyone else making less than $100,000 cannot afford to live in it? Where will the people making coffee for the tech workers in the Mission live if only 4 percent of one-bedrooms in the neighborhood cost below $2,500 a month, making the area essentially off-limits to working-class people? Rebecca Solnit calculated that back in the 1950s and 1960s artists had to work about sixty-five hours a month at minimum wage to afford an apartment. San Francisco's minimum wage today is high for the United States, at $12.25, but a $2,500 apartment (which is on the very cheap end these days), would account for about 200 hours of minimum-wage work. That's more than a full-time job, just to pay the rent.

San Franciscans' complaints—that the culture of the city is being crushed by its rents, that the people who make the city function can no longer live within its borders—seem to go unregistered at city hall. While prices rose and tech firm after tech firm came to the city, its politicians chose to use the city's limited resources to court even more investment. Ed Lee, the current mayor of the city, has been accused of having corrupting ties to the real estate industry here. Three people who have done fund-raising for Lee have been charged with felonies for accepting bribes from undercover agents who were looking for favorable access to real estate deals. And while Lee hasn't been convicted of anything, his public actions have been enough to elicit protests. At virtually every public speech the mayor gives these days, he's booed by activists for actively courting the tech industry and ignoring its impact on everyone who works outside of it. Lee's most infamous tax break was a $30 million deal to Twitter to locate its office in already booming downtown San Francisco. In 2016, when the Super Bowl came to Santa Clara, about thirty miles south of San Francisco, the city threw a party for the National Football League. To get its streets ready, Lee increased police patrols, spent city money on banquets for NFL officials, and pushed homeless camps out of the downtown area. To activists, the event highlighted everything wrong with the new San Francisco, a city more concerned with the welcome offered to outsiders than with the lives of the city's most vulnerable. Hundreds took to the streets.

"You have mass displacement, you have homeless people being pushed from one neighborhood to another," Miguel Carrera, the housing justice organizer for the Coalition on Homelessness, told me. "And the mayor throws a party."

This is in many ways exactly what the city asked for. The tech industry here is for the most part greeted with open arms. People recognize the problem of gentrification, but this is a company town, and anything perceived as anti-tech gets blasted by well-funded industry groups, by the mayor and most of the city council, and usually by many of the city's residents. A ballot measure that would have limited Airbnb rentals in an attempt to preserve housing for people who actually live in the city failed to garner enough votes in 2015. So did one that would have put a temporary moratorium on development in the Mission. A proposed 1.5 percent tax on tech companies that would have raised millions for affordable housing was killed even before it made it out of the Board of Supervisors' finance committee. San Francisco has decided not to bite the hand that feeds it, even if that hand is also signing its eviction papers.

- - -

I met Hugo Vargas, a sixteen-year-old who grew up in the Mission, when I was wandering around the neighborhood one day. Hugo was volunteering at a local community center and agreed to show me around. He grabbed his fixed-gear bike and walked me down Mission Street, past the dollar stores and fresh fruit stands and the smattering of hipster-filled coffee places and bars. Hugo told me about his parents: one's a barista, the other's a cook, and both work at Blue Bottle Coffee, one of the hippest and most expensive coffee chains in the city. They each make about $45,000 a year, yet Hugo and his family are constantly thinking about leaving the city, maybe for Richmond, about an hour north, maybe for somewhere else even farther afield. The idea that he might have to leave is constantly at the back of Hugo's mind. As we walked, I wondered how two good salaries could equate to a life of precariousness—until Hugo showed me what $90,000 a year gets you in San Francisco.

We stopped in front of a four-story building and Hugo rang the bell. A security guard let us into what turned out to be SRO, or single-room occupancy, housing—buildings divided into rooms big enough to fit a bed, a dresser, and not much else. San Francisco's SROs have been a backbone of the city's housing stock since the gold rush. They've housed transient workers, new immigrants, the homeless, and, increasingly, working families. SROs were once much more common throughout the United States—they aren't exactly ideal affordable housing, but they nonetheless were and are important sources of housing for low-income people. But since the 1970s, more than 1 million SRO units have been demolished across the country. They've been replaced mostly by market-rate housing. San Francisco still has some 30,000 SRO units. That's enough to house about 5 percent of the city's population. The city has a law requiring any SRO owner who converts a building to market-rate housing to pay a fee to the city to build new affordable housing, but that hasn't stopped dozens of demolitions.

Hugo's parents had rented two SRO rooms here, one for themselves and one for Hugo and his younger sister. Hugo showed me his room, which was about twelve by eight feet. His sister was there watching a small TV, holding their little Chihuahua, Novio. Clothes and books were piled everywhere, though the room was not messy—this is just what it looks like when you need to fit the lives of two teenagers into less than 100 square feet. His parents' room, upstairs, was the same size. They pay $1,900 a month for the two rooms.

Hugo's living situation was not ideal, but that wasn't what made him the angriest about the city changing around him. That wasn't what turned him into a young community activist. In the fall of 2014, Hugo and some friends were playing soccer at a local city-owned field when a group of white men came over and started explaining to the kids, who like Hugo were all Latino, that they'd paid $27 an hour to reserve the field via a city website. They asked the kids to leave, arguing that the field should go to whoever followed the rules and paid the fee. One of the older kids asked the men how long they had lived in the community.

"Who gives a shit?" the man responded. "Who cares about the neighborhood?"

A video taken of the incident went viral, and journalists discovered the men mostly were employees of Dropbox, a web storage company, and Airbnb, the apartment-sharing service that many here accuse of profiting off of real estate that could otherwise be used to house full-time residents. If you watch the video, it's obvious why it became so popular: it showcased the sense of entitlement among many gentrifiers, and it encapsulated the mounting tension between the new and old San Francisco—the community on one side and the tech sector on the other. It also highlighted a huge philosophical gap that's at the crux of gentrification: the kids believed that because they'd been in the community longer, because this was their routine, because they were on the field first, they had a right to play soccer there. The tech workers believed that because they'd purchased a ticket to the field, it was theirs. In the minds of the tech workers, it seemed, everything was a commodity—not just tacos and apartments, but the city itself. They had the technological access, the know-how, and the money to buy it. The kids did not.

This mentality is what New York–based writer and activist Sarah Schulman has called "the gentrification of the mind." As our cities' landscapes have changed, we have too, increasingly viewing ourselves not as community members with a responsibility to each other but as purchasers of things and experiences. This is what pissed off Hugo the most—the idea that these people felt they had more of a right to space than he and his friends; that the amount of time spent in a community and the traditional ways of doing things, of accessing public space, did not matter, and only money did.

8

Growth Machine

What's happening in San Francisco is not an anomaly, but simply one of the most extreme examples of what's happening in nearly every city in the United States. President Ronald Reagan cut taxes on the rich from around 70 percent to about 30 percent, and, along with cuts to spending on housing and transportation at the federal level, that's forced cities to figure out how to fund themselves. As we saw in Detroit and New Orleans, that means cities are now trying to attract as many rich people as they can in order to feed their budgets for infrastructure, education, pensions, and everything else. And because cities must borrow heavily to do these things, they are beholden to ratings agencies such as Standard & Poor's, which determine whether a city is financially healthy enough to take out loans or too risky an investment.

But gentrification today goes beyond an accounting trick. It's become a theory of governance that places the needs of capital over people. One could argue that a poor city such as Detroit might need gentrification to fill its budget gaps. But what about San Francisco? The city doesn't *need* to keep attracting rich people; it was not in economic crisis before the tech wave crashed on its shores. The city's budget was already relatively balanced before the tech boom. Yet city administrators keep zoning for more condos and more high-rise office buildings and handing out tax breaks to companies; its mayor keeps courting the big tech players at conferences and in corporate boardrooms as if San Francisco were desperate for their money, even though the city is expected, at least by one estimate, to have a $10 billion budget surplus by 2017. This is the city as growth machine.

By now, we've come to expect that economic growth, at all costs, governs most industries and businesses in America, from finance to oil to real estate. And we've seen what happens when those sectors are left with little to no regulation. But it is only in the last few decades that economic growth has become the driving force in the governing of cities, to the exclusion of every other metric of well-being. Mayors are now often elected on the idea that they will run cities like businesses. In *Urban Fortunes*, their foundational work on the economies of cities, urban theorists John Logan and Harvey Molotch argue that the people running American cities no longer care about affordability, a city's ability to educate children, or the happiness and health of its residents; rather, they are only interested the amount of money a city is able to generate. This focus is not the result of a philosophical bug that's somehow spread to the brains of city managers everywhere. People such as Richard Florida make the city-as-business philosophy seem appealing, but there's something bigger going on. Logan and Molotch argue that the city-as-growth-machine is an inherent feature of late capitalism in the United States. Cities, more than being places for people to live, have become ways to produce, manage, attract, and extract capital.

Under capitalism, there's an inherent tension between what Marxist academics call "use value" and "exchange value." Use value means the value a place is given by being useful to people—because it houses them, because it gives them a sense of community, a place where they can work, a sense of identity. Exchange value is a place's potential economic worth. In a society in which land can be bought and sold, every place has both a use value and an exchange value. The inherent problem with this setup is that the poorer you are, the more likely it is that places that provide you with use value don't offer an increased exchange value for anyone else. Molotch and Logan point out that in the heyday of urban renewal—when highways and housing projects were forced on top of low-income neighborhoods, displacing tens of thousands—the main metric for deciding where these projects should go was not crime, education, or the health of its residents, but whether those areas could be used for more profitable things. Detroit destroyed an area of the city based on the fact that the area's residents took more tax revenue in the form of government services than they produced in the form of property taxes. And while it's not usually as explicitly stated as it was in Detroit, poverty and race are often the lines along which infrastructure decisions fall. There's a reason new highways and new industry go in poor, often black and Hispanic neighborhoods: sections of cities with lower real estate values have less tax base to be destroyed. Pushing a highway through a rich neighborhood wouldn't only cause more opposition, it would lose a city more money.

Gentrification can be subtler than ramming a highway through a neighborhood, but its effects and—in the logic of the growth machine—its intents are often similar: when a poor neighborhood is viewed as having more potential for profit, politicians and industry work hard to change how that neighborhood is used so as to increase its exchange value. Let's take Leticia Rios's house as an example. Its use value is that she can live there, raise a family, and build a community in San Francisco. Its exchange value is that it's worth much more without her in it.

In urban planning circles, use and exchange value are not controversial terms. Conservative economists and planners call the process of exchange values trumping use values "highest and best use," the idea being that amenities and residences that are most profitable will naturally find their way into the desirable neighborhoods. In market logic, housing poor people at the center of a city is not a "highest and best use" because it is not as profitable as housing rich people or a bank at the center of a city. Even rich gentrifiers embody both use and exchange values. But the richer you are, the less likely it is that the use values of the land you use and the exchange values of it will be in conflict. A rich person gets many of the same use values out of a city as a poor person might: a place to live, community, identity. But in an era in which proximity to a city center heightens exchange value, gentrifiers simply have a better leg to stand on. "The crux of poor people's urban problem is that their routines—indeed their very being—are often damaging to exchange values," Molotch and Logan explain.

This is capitalism's constant urban conundrum: what makes cities profitable is inherently at odds with the needs of the poor and middle classes (who are needed for a city to function), and centrally located land has inherent value if it can be made amenable to the rich. Gentrification may be a new expression of this conflict between land value and the needs of the poor, but it's a problem as old as capitalism itself. Friedrich Engels essentially predicted gentrification in 1872:

> The expansion of the big modern cities gives the land in certain sections of them, particularly in those which are centrally situated, an artificial and often enormously increasing value; the buildings erected in these areas depress this value, instead of increasing it, because they no longer correspond to the changed circumstances. They are pulled down and replaced by others. This takes place above all with centrally located workers' houses, whose rents, even with the greatest overcrowding, can never, or only very slowly, increase above a certain maximum. They are pulled down and in their stead shops, warehouses, and public buildings are erected. . . . The result is that the workers are forced out of the center of the towns towards the outskirts.

In other words, Engels was saying, in a society in which land is privatized and can be made more and more profitable, the low-wage worker poses a dilemma for those who own and control land: even if jammed in overcrowded high-rises, poor people can only afford cheap apartments, and cheap apartments do not produce a lot of profit, or at least not as much as pricey ones do. Market logic dictates that the most profitable land (land near city centers, transportation lines, parks, etc.) goes to more profitable uses. Is there a conscious conspiracy to do this—to replace low-wage workers with higher-earning ones? It's not necessarily as deliberate as that, and it doesn't need to be in order for the system to have devastating impacts on the poor. Rather than the effect of individual or institutional actions, gentrification is a logical consequence of a system in which real estate is viewed as an unrestrained commodity. In cities that function as growth machines, where economic growth is prized above all else, the needs of the poor and middle class are eclipsed by the desire to inflate the value of land.

Late nineteenth-century theorist and activist Rosa Luxemburg hypothesized that under capitalist economies, cities would inevitably be used as ways to absorb capital—that in systems in which there is surplus money floating around (i.e., a society with rich people), cities become a mechanism, like luxury goods, to open the pockets of the rich. Luxemburg saw grand architecture, monuments, parks, and beautiful streetscapes as ways to attract the rich and beef up a city's tax base. In that way, those features of cities were the first version of Richard Florida's urban amenities. We're still doing the same thing; we've just replaced statues and plazas with coffee shops, streetcars, and art galleries. They're all just ways to boost the value of the land and to convince people with disposable incomes to come spend their money.

The problem with gentrification is it's a more complex, less obvious form of capital attraction, destruction, and creation. While urban renewal, the suburbanization of cities, and other forms of capital creation are easy to spot (a highway built through a neighborhood is a relatively obvious event), gentrification is more discreet, dispersed, and hands-off. As Rebecca Solnit writes: "Redevelopment is like an oil spill, with a single cause and a responsible party; gentrification is like air pollution, a lot of unlinked individuals make contributions whose effect is only cumulatively disastrous." Just like air pollution, gentrification may come from disparate sources, but those sources are simply signs of a larger, underlying system. With air pollution, that system is an oil-based economy; with gentrification, it's a real-estate-based economy.

The dispersed nature of gentrification could explain why gentrifiers seem unconscious of the desires that undergird their move to a neighborhood, the role they play in displacing people, or how to stop it. In my experience talking with gentrifiers, it's not that they don't care about what they're doing; it's that they don't know what they're doing. They see everything as an individual choice ("I moved here because it was affordable and there's a good coffee shop"), not as a symptom of a process with definable causes. But this ignorance naturally benefits those who profit from gentrification. What would happen if gentrifiers saw themselves not as consumers but as active members in a community, or as actors in a larger system, able to fight against what enables their presence to be a harmful one?

- - -

While gentrification is an issue in nearly every industrialized nation these days, it is a crisis, displacing tens of thousands, only in countries without sufficient housing regulation. In other words, it comes down to policies and politics. You could draw a predictable inverse graph with the amount of displacement on the Y-axis and the strength of progressive housing policy on the X-axis. The United States would be first, with the most displacement and the least progressive policy; England and Canada, countries where land markets are more regulated but are going through crises thanks to recent conservative political wins, would be next; after that would come the capitalist countries with a socialist bent (Sweden and Germany, for example); and the most socialized countries, with the least displacement and the most progressive policy, would be last.

In nearly every other industrialized nation besides the United States, there is near-consensus that purely private land markets will not meet the needs of the poor, and so measures have been taken to ensure that at least some land remains off the market or subject to regulations that make it affordable. In Hong Kong, for example, which has economics that mirror those of other global cities such as San Francisco and New York, 60 percent of all new construction has been set aside for low-income people. In Sweden, local governments have much greater control over land use decisions. In Stockholm, virtually every piece of undeveloped land is owned by the municipal government. In Berlin, which is gentrifying relatively rapidly for a European city, legislators recently approved a law capping new tenants' rent at a maximum of 10 percent above the area's average rent, so landlords cannot inflate rent as soon as an apartment becomes vacant, and have little incentive to evict long-term tenants. Though the governments of Sweden, Hong Kong, and Germany are by no means anticapitalist, they have accepted a truth that few in the United States are willing to grapple with: unregulated capitalism cannot provide a complete solution to the housing question. There are only 6,000 units of public housing in all of San Francisco, a city of 864,000 in which thousands are being displaced each year. We lose 10,000 units of subsidized rental housing a year in this country.

Housing for the poor in the United States arises largely through happenstance, not through any kind of planning. It is never the priority for growth-obsessed city or state governments. Less-profitable land goes to the poor. If that land happens to be in inner cities, as it was in the 1970s, so be it. If it happens to be in the suburbs, as it increasingly is, then the poor must move there.

This freewheeling system of real estate capitalism means that centers for capital and centers for culture are always shifting. The poor, artists, and activists, who are never stably housed in this country, are constantly fleeing the wave of capital searching for its rate of highest return. Every "golden era" for culture and art in cities—for example, New York in the 1970s and San Francisco in the 1960s—was possible only because artists and activists were able to find cheap real estate in those cities. Put another way, the use value of New York and San Francisco for artists and activists in those years—that they had creative communities, were tolerant of "alternative" lifestyles, and had public transportation networks—just happened to line up with exchange values favorable to low- and middle-income residents. As soon as the exchange value of land in New York and San Francisco changed, the artists and activists were out. Under our current system, the exchange value of places is in constant flux, and so artists, activists, and other low-income people will always be pushed around. That's why Sun Belt states such as Florida, where land is much cheaper, are currently seeing an influx of poor people, and why artists seem to be fleeing from New York to places such as Detroit and New Orleans (and then to the next "up-and-coming," even cheaper places).

If land markets in the United States remain largely unregulated, or regulated in favor of higher and higher exchange values,
then we can expect this process of displacement via heightened exchange value to continue ceaselessly. Capital will constantly find
places with large enough rent gaps (where land is cheap and can
be made more expensive) to gentrify, and the people who were able
to live on that cheap land will be forced to move, settling (but only
temporarily) in places with lower exchange values.

I often get asked why so many natives in New York see every
new coffee shop, bike lane, or apartment building as a bad sign, why
we're so "anti-change." As I was writing this book, New York mayor
Bill de Blasio proposed a new streetcar line that would go right by
my house, and my first thought was, "Well, guess I have to move."
Even if they don't call it gentrification, and even if they don't understand the economics underlying it, I think people have subcon-
sciously learned the consequences of an unregulated land system:
a coffee shop is not just a place to get a cup of coffee, and a new
streetcar is not just transit. Both are signs that your neighborhood
will all of a sudden be valuable real estate, and therefore you might
not be able to live in it. People in other cities told me they felt something very similar. Anabelle Bolaños said she used to welcome every
tree planting in the Mission, greet every street beautification project
as a chance to make her neighborhood nicer. The Mission could use
more trees, she used to think. "I used to be hella friendly," she said.
"Then I started to feel like I was taking the smallpox blankets."

Of course poor neighborhoods should have trees and nice
streets and public transportation. But under our current land use
system, upgrading a neighborhood almost always signals displacement. Only if we institutionalize a system that keeps some land affordable to the poor, or at the minimum if we provide for people
who cannot afford to rent when land gets expensive, will residents
of cities in the United States become more stably housed. To a certain extent, the United States already does this: public housing is
a way of keeping land affordable no matter what happens around
it, and the Section 8 program is a way to subsidize rents for people
who cannot afford what the market dictates they pay. But both of

these programs are woefully underfunded and mismanaged. In most cities, waitlists for Section 8 vouchers are years long. Section 8 also doesn't challenge the fundamental problem of rent increases. Rising rents mean Section 8 covers less and less of each city, and so the poor are pushed farther and farther out.

The same goes for public housing. New York is the only city in the United States with a significant public housing stock left, but even in New York there's not enough of it, and the current stock is in such disrepair that the city now plans to lease parking lots and grasslands surrounding public housing to private developers to build a mix of market-rate and affordable housing (though none of the apartments will be as affordable as traditional "project"-style housing). Our approach to housing in this country is scattershot at best.

If we are serious about moving toward a saner housing future, the options in terms of federal policy are relatively clear: we can prevent land from becoming subject to market forces, either through government ownership of land (housing projects) or through heavy regulation (rent or land-price control), or we can prevent the ever-increasing value of land from displacing people (programs such as Section 8 vouchers would fall in this category of solution). Instead, we do almost nothing and hope the market works it out. Without major new regulations, we can expect what's happening in San Francisco to continue in virtually all major US cities. In the same way that the suburbs were once inaccessible to the poor, in the near future American cities will become gilded jewel boxes, and the exodus of the poor to the suburbs will continue unchecked—that is, until the rent gaps in cities become too small to make gentrification profitable, and a new form of spatial filtering begins.

9

The New Geography
of Inequality

The suburbs were the prototype for gentrification, not aesthetically but economically. Suburbanization was the original American experiment in using real estate to reinvigorate capitalism. Gentrification can be understood as a continuation of that experiment—suburbanization part two. The suburbs are also a good reminder that housing, planning, and economic policy in the United States is deliberate, and that its main purpose is to produce money, not adequately house people. It's harder to see gentrification in this way because we're still in the middle of the process. But if we can identify the motivations behind the creation of suburbia, we can find corollaries in current urban policy that can help determine the future of cities.

Gentrification does not mean that the suburbs are over. They will still exist. But because they are no longer as profitable as cities or as desirable for the wealthiest Americans, who now populate cities, suburbs have become the leftover spaces in which we house the poor and the middle class. The suburbs are being reused, reconfigured, and repopulated. They are becoming poorer, and that has wide-ranging implications for policy and the lives of lower-income people.

- - -

After I walked around the Mission with Anabelle Bolaños, she told me that if I wanted to understand the future of the Bay Area, I had to go east, past San Francisco, past Oakland, under a mountain, over a highway, and to Concord, the biggest city in Contra Costa County. The area, which was once mostly farmland, has become a sprawling mess of suburbs, exurbs, and car-centric mini-cities. I agreed to take the trip, but first I had to get over the bridge connecting San Francisco to the East Bay, which turned out to be a lesson in itself about the Bay Area's new economy. Every bridge connecting San Francisco to the rest of the Bay Area has seen a double-digit rise in commuters over the last five years—a good indication, before census statistics catch up, that the region's population is growing. On the Bay Bridge, which connects Oakland and the rest of the East Bay to San Francisco, rush hour now starts at 5:00 a.m. This is what happens when you create an urban economy that people cannot afford to live in.

Anabelle told me to go to Concord because her best friend, Oscar Perdomo, lives there. Oscar, forty-five, gay, Latino, and raised in San Francisco, has good reasons to dislike living in Concord, which is ugly, sterile, cultureless, very straight, and relatively white. But this is where he could afford to buy a home without leaving the Bay Area completely, so this is where he is.

Oscar grew up in the Mission. He and his mom lived in the same apartment for twenty-five years. It was a two-bedroom in an old Victorian with lots of wainscoting, vaulted ceilings, and creaky wood floors. He remembers loving getting dressed up for church as a kid, then going to the park with friends afterward. His family was neither destitute nor rich, and the Mission felt like a great way of life.

"I was raised there, I wanted to stay there, that's all I know," he told me, sitting outside a chain coffee shop on one of the empty downtown streets of Concord. "It was a bunch of brown faces. It was a community. Everyone knew everyone."

But his mom's apartment was falling apart. Several of the rooms had black mold. They paid $800 a month for it, but the landlord wouldn't repair anything. It's unclear if their apartment should have been rent-regulated, but Oscar and his mom, who has health issues, did not fight when the landlord started threatening them with eviction. The struggle just did not seem worth it. The landlord turned the apartment into a one-bedroom, got rid of the high ceilings and wainscoting to make it more modern, and raised the rent to $3,000. That was in 2011; it likely costs even more now.

So Oscar did what's become known in real estate circles as "drive until you qualify": he searched for two-bedroom condos for himself and his mother farther and farther and farther from San Francisco until he found one that he could afford, here in Concord. The trip between Concord and San Francisco can take thirty minutes or more than an hour, depending on the traffic.

There is little in the way of culture or community here. Oscar said he felt at home in the Mission, when people would wave to him on the street. He felt at home in the gay bars, in his church. He does not feel that in Concord. "The neighbors keep to themselves at the grocery store here," he said. "If you're hungry, there's nothing at 10:00 p.m. Foot traffic stops at 7:00. Car traffic stops at 9:00. There's no good taqueria, no good gay bar. You open up Grindr and see the same five people, and they're all picky."

After our coffees, Oscar took me on a walking tour of Concord. The downtown is a block long and, with the exception of the coffee place and a few small restaurants, nearly empty. Then the city sprawls outward and quickly begins looking like so many other parts of the United States. The sidewalks are narrow, the roads wide, the intersections far apart. There were some strips of sad grass separating Oscar and me from Concord's multilane roads. We passed about two people in our twenty-minute walk. During the walk Oscar told me he had recently been laid off from his job as a graphic designer at a business news site in San Francisco. He's still applying for new jobs, but the move out to Concord, coupled with the time needed to take care of his mom, has made it tough for him to keep in touch with potential employers in the city. He now works part-time at a local Home Depot.

We kept walking. We passed a strip mall and another one, and another one, and then we stopped at a large four-way intersection that wouldn't look out of place in Florida, Ohio, or anywhere else. Oscar pointed to a set of newish condo buildings across the intersection, next to a park—"at least there's a park," he said, and he told me he sometimes watches the birds on the pond there—and said his condo was just beyond those. There was a brief lull in car traffic, but Oscar wouldn't cross against the light—apparently the cops here delight in handing out jaywalking tickets. So we waited in silence for the cars to stop rushing down the road's many lanes, and then Oscar walked toward what is now his home.

- - -

The suburbs were not built for poor people. Really, they were not built for anyone. They were built to reinvigorate capital. But they were especially not built for poor people, for people who rely on community, nonprofit service providers, and public transportation. They were built for a life of secluded individuality. As Jane Jacobs wrote: "The well-off have many ways of assuaging needs for which poorer people may depend much on sidewalk life—from hearing of jobs to being recognized by the headwaiter. But nevertheless, many of the rich or near rich in cities appear to appreciate sidewalk life as much as anybody. They capriciously desert, after only a few decades of fashion at most, the monotonous streets of 'quiet residential areas' and leave them to the less fortunate."

What does it mean that low-income people are now inhabiting these spaces built for the middle and upper classes? Both academics and social service providers are still catching up to the newness of the phenomenon. Poverty is still by and large considered an urban issue, and so the poor live relatively under the radar in their new geographies, disconnected not only from meaningful community but also from many of the services they relied on in the city. We do not know how this affects people—how the suburbs add to stress, how they change the ability of people to organize social and political movements. Suburban geography is not built for protest; it is not built for collective action. What we do know is that for the foreseeable future, the poor will be moving to the suburbs at unprecedented rates.

For the first time in US history, the majority of poor people in metropolitan regions live in the suburbs. In eastern Contra Costa County, just to the east of San Francisco, there was a 70 percent rise in poverty between 2000 and 2010. During the 2005 school year, 38 percent of students received free or reduced-price school lunch; by 2010, that number was up to 50 percent. These stats are not simply features of broader trends in income inequality or purely consequences of the recession that began in 2008. Yes, poverty has increased everywhere, but in the suburbs it increased at twice the rate it did in cities in the 1980s and 1990s. Fifty-five percent of poor people in metropolitan areas now live in suburbs, and 63 percent of the near-poor (those with incomes of up to twice the federal poverty level) live in the suburbs.

Ethnic demographics have shifted too. The percentage of poor black people in urban centers in the Bay Area decreased by 11.3 percent between 2000 and 2009 and increased in the suburbs by nearly 20 percent during that same period. The typical path for immigrants is no longer coming from abroad to the center of cities either, but to go straight to the suburbs and exurbs of those cities. This is another way that gentrification studies and displacement statistics do not accurately reflect the realities of gentrification, as those who ten or twenty years ago might have moved to the city center but who now move to the suburbs are not counted as displaced. Just over 50 percent of first-generation immigrants now live in the suburbs, and only 33 percent live in cities (the rest live in rural areas).

When people fall on hard times in San Francisco, the cost of real estate means there are fewer and fewer places to go. Rent vouchers via Section 8 do not cover the cost of apartments here, and charities cannot afford to build or subsidize housing in the city.

"We're now essentially a broker for the suburbs," Jeff Bialik, the executive director of Catholic Charities in San Francisco, told me. "[People] move into crisis, we move them into a shelter, and then move them out of the city. It used to be Oakland. Now it's Antioch, Brentwood, Vallejo. And then of course when that happens they lose their entire support structure. Sometimes we feel really desperate, but what are we supposed to do?"

For those without cars, living in the suburbs is even harder. Public transit tends to be so bad that an average resident of a low-income suburb who is reliant on public transit can reach only a fraction of the jobs available in that metro region: only 4 percent of jobs are reachable with a forty-five-minute commute on public transportation, and if that commute is extended to ninety minutes, still only 25 percent of a metro area's jobs are accessible.

There are only four commuter lines in the Bay Area. Outside San Francisco, the stops for each are far between and the trains run relatively infrequently. One day, a San Francisco Bay Area Rapid Transit employee tweeted from the company's official Twitter account that "BART was built to transport far fewer people, and much of our system has reached the end of its useful life." Another tweet characterized the transit agency as overwhelmed by the tech boom. It was a rare candid moment—an agency essentially admitting there was a problem it could not fix, and no easy way out.

There's also evidence that poor students do less well in the suburbs than in inner cities: low-income students in Antioch and Pittsburg, two far-flung Bay Area cities absorbing much of San Francisco's population exodus, were found to underperform their counterparts in San Francisco.

While poverty overtakes many suburbs, the systems we have set up to grapple with poverty have remained within urban cores. Nonprofits in the suburbs operate over much larger geographical areas than their urban counterparts, and their funding sources seem to be more precarious; consequently, as more and more poor people move to the suburbs, the resources of those nonprofits are stretched thin. which keeps them off the table for many suburbs. Nonprofits are struggling too.

"What they're dealing with is extremely weak public infrastructure and primary services, and we're trying to build that out but we have much more experience and expertise in the urban center," Dawn Phillips, a program director for Causa Justa/Just Cause, one of the biggest Latino activist groups in the Bay Area, told me. "For us, it's not a question of whether or not to expand. This is part of the regionalization of life. We didn't feel like we had a choice, but we're still reckoning with it."

Even basic services are hard to find in the new exurbs of the Bay Area. Many poor people are moving to unincorporated towns in the middle of the desert that don't have sewer systems, or even clean drinking water.

"It's like people are living in colonies of the United States," one activist told a local news website. "Living in a Third World country, that's close to what you see here today."

This is the new geography of the Bay Area: people living in trailer parks in dusty towns with no centers and no clean water.

- - -

Suburbs and sprawl simply don't make sense for low-income people who depend on public infrastructure and programs for survival. When you think about it, suburbs make it difficult for people of any income level to build community, which is at least part of the reason people raised in suburbs seem to dislike them enough to move into cities. But for decades, suburban life has been representative of all the American dream has to offer. It's worth asking how and why that happened, and why suburbs were developed in the first place.

One of President Roosevelt's main advisors on housing and geography, Rexford Tugwell, explained his plan for a new urban geography. "My idea is to go just outside centers of population, pick up cheap land, build a whole community and entice people into it," he said. "Then go back into the cities and tear down whole slums and make parks of them." Roosevelt was not a conservative. He was a supposed champion of the poor. The fact that one of his most powerful housing advisors had such a negative view of cities suggests just how anti-urban US housing policy is at its core.

Since they began being planned on a massive scale in the early 1930s, suburbs have always been envisioned as a way to fundamentally alter the way Americans interact with each other. They were never just about space. They were about reinvigorating the economy, yes, but they were also about more than that. The suburbs were a way to reinforce a specific way of life more favorable to the country's ruling class. Engels had warned that mass homeownership would have the effect of "chaining workers" to the factories in which they work, therefore lessening the chance they could rebel against factory owners. Engels was a communist, but plenty of capitalists admitted that was the intent of the creation of the suburbs as well. One railroad baron in the nineteenth century said he was happy when workers owned their homes because they "therefore cannot afford to strike." Perhaps the man most synonymous with the suburbs, William J. Levitt, who built the 50,000 houses in the all-white suburb of Levittown on Long Island, felt much the same way. "No man who owns his house and lot can be a Communist," he said in 1948. "He has too much to do."

Joseph McCarthy, the senator who became famous by going after Hollywood liberals he suspected were communists, actually first made a name for himself by linking multifamily housing in general and public housing in particular with communism. When the federal government funded a housing project for veterans in 1948, he said they'd just paid for "a breeding ground for communists."

Suburbs, to McCarthy and so many others, were capitalistic not just in an economic sense but in a moral and philosophical one as well. Take Robert Moses, the man who through various New York governmental agencies, mostly the Parks Department, did more than anyone else to suburbanize the Northeast. Moses was virulently anti–public transit, anti-poor, and pro-automobile. Nearly all of the hundreds of bridges Moses commissioned from New York out to its suburbs were built too low to accommodate public buses, which Moses saw as the main transportation choice of poor people and black people.

In 1942, Moses wrote an appraisal of the mid-nineteenth-century reconstruction of Paris. That reconstruction, carried out by Georges-Eugène Haussmann under Louis-Napoleon Bonaparte, turned Paris into the "city of light" we know today, with its wide boulevards. The reconstruction of Paris had three explicit purposes: absorb the surplus money floating around the empire; jump-start the working class, which was facing high unemployment; and take away momentum from the leftist social movements brewing in Paris's urban core. The plan worked. Neighborhoods were razed, disaffected workers were put back to work (and therefore less likely to join revolutionary movements), Paris turned from a provincial working-class city into a consumer- and tourist-friendly city, and Haussmann proved that urban planning was a tool not only for economic growth but also for social and political restructuring. Like many capitalist projects, the win was unstable: fifteen years later, the French economy came crashing down, largely thanks to the grand ambitions of builders such as Haussmann, and a revolutionary socialist movement rose up in the center of Paris. But despite the eventual failure of Haussmann's project, Moses pushed a similar countrywide infrastructure project in the United States and city planners followed suit.

The 1940s were precarious times for ideological conservatives in the United States. While World War II had solved the economic problems of the Great Depression, culture and politics were in upheaval. Women were working more than ever and becoming increasingly independent of men both politically and economically. There was a brewing gay movement in many major cities, particularly San Francisco and New York. Union membership was high. The United States seemed to be heading toward liberalism. The suburbs became a way to reestablish conservative values.

The suburbanization of the United States pushed whites into a privatized, anti-communal form of living, encouraged more traditional gender roles (women as housewives, men as breadwinners), and reified racial boundaries—keeping white people separate from black people, Latinos, and other ethnic groups.

In place of collectivism or urbanism, the suburbs offered consumerism—a life in which meaning is built through buying things. When Herbert Hoover, in one of his best-known moments, promised Americans "a chicken in every pot and a car in every garage," he was offering not just prosperity but a vision of a future America in which nuclear families lived in detached housing with well-appointed kitchens and garages.

The suburbs were a very particular and peculiar idea from the outset, but they were a necessary project if the United States was to maintain itself as a hypercapitalist, individualistic, patriarchal, and racist society. They were by no means a natural or even logical creation. Even the rich had to be convinced to move to the suburbs.

The idea of moving farther away from one's work to isolated communities in the middle of nowhere was a hard sell. And so unprecedented measures, both cultural and economic, had to be taken to convince consumers that a less-convenient life was in fact in their best interest. Ads for suburban homes filled magazines of the 1940s and 1950s, selling Americans on the idea that the suburbs were a moral good, a cure-all for the pestilent life of the urban core. Some ads were placed by homebuilders, including Sears, which sold books that helped you design your own home that Sears would then build. Others pushed the idea of the suburbs in order to sell all the things required for a suburban home to function—toasters and dishwashers and new refrigerators. In one General Electric ad, a woman sitting on a bench is pictured hugging a serviceman who is drawing with a branch the outline of the typical suburban home—a square box with a triangular roof—in the dirt beneath their feet. The ad implores women to buy war bonds as an investment so that when their husbands get home from the war, they'll have enough money to buy a house and fill it with GE appliances. The suburbs may have been inconvenient, expensive, and boring, but they were also Americans' patriotic duty.

Television was the biggest tool for selling suburban culture. It's no coincidence, Yale architecture professor Dolores Hayden argues, that TV's rise coincided with the suburban boom of the 1950s. TV sets were a way to convince people that the idea of suburban living was popular, natural, and American, with sitcoms and dramas providing images of happy housewives using new appliances and men driving new cars to their far-off jobs (those appliance and car manufacturers would also advertise on the same programs). "The person sitting in the living room window watching the set was a kind of minor-league star as well as a spectator," cultural critic Karal Ann Marling wrote. "Look at me! Look at my house and my new color TV!"

After the war, suburban culture became a weapon in the Cold War fight against the Soviet Union. In 1959, in an iconic moment of television, Vice President Richard Nixon debated the merits of American culture with Soviet premier Nikita Khrushchev in front of a model American home decked out with every modern appliance available, in what came to be known as the "kitchen debates." These material goods—the toaster and the television, the canned foods and Pepsi products—Nixon argued, were the best proof yet that Americans were living a lifestyle superior to that of the communist Russians.

Hollywood got in on the propaganda too. In 1961's *Bachelor in Paradise*, Bob Hope plays a critical essayist who goes to a California subdivision to write an analysis of suburban life, only to fall in love with a real estate agent and move there. In 1948's *Mr. Blandings Builds His Dream Home*, Cary Grant plays an ad executive who gets tired of New York City and moves his family to the suburbs. Things go awry at every step of construction (these mishaps, at least one film historian argues, were a way to show the perils of unionized labor right as the United States was subsidizing housing construction at unheard-of rates), but the family ends up happily in the suburbs in the end. The film served the dual purposes of convincing Washington in the McCarthy era that Hollywood was pro-American and of selling the consumer dream of the suburbs. The movie even employed corporate tie-ins with General Electric, as well as paint, carpet, and steel companies. Several replica "Mr. Blandings homes" were built by real estate developers to sell people on the suburban lifestyle around the country. (A sequel by the writer of *Mr. Blandings*, in which the main character gets sick of the suburbs and moves his family back to the city, was written but never filmed.)

But culture alone couldn't sell the suburbs. The mass exodus from cities in the mid-twentieth century required hundreds of billions of dollars in incentives, which came in the form of highways, home loans, and myriad smaller, more subtle supports of subsidization. The FHA and VA mortgage programs were the most effective subsidies to the suburbs. Those loans not only trapped low-income Americans, especially blacks, in the center of cities but encouraged the rest of the cities' populations to move out into the suburbs. In the 1950s, one-third of all private housing was financed with FHA and VA loans. While not all suburban homes were financed through those agencies, the magnitude of the subsidy depressed the market for low- and moderate-income housing, with the result that nearly all new investment in housing went to single-family homes. Home mortgages are still subsidized today via tax deductions that rise with the expense of a new home. These tax breaks end up costing the federal government four to five times what it spends on public housing each year.

The highway system functioned similarly, providing people with an illusion that it was cheap to move out to the suburbs. The United States' interstate highway system is one of the biggest infrastructure projects ever created, spanning some 48,900 miles. Ninety percent of it was funded by the federal government. Roads are still heavily subsidized by the feds: one study found that drivers pay only half the real cost of driving.

Even today, the suburbs remain such an illogical system of living that they require immense subsidy in order to function (and they still function poorly). For the privilege of enduring traffic, air pollution, isolation, and monotony, Americans subsidize the suburbs to the tune of $100 billion a year. Without massive highway funding as well as fuel and mortgage subsidies, the suburbs could not exist. These subsidies to the suburbs have given us the twin illusions that the American city was in some sort of natural tailspin for decades and that the suburbs are inherently more desirable, when in reality the suburbs are just better funded.

- - -

Given the extreme illogicalness of the suburbs—the fact that only with hundreds of billions of dollars in incentives did it make sense for so many Americans to move out of cities and to the suburbs—it seems predictable that their drawbacks would manifest relatively quickly, and that those who could afford it would eventually find other ways of living. That's exactly what's happening: children raised in the suburbs have decided their lives would be better elsewhere, and if they have enough privilege, they have mostly decided to settle in city centers instead.

This desire to escape the suburbs is not in and of itself a bad thing. The suburbs are a terrible way to house Americans. From a progressive urban planner's perspective, an ideal world wouldn't even contain American-style suburbs. Everyone would live in denser environments surrounding public transit hubs. This is not outlandish fantasy but how much of the world looks: as Kenneth Jackson points out in *Crabgrass Frontier*, if you take a twenty-minute train journey from most European cities, you'll be in the country. And if American cities were built to accommodate everyone—the poor, the middle class, and the upper class—the influx of people and wealth back into city centers would likely be perceived very differently. After all, we cannot fault the children born into suburbs for abandoning an illogical, environmentally harmful historical anomaly in favor of something much better.

But cities in the United States are not built for everyone, and so the suburbs are not going anywhere. For one, the National Association of Realtors is the second-biggest lobbying group in the country, right behind the US Chamber of Commerce, and they have a vested interest in keeping the market for single-family homes strong. But the bigger problem is that there isn't enough equitable housing in cities. Everyone should have a right to live in a city, but with housing stock limited and poor regional planning the norm, those with a higher economic status are granted more choice in where they live. And with few protections for the poor, we can expect urban geographies to continue to be remade—the suburbs will continue to be abandoned by the rich, who will continue to move into urban centers, and the poor, who are never stably housed in this country, will get pushed out, forced to take whatever housing's left.

Soon most major metropolitan areas could start to look like the Bay Area does now. If you go to the central neighborhoods of San Francisco today, there are almost no people of color walking the streets. There are few stores with affordable food. The Castro seems more frequented by tourists than by gay residents. The city has become a sterilized, whiter version of itself.

To see San Francisco's former self, you now have to go outside it—to BART stations in the East Bay overflowing with passengers, to the highway leading to the Bay Bridge during rush hour, to the shared apartments and trailers in the exurbs of San Francisco. In these outer suburbs, there is no public transportation and no density, and community is hard to come by. This is what a gentrified city looks like: nothing like a city at all.

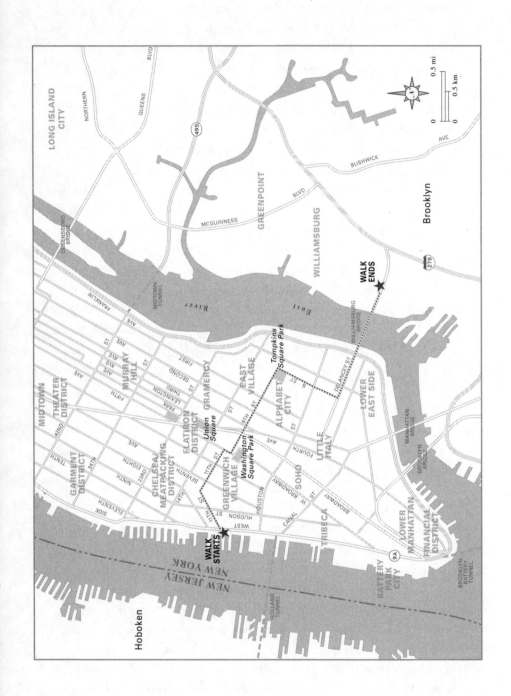

Part 4

New York

10

An Elegy

Who has the right to space? I feel like I deserve to be in this city, to see it, in some respects, as *my* city. To a certain extent, this makes sense: I was born in New York, I was raised at its heart, my family has roots here. My memories were made here. My connections are here. I see the world through a New Yorker's eyes (a former boyfriend would always complain when we visited other cities about how I'd compare everything—the food, the architecture, the people—to New York). But I'm also a gentrifier, and I come from a family of gentrifiers. I live a life of relative privilege. I provide New York with little of the authentic flavor and grittiness sought by writers who reminisce about the good old days of creativity and parties and queer chaos in the *real* New York. My life is pretty boring. I enjoy fancy coffee from time to time. But the New York that increasingly engulfs me seems even less interesting than I am. In the coffee shops filled with out-of-towners in Bushwick and Bed-Stuy and Prospect Lefferts Gardens, at the media meet-ups at bars on the Lower East Side, at parties, even in gay bars, I sense that I'm—to be quite honest—cooler than what surrounds me. Sure, that's a brag, but it's one I'm willing to defend: New York has given me a personality and an inner life that I cherish, and every day I can see that personality stand in increasing contrast to what New York is becoming. I feel the way Jimmie Fails and Joe Talbot felt in San Francisco: like a relic.

Maybe that's why my favorite days in New York are when I'm alone, on a long walk that gives me the space to ruminate on how I am connected to this city, how its identity is mine, how its changes have changed me. I need the distance from other people in order to fully take in its vastness and appreciate the immensity of its losses, to internalize its transformation so it doesn't overwhelm me.

I've begun taking these long walks through Brooklyn and Manhattan, sometimes tracing my childhood, sometimes exploring neighborhoods I do not know, seeing what's closed and what's opened, what block seems to be popping on a given day and what seems weirdly unchanged. There are a few times where I'll catch a glimpse of the city's former self—a block where there's garbage on the street, one or two delis, no new coffee shops, and maybe a couple of people in puffy winter jackets minding their own business, looking down at the sidewalk as they walk. These kinds of scenes trigger memories of a former city, and for a moment I can apply this scene, this sense memory of this old New York, to the rest of the city, as if my eyes were an X-ray machine; I can see briefly underneath the newness that's been plopped in gaudy layers on top of my home, and fantasize about peeling the layers off like dried Elmer's glue.

On a recent walk I decided to start at my childhood home, where my parents still live, and walk to Brooklyn, where I currently live. I began on West 11th Street, at the last building before the West Side Highway and the waterfront piers on the Hudson River. The piers were once an industrial and crumbling complex of concrete and now have been beautified with plants native to New York and bike paths.

This is where I grew up. My mom's parents, Holocaust survivors, came to New York after World War II and settled in Williamsburg, Brooklyn. They opened a fabric store in downtown Manhattan, built up the business, and then, like most middle-class people back then, upgraded their lives by moving out of the city, in their case to New Jersey. Eventually they moved back to New York, to a nice apartment in a doorman building near New York University. The fabric business had done well for them.

My mom met my dad, whose family had also had a long history in New York City but who had settled in upstate New York, in the late 1960s, when they, like the city, were broke. They were hippie college students who became psychology graduate students. Their first apartment together was on West 10th Street. They paid $65 a month. Right after my older brother was born, they moved into their current place on 11th Street. Back then, in the early 1980s, the building was one of the only residential structures on the block. Most of the others housed garbage trucks, and I remember waking up some hot mornings to the smell of the city's rotting leftovers, which would drift through the loft's open windows. Back then, this wasn't many people's idea of a good place to live, and so my parents got it cheap: $90,000, some $170,000 under the asking price.

It's hard to not sound nostalgic when talking about growing up in the West Village. My childhood home was just a few blocks from where Jane Jacobs wrote *The Death and Life of Great American Cities*. And even though I was born years after that book was published, its lessons felt applicable—I could have been a character in Jacobs's book. Jacobs wrote about how sidewalk life provides many of the things people in suburbs have to pay for—namely, safety and community—and that's what the Village provided me. I was able to walk on my own to elementary school on Hudson Street (now christened Jane Jacobs Way by the city) when I was ten years old, because I knew people on the route. My parents never worried. If they were late to pick me up from school, I could wait with Ernie, the friendly sandwich man down the block, or at the pizza place, where they'd give me free slices. Sure, I went through normal bouts of angst growing up, but the neighborhood I grew up in felt like a real-life Sesame Street in a lot of ways.

From an early age, though, I could that tell something was missing, that there was a shadow of a former New York casting a pall over the Village's aseptic, family-friendly aesthetic. There was some other city, maybe a seedier and more exciting one, that felt completely inaccessible to me, both because I was privileged and led a somewhat sheltered life and because it was already rapidly dying by the time I was coming to the age I'd need to be to enter its orbit. The piers on the Hudson River, which my parents' apartment overlooked until someone built a condo in front of their windows, were the same ones that New York's gay scene largely revolved around in the 1980s; where the famous documentary about voguing, *Paris Is Burning*, was filmed; where the queer artist David Wojnarowicz had sex with countless men and wrote about them all in one of the books I relied on most during my coming-out journey, *Close to the Knives*. But by the time I was fifteen, there were no more gay men on the pier. Down on Christopher Street, just a few blocks south, a huge black and Latino gay scene had flourished for decades. When I was a kid and a teen I'd see trans and gender-nonconforming sex workers walking Washington Street and flamboyant gay men hanging out on Christopher Street's stoops. I knew I was not part of this New York. I was too young. It was a different era. But I relished being raised within it, or at least beside it. But then the changes started to hit faster and faster. Every year I'd see fewer sex workers walking down Washington Street at night. A gay bar on Christopher would close, then another one. I'd been here long enough just to see the tail end of a world I'd heard so much about in books and movies.

I thought this was the end of the process. Even in my young brain it made sense to me that a gayborhood couldn't last forever—that people grew older and moved elsewhere and had kids and that things would change accordingly. But then the change kept going, and even accelerated. Even the family-friendly, middle-class neighborhood joints started closing: the cheap diner, the secondhand jewelry shops and antique stores where I'd browse after elementary school, the video store where my brother worked as a kid, the deli where I bought cigarettes when I was sixteen, the Chinese place (the better one), then the other Chinese place (the worse one), the pizza shop, the sushi place, a bar, the bakery, a laundromat, a grocery store, a pharmacy—all closed within about five years.

And then the people started leaving. I remember the day a gay guy moved out who'd lived in my parents' building since I was born. The Village was no longer the gayborhood, so what was the reason to stay? Soon after, the remaining artists in the building were gone. The monthly maintenance in the building had gone up. There were almost no more art supply stores or galleries downtown. Then some of the professional yuppie types left. What's the point of living in a relatively cramped place instead of the suburbs if they increasingly provide the exact same things? Then even some of the rich left. Gentrification has a way of creeping up on you. The white, hippieish middle class doesn't notice when the black queer kids go missing; the professionals don't notice (or don't care) when the hippies leave; the rich don't notice when the young professionals leave. And then you're left with the Village today: an upscale mall for international oligarchs.

At one point I noticed it was just my parents and my brother and me, plus a couple of older residents—the holdouts—mixed in with the new people, who seemed very different. They were the types who wouldn't say hi to me in the hallway; who would quickly close the front door on the way into the building out of fear someone would follow them in; who I would later learn worked for investment banks and as defense contractors and as corporate lawyers; who would spend millions from the communal co-op pot (which every apartment pays in to) in order to add security cameras to the hallways and renovate the lobby with hideous dark-metal finishes and expensive stonework; who in 2015, for the first time in the building's history, hired private security during the Village's annual gay pride parade to check people's IDs at the front door. The neighborhood felt like it was slipping into a new world, one in which everything except sterile aesthetics and expensive clothing and food was a threat. The rich had taken over the neighborhood, and their obsession with security made it clear they had no intention of giving it back.

A collection of small Marc Jacobs stores replaced the antique shops on Bleecker Street, an expensive tapas place replaced the good Chinese food place, a wine bar replaced one deli, an expensive deli replaced the other one, a bank replaced the other Chinese food place, and some kind of toy store that is so expensive I don't really even understand what they sell replaced the video store where my brother worked. Gay people no longer really hung out on Christopher Street, and the pier where I saw gay guys lying naked when I was a kid was renovated with millions in city funds and is now heavily policed and filled with joggers and babies. And over and over again I try to explain to people who aren't from here, who do not

carry the same mental geography of loss as I do, how it feels to see
the Village like this, and all I can say is it's sad, and that they'll never
understand.

That old New York, the one that I was too young to know but
which still felt tangible and real, even if I only knew its shadow,
now feels like it had to have been a dream. Standing on the corner
of West 11th Street with words by my favorite New York authors—
Sarah Schulman and Allen Ginsberg and James Baldwin—in my
head, it's hard to bring together their world and this one. It seems
impossible now, as I walk the streets—past the Michael Kors store
and the Marc Jacobs stores, past the hordes of tourists brunching
on $20 omelets, past the people who seem not to know how to walk
down sidewalks without blocking the people behind them, who
glare at the architecture in the neighborhood as if it were a luxury
good in a window at some store I cannot afford to shop in—that this
is the same place that could have inspired writers and artists. Whom
can this place inspire?

From my parents' building I look east, toward the rest of the
Village and Manhattan. One block north of me is Westbeth, the
first federally subsidized artists' colony in the country. The building
is old, tall, and gray and filled with aging artists reluctant to leave
the only place they can still afford in this city. A block south are
three glass condo buildings designed by "starchitect" Richard Meier.
When they opened in 2004, they were a sign that things were about
to change rapidly in the neighborhood: the first and second and
third waves of gentrification were over, and a fourth one, filled with
people who can afford $15 million apartments, was here. The Meier
buildings were also some of the first glass-fronted buildings in the
city. Now Manhattan and Brooklyn are filled with blue and green
glass knockoffs. One block to my east is a complex of low-slung
brick houses. Several of my childhood friends once lived in them.
They were at one point reserved for middle-income people through
a state program called Mitchell-Lama, which gave tax breaks and
low-interest loans to landlords willing to rent at below-market rates.
Then an investment firm called Island Capital bought the complex,
and New York governor Andrew Cuomo—who worked for Island

Capital before becoming governor—brokered a deal to take the apartments out of the Mitchell-Lama program and convert them to market rate. Several other Mitchell-Lama buildings are now going through a similar process. There were originally 70,000 rental apartments available through the program; that's now down to 35,000.

A little farther north is the meatpacking district, which was, quite literally, where they packed meat. I remember seeing bloody cow carcasses hanging from hooks and men in white smocks smoking outside the one diner there when I was a kid (the diner, inexplicably, has managed to stay open even as everything around it has closed). The High Line, once an abandoned elevated railway, has been turned into a park partially funded by the city but managed by a private group. It's closed at night. It would be a nice space to hang out in were it not a conveyer belt for tourists who start in Midtown, walk briskly down the extensively policed High Line, and end up on the streets of my neighborhood.

Beyond the meatpacking district is West Chelsea, which used to be mostly industrial as well. In 2005, the city used its most powerful urban planning tool—zoning—to turn West Chelsea's photo studios and warehouses into some of the most expensive real estate in the city. The Michael Bloomberg administration rezoned large swaths of the city, mostly from industrial and commercial to high-density residential. Developers were given free rein in these newly zoned areas. Most buildings were not required to provide any affordable housing, and in those that were, the percentages were low enough, and the definition of affordable loose enough, that they made virtually no impact.

And so multimillion-dollar condos fronted by twisted blue and green frosted glass have sprouted in Chelsea, in Midtown, and along every other corridor where the city has allowed height limits to be raised and zoning to be changed. Given the height of these buildings, you'd think street life in West Chelsea would be busy, but the neighborhood is still largely a dead zone. And that's because these buildings, like many in New York nowadays, are not so much places to live as places for capital to grow. Entire neighborhoods are becoming stash pads for the global elite who see real estate as a safer

investment than the stock market. Often few people are really living in these buildings, except for maybe a month or two out of the
year. Chelsea's not even the worst: a *New York Times* investigation
found that on a single three-block stretch in Midtown, 57 percent
of apartments are vacant for at least ten months each year. Absentee homeownership has grown by 70 percent in Manhattan since
2000. Even if you believe that attracting billionaires to New York is a
good idea, it's hard to understand why these apartments are assessed
at rates 1/100th of what they are worth. Because of New York's tax
code, a $100 million apartment in one of these new, super-tall glass
buildings is usually only taxed as if it were worth $3 million or $4
million. And even Mayor Bloomberg's more progressive successor,
Bill de Blasio, has done little to challenge this status quo.

As I walk east, I pass through the rest of the West Village and
Greenwich Village, thinking of Jane Jacobs and how she saw here
an example of what every city should be: a mix of residential and
commercial, old and new, lower- and upper class. A line from her
book pops into my head: "I am afraid people who do not [know the
neighborhood now] will always have it a little wrong in their heads,"
she wrote, "like the old prints of rhinoceroses made from travelers'
descriptions of rhinoceroses." The people who never knew what it
was will never understand what it can be. They see the current Village as a static place, not one that once meant something more to
the poor and the working and middle classes.

Seeing what it has become, I think of another Jacobs maxim:
extraordinary amounts of money, forethought, and policy are required to make a place feel so monotonous, sterile, and vulgar.

I walk along tree-lined 11th Street (one of the prettiest streets
in New York, if you ask me), past Magnolia Bakery, where dozens of
tourists perpetually stand outside to partake in their own personal
recreations of a *Sex and the City* episode that aired nearly twenty
years ago. I hit Seventh Avenue, and in front of me is St. Vincent's,
or what used to be St. Vincent's—the neighborhood hospital that
everyone in my family made use of at least once. It closed down to
make room for a condo development that now takes up the entire
block and where apartments go for $20 million. Down the block was

a good vegetarian Chinese restaurant that recently closed when its rent was raised from $5,000 to $25,000 a month.

Continuing on 11th Street, I hit Sixth Avenue, and then Union Square. One of the only open, European-style plazas in the entire city, Union Square was well on its way to being gentrified when I was growing up, but now it is essentially a shopping mall. If you've never been there, imagine a big town square like a piazza in Italy, but instead of government buildings and stately architecture flanking each side, there are stores: DSW and Walgreens and Nordstrom Rack and Best Buy, to name a few. It's a hypercapitalist's version of a stately plaza. This area did not naturally evolve to become an outdoor shopping mall. It took concerted effort.

During the 1950s, '60s, and '70s, Union Square was a site for protest and a gathering spot for New York's art scene. Andy Warhol's Factory was nearby, as were famous nightclubs such as Max's Kansas City. But after New York City went bankrupt in the 1970s, a consortium of business leaders, including the chairman of the board of Con Edison (New York's main electric company), proposed redeveloping Union Square as an essentially private enterprise. A business improvement district, or BID, took over Union Square, replacing city control. BIDs aren't unique to New York, but they wield a lot of power here. Business improvement districts in New York often do the work that a robust city government would do on its own, planning streetscapes, cleaning up trash, and policing the area. But a BID's employees are nonunion workers and get paid low wages, and BIDs have no special laws governing them, meaning they cannot be held accountable to voters/citizens in the same way that a government agency theoretically could be. BIDs are accountable to no one except the neighborhood businesses that provide 100 percent of their funding. Member voting rights in a BID are assigned to each business based on that business's land value. Today, Union Square is often blocked off by BID-sponsored barricades, its grassy areas protected with BID-approved netting, its security and cleanup paid for by the BID. Sure, thanks to the BID, Union Square is less dirty than it once was, but it's also no longer a public space in any true sense. "We're constantly trying to attract a specific demographic: young, moneyed consumers who know New York City from *New York Magazine* . . . and who watch *Friends*," a spokesperson for the Union Square BID (called the Union Square Partnership) once said. "We can train these young consumers to think of urban living on Union Square."

Harlem's 125th Street "revitalization" has a similar story: a cabal of development-friendly nonprofits has worked to bring in chain stores and luxury housing. Meanwhile, the media report on the "new" Harlem as if its progression to luxury and whiteness is somehow natural.

I take a right on Fifth Avenue and walk down to 9th Street, which is where my grandparents used to live. This block, unlike so many others, looks relatively unchanged. The mediocre restaurant is still on the corner. There's a Chase Bank, but that's been there for decades. Right below it, though, is 8th Street, which farther east turns into St. Marks Place—the locus of much of New York's punk scene in the 1980s. St. Marks is now mostly chain stores and restaurants that cater to NYU students. CBGB, the famous concert hall where a lot of big punk acts first made a name for themselves, is now a John Varvatos shoe store.

Farther to the south are Washington Square Park and New York University, which has been involved in its own gentrification battle for the last decade as the school has tried to expand its already ample real estate holdings into historic parts of the West Village. The school has become more corporation than educational institution, buying up real estate, raising tuition, and compensating its leaders with salaries in the millions of dollars. In exchange, the city has given it political support and free land—recently the school was sued for taking up three sections of public parkland in its proposed expansion, which the city agreed to.

And beyond that is SoHo, the original gentrified neighborhood. SoHo is often used by urban planners as an example of how neighborhoods can adapt to postindustrial capitalism—from factory to loft, from industrial to retail. But this ignores the fact that the neighborhood's "adaptation" was a forced one. In her study of lofts in SoHo in the 1980s, Sharon Zukin found that most industrial manufacturers in SoHo would have stayed if they were allowed and could afford it. Instead, the city rezoned the area to permit artists to live in formerly industrial spaces, and provided tax breaks for conversions to residential housing.

From 9th Street and Fifth Avenue, you can also see past Washington Square Park, past SoHo, all the way to the tip of Manhattan to Freedom Tower, or 1 World Trade Center—what once was the Twin Towers. The site is rarely criticized today because the buildings occupy hallowed ground, but before September 11 the Twin Towers were considered examples of terrible urban planning. And they were one of New York's biggest "urban renewal" projects: to make way for the massive structures, some 33,000 workers and small-business owners were displaced.

Planners and politicians often like to pretend we've moved past the urban renewal era—when highways and super-tall buildings were rammed through neighborhoods (most often majority-black ones, though in the case of the original World Trade Center many of the displaced were Syrian) in the belief that whatever came next would be more profitable and less social-service-intensive than what was there before. But New York has undertaken several projects in the past decade that have bulldozed mini-neighborhoods and replaced them with "higher-use" ones that are reminiscent of the first construction of the Twin Towers. On the far western edge of Manhattan, Hudson Yards is being billed as the largest real estate project in American history. It is its own neighborhood, with offices, apartments, and retail space. At least 20 percent of the housing will be affordable, but not much of that has materialized yet, and when it does, it'll largely be made up of 400-square-foot studios and 600-square-foot one-bedrooms in separate buildings. And it's not clear how affordable they'll actually be: the city uses the entire New York City region as its base for determining median income, including New York's rich suburbs. That means the area median income of New York is currently about $86,000. So if a new, affordable housing complex is set at 60 percent of AMI, that means it will be affordable to those making about $52,000 a year. The city is also on the hook for $650 million in bonds used to finance a new subway station for the area.

The most egregious example of recent redevelopment planning is Atlantic Yards, across the East River in Brooklyn. The project, recently renamed Pacific Park, includes thousands of apartments and a new arena for the Nets basketball team. It was spearheaded by the Empire State Development Corporation, a state agency that isn't required to elicit the same kind of public input for projects as a truly public project would. State land in downtown Brooklyn was given away to developer Bruce Ratner at under market price, but the thousands of jobs promised never materialized, and the new arena has had gentrification ripple effects throughout much of downtown Brooklyn, Fort Greene, Prospect Heights, Boerum Hill, and Park Slope, forcing independent stores to close and be replaced by chain stores that can afford higher rents, and pushing up rents for residents anywhere in the vicinity of the project. The city and state subsidized more than $2 billion of the deal. The city's own Independent Budget Office found that Atlantic Yards would cause a net loss to city revenue, but nearly every politician in New York approved of the project anyway. The borough's vice president at the time, Marty Markowitz, even took a trip to China to find investors for the project. "Brooklyn is 1000 percent, 1000 percent behind Atlantic Yards," he said. "There's nothing better than China and Brooklyn together."

Next on my walk, I take a left on 9th Street and pass through the detritus of the East Village and the Lower East Side. I never knew the old East Village, so it's hard for me to mourn its death properly, but I know the new neighborhood, and it's easy for me to imagine how anything would be better than this—an outdoor mall filled with recently graduated Goldman Sachs boys who can afford nights of $200 binge drinking, new condo buildings that block the skyline, and tourist-oriented shops that locals have no reason to go to. This is the area that was once home to punks, to anarchists, to social movements, to Latino rights organizations, to a street culture of protests and stoop-sitting. I know very few people who can afford to live in the East Village now. The Hispanic population in the East Village recently fell below 50 percent for the first time since 1980. East of Avenue B, an area often referred to as Loisaida because that's how Puerto Ricans would pronounce "Lower East Side," the Hispanic population dropped by 10 percent between 2000 and 2010. The neighborhood is just a microcosm of what's happening all over the city: for the first time since the era of white flight, the city's white population is now rising faster in Manhattan than it is in the suburbs, and the black and Hispanic population is rising faster in the suburbs than it is in Manhattan.

I walk through probably the most famous (and infamous) piece of land in the area: Tompkins Square Park, a block-long city-owned property that was a favorite hangout of heroin users and political activists back in the 1980s. It was also home to one of New York's first fights against gentrification: in 1988, demonstrators filled the park to protest an increased police presence there and the upgrading of buildings surrounding Tompkins Square into fancy condos and rentals. "Gentrification Is Class War," one banner read. Police attempted to corral the crowds with netting and batons, and eventually the park erupted into a mini-riot involving hundreds of protesters and 450 police officers. The city's Civilian Complaint Review Board received 121 complaints of brutality following the event.

Activists used the event as a way to highlight the police's complicity in gentrification: while there's no official NYPD policy, it seems that as soon as a neighborhood begins gentrifying, black and brown bodies are subject to increased violence and arrest at the hands of officers in New York. Bill Bratton, police commissioner under Mayor Rudy Giuliani in the early 1990s, popularized a style of policing known as "broken windows," which is the idea that arresting and ticketing people for minor, "quality of life" crimes such as littering and jaywalking prevents more major crimes. This style of policing, predictably, disproportionately impacts people of color and the poor, but New York's mayors, even the most liberal ones, such as Bill de Blasio, have doubled down on the strategy. It's important to note that the displacement that accompanies gentrification and policing are intimately related: there are 120,000 black men who would live in New York City today who are instead locked in prison, leaving their communities destabilized and more easily infilled with whites and outside wealth.

After the 1988 protests, Tompkins Square Park was dramatically altered to serve the police: it was redesigned by the city so that fences block off every grass area and paths wind in a way that prevents large groups from gathering. The one open space in the park that would theoretically be big enough for any kind of protest has been designated a dog run.

After Tompkins, I turn right on Avenue B and walk down about ten blocks to Delancey Street and past another city-supported development that is under construction. Essex Crossing will place thousands of glass-fronted condos at the intersection of the Lower East Side and Chinatown. This is, or was, one of the most culturally dense sections of New York. Essex Crossing will be at the entrance to New York's still vibrant but rapidly gentrifying Chinatown. It'll sit on top of a forty-year history of music and art that was birthed in the East Village. It'll further displace the Latino communities here that have managed to hang on. I look at it, turn left, and walk up and over the 7,000 feet of the Williamsburg Bridge, to Brooklyn.

- - -

Brooklyn, like the West Village, again makes me think of gentrification's ability to erase collective memory. I cannot imagine what people who aren't from New York think when they move to Brooklyn. Do they know they're moving into neighborhoods where just ten years ago you wouldn't have seen a white person at any time of day? Do they know that every apartment listed on Craigslist as "newly renovated" was once inhabited by someone else who likely made a life there before the ground under their feet became too valuable? It's hard not to feel guilt living here, and I wonder if other gentrifiers feel the same way. I represent the domino effect. I was priced out of Manhattan, but I know my existence in this borough comes at the cost of the erasure of others' cultures and senses of home. I know the woman with the Gucci bag in the West Village elicits the same kind of angst within me as my presence does for a native Brooklynite. I try to stay away from the hippest joints and I try to support long-established businesses, but I often fail at doing these things, and I know that even when I'm successful at trekking this increasingly narrow path, I've only done so much. Brooklyn, like the West Village, is irrevocably changed, and I know I'm part of that.

The question is, how do I stop it when the process is so much larger than me and has already progressed so far? Mass displacement means that there are fewer and fewer people left to act as historians for their borough, and so people coming to Brooklyn now know only that it's hip and expensive and has good brunch. As Sarah Schulman writes, gentrifiers "look in the mirror and think it's a window, believing that corporate support for and inflation of their story is in fact a neutral and accurate picture of the world." It's a circular logic that dictates Brooklyn is Brooklyn because it's *Brooklyn*—the brand mimicked by hipsters all over the world and mocked in hundreds of tired late-night parodies. What gentrifier sees Brooklyn not as it is but as the consequence of a powerful and violent system?

"There is something inherently stupid about gentrified thinking," Schulman writes. "It's a dumbing down and smoothing over of what people are actually like. . . . Gentrified thinking is like the bourgeois version of Christian fundamentalism, a huge, unconscious conspiracy of homogenous patterns with no awareness about its own freakishness. The gentrification mentality is rooted in the belief that obedience to consumer identity over recognition of lived experience is actually normal, neutral, and value free."

I see this mentality every day and also wonder if it's infected me—when I'm walking down the street on my way to a bar, glaring at my phone, am I the person Schulman is talking about? While gentrification cannot happen without state support, I think it also requires this learned or willful ignorance adopted by gentrifiers. If people saw themselves as part of a system perpetuating white supremacy and economic cleansing of neighborhoods, brunch would be less fun, and the logic of paying $3,000 for a studio apartment deep in a borough with inconvenient transit options would start to seem suspect. Individuals are not responsible for gentrification, but they—we—can be complicit in it.

It seems gentrification has always taken place in this mind-set. History professor Suleiman Osman points out that as Park Slope gentrified in the late 1950s and 1960s, magazines and newspapers were filled with embarrassing but telling quotes from gentrifiers who waxed ignorant about the charms of their new neighborhoods. One Greenwich Village expat complained in a local paper about the lack of coffee shops, a good jazz club, or "spring art shows along the promenade." Another article in *Vogue* described a woman meeting her electrician neighbor, "a lively young Italian with a warm, quick face and a pleasant way of whistling operatic arias while on the job." The electrician invited her over for some provolone and salami. "It is strange in New York to find yourself living in a real neighborhood," the transplant said. You'd be hard-pressed to find someone writing similar sentiments in today's Brooklyn, for two reasons: the borough is already so gentrified that finding any local character is a challenge, and because gentrifiers in New York are better-trained mediawise than they once were, self-conscious of their role in the destruction of the borough—or at least of the overhyping of it in the *New York Times*. But the articles and sound bites coming out of Detroit and New Orleans today sound remarkably similar, with gentrifiers praising the grit and local flavor of the people in their newly discovered homes. The continuousness of this mentality serves as a reminder that since the beginning of gentrification the process has involved the commodification of people and neighborhoods, and the transmogrification of normal neighborhood life into a story that can be sold like a play for the enjoyment of gentrifiers.

The only difference is that now those same ignorant attitudes are being backed by considerably more state power and global capital. Take Williamsburg, for example. While the media pumped out article after article about the surprising rise of hipster culture there, few reported on its real cause: in 2005, the city rezoned 170 blocks of Williamsburg and Greenpoint (essentially the entire waterfront), allowing high-end condos and rentals to replace factories and warehouses, and guaranteeing increased rent pressure on the area's low-income population. Private companies such as Clear Channel donated money to the Parks Department to turn a park on the neighborhood's waterfront into a quasi-public concert and food stall venue. And the L train, once bemoaned for its lack of service, was upgraded to run every few minutes during rush hour. Sure, Williamsburg was gentrifying before these interventions, but without them, it would have been literally impossible (legally because of zoning, and monetarily because of a lack of reliable transportation) to turn the neighborhood into a Miami Beach–esque bonanza of consumerism. The city repeated this successful gentrification-promoting rezoning in many other Brooklyn neighborhoods. In total, under the Bloomberg administration, more than 40 percent of the city was rezoned.

"The Bloomberg administration was kind enough to rezone most of Brooklyn, and enable developers to do large scale development," one real estate developer told a local news publication in 2015. "And in turn, people come to create life, to create families, to work and to do everything that we're doing."

With no one putting the brakes on the system—with no new rent control, no Works Progress Administration–era levels of new affordable housing—the process propels itself into illogical loops: parts of Brooklyn have become more expensive than lower Manhattan, and the borough has become the least affordable housing market in the entire United States. The new, progressive mayor of New York who won in a landslide with promises of affordable housing has now promised to rezone large sections of previously affordable neighborhoods such as East New York, with the caveat that some of the apartments there will be made affordable. But again, because of the area median income system, it's unclear how affordable they'll actually be.

And even though the prices keep rising, the commuting distances get longer and longer, and the little unique culture left gets trounced on by chains and upscale restaurants that serve more of the same, people keep moving here, even though no one seems to enjoy living here. There's an old semi-humorous line by a nineteenth-century historian about how the British Empire was not the result of some genius planning but instead was acquired in a fit of absentmindedness, and I sometimes wonder if gentrifiers go about their day with a similar distracted destructiveness. In 2014, a listicle posted on MTV.com with the title "17 Ways New York City

Makes You Want to Be Basic as Hell" went viral. It contained pictures of yards and laundry rooms, barbecue grills and a driveway, with the author lamenting all the ways in which New York was such a challenge compared to suburban living. And I wondered, as the article was shared over and over again, "Then why the fuck are you living here?" If gentrifiers do not even enjoy Brooklyn for what it is, then is it worth it to push those who live in it to its edges, past the areas that have become too hip to be affordable, or out of the city altogether?

Instead of leaving, these newcomers plant themselves in the borough, bring with them an internalized suburban logic, and then dispense that logic onto the borough's streets, insisting on expensive food and sterile streetscapes, Targets and Walgreens and apartment buildings that feel more like gated communities than like city-born edifices, replete with gyms and spas and sometimes even tennis courts, so that at the end of the day there are no winners in Brooklyn. It has been amenitized to a cultural death that has also ruined its affordability. The people who made the borough what it is can no longer live here, and the people who made the borough boring no longer want to. If this is what we get with gentrification, what's the point? The borough's destruction is so complete that even Mary-Anne Gilmartin, the CEO of Forest City Ratner, the group that developed Atlantic Yards and much of the rest of the borough, has complained about Brooklyn becoming too sterile to be sellable.

"You don't want Brooklyn to become so diluted and watered-down that it loses its edge," she said. "Could you have all this prosperity, all this growth, and still keep the ethos of the borough?"

It's become obvious the answer is no.

11

New York Is Not
Meant for People

In 2016, my brother and his wife, who have a three-year-old kid, were informed they'd have to leave their apartment in Williamsburg. They'd lived there for twelve years. The apartment—small but affordable—was being converted into a condo and sold for an amount of money they could not afford. Their next-door neighbor, who happens to be my ex-boyfriend, was also told to leave his one-bedroom apartment. The building's board gave him thirty days to get out. He's now subletting around the city, trying to find a permanent place to live that's within his budget. A few months later, fearing a similar fate, I tried to find out whether the apartment I was living in should be rent-stabilized. I filed a petition with the state, which starts a process that requires the state to inform the landlord of my petition. The landlord decided it was in his best interest not to renew my lease. I now rent the apartment month-to-month as I await a decision from the state, which could take years. My brother's family, my ex, and I are all middle-class people, and staying in this city is a struggle.

Around the same time, Baruch College and New York 1 (a local news station) conducted a survey that found 65 percent of all New Yorkers feared being priced out of their homes in the next few years. The findings cut across economic and racial lines: low-income residents, Latinos, and black New Yorkers were more likely to be worried about rising rents, but everyone, including a majority of people making over $100,000 a year, feared they were next in line. This is what a housing crisis looks like.

If the middle class and even some upper-income people can barely afford New York, what does it mean for the working class and the poor? My brother and sister-in-law are lucky they're able to afford more, even if it does strain their budget to remain in this city. I am flexible. I'm young, I have money, and I have no immediate family. I can figure it out. Others only have one option: fight back.

- - -

On Schaefer Street, deep in Bushwick, is a vinyl-sided three-story building. Ten years ago, most transplants would not consider moving into this neighborhood. Five years ago a few would, the "pioneers" maybe. Crime was high and the streets were dirty, but this is a nice neighborhood, located a few blocks from the L train, which takes you straight to Bedford Avenue in Williamsburg and then into Manhattan. And Schaefer Street is tree-lined, near a park, quiet, across from a school. There's plentiful parking. With gentrification encroaching from the west (the average rent for a one-bedroom in Bushwick is already up to $2,150), this building, like many buildings in the neighborhood, was an obvious choice for a mass eviction. Except its tenants wouldn't leave.

It started with a notice one day over the summer, slipped under each of the tenants' doors. "The building has been sold," it said. "Please direct all of your rent to the following address." Karen Genetta, thirty-six, immediately knew they were in for a fight. Genetta is the second-newest neighbor in the building, having moved in eight years before the notice came. The building was a mess—the hallway was literally falling to pieces, its front door wouldn't lock—but the rent was cheap, $1,000 for two bedrooms. And every one of the six apartments in the building was rent-stabilized, meaning rent could only legally be raised by a few percentage points each year. Most buildings built before 1969 with six or more apartments are covered by rent stabilization, but that hasn't stopped landlords from going

into hundreds of apartment buildings in Bushwick and kicking everyone out. There's not much data on how many people have been
illegally removed from rent-stabilized buildings, but a walk around
Bushwick suggests that the number is high: if you see an entire old
building being gut-renovated in Brooklyn, you can bet the tenants
did not leave without being illegally forced out. Sometimes landlords will offer buyouts of $5,000, $10,000, $50,000, even $100,000.
Many of those who take these buyouts do not realize how quickly
this money will disappear. If your rent goes from $800 a month in a
rent-regulated building to $2,000 a month in a market-rate building,
$50,000 only buys you a few years in your new apartment. But the
money can seem like a lot to those struggling to get by.

In this case, money did not matter, because the tenants knew
that at this point in New York's history, they'd have nowhere else to
go if they left. Their old landlord was a nuisance. He rarely made repairs, rarely cleaned, and came late to collect rent. But Genetta and
her neighbors put up with him because they knew they were getting
a good deal, and they suspected that everything would change if the
building was sold.

Then, without warning, the notices showed up under the door.
Soon after, two men appeared at the building, saying they wanted to
introduce themselves. They pushed their way into Genetta's apartment and asked to see her bedrooms. She could tell they were as-
sessing how much every apartment might be worth. She couldn't
tell much else: the men told her their names, their company had no
website. They gave no clue about what else they did. A few weeks
later, official-looking forms started arriving from the duo's LLC.
One said all the tenants would have to reapply for their apartments.
Another claimed each apartment owed $7,000 in back rent. This
would usually be the point in the story when tenants, not knowing
their rights, might start leaving. But one resident of the building
called a local nonprofit, the Ridgewood Bushwick Senior Citizens
Council (RBSCC), which has been in the neighborhood for decades
and has recently hired more lawyers to fight evictions.

The building's tenants started getting their paperwork in
order—rent receipts, proof of money orders from years back, their

leases. They started an email thread to send updates on the latest forms of harassment from their new landlords. One week they noticed the building's trash being thrown into the park across the street, and they suspected the landlords had instructed the super to do that, in order to get residents in trouble with the Department of Sanitation. Another week they noticed new security cameras in the building, pointing not at the hallway but directly at each tenant's doorway. The residents started relaying all the communications to RBSCC. The steps the tenants took were relatively simple, but far beyond what most people do. The only reason landlords buy rent-stabilized buildings is because they know in most cases they can get the people out. Next time one of the new landlords called, Genetta was prepared.

"I told them, 'If you need anything from me, call my lawyer and talk to him,'" she said. "He was speechless."

Genetta and her neighbors are not activists. They simply have no choice but to stand up for themselves if they want to stay in their homes. Genetta has a real estate agent friend who has been showing apartments across the street that are similar to hers for $2,500 a month. They know this is the only place they can live in the city. But she and her husband, Jakob, are the lucky ones: they don't have kids, Jakob has a steady job, and because their work is flexible (Karen works in e-commerce) they can always move to Berlin, Germany, where Jakob is from. That city has better rent control laws. Other residents have no plan B.

There's Lynn and Ramsey, who've lived in apartment 2L for twenty-five years. There's Ray, who grew up in the building. And there's Heidi Martinez, who lives upstairs and whose life is made more stressful daily by the goings-on in the building, but who stays anyway; Heidi, now thirty-eight, grew up just a few blocks from Schaefer Street.

"I clearly remember being five, six, seven, eight, nine, driving on Bushwick Avenue, being in the projects," Heidi told me. "And it felt like a Third World country back then."

Her family moved around and eventually settled in the Bronx. Six years ago, when Heidi was looking for an apartment for herself and her son, a senior in high school, she found the building on Schaefer Street. Even back then it was different from how it is today. Heidi remembers gambling in the hallways, a constant smell of weed. The first week she moved in, she heard people outside her door, looked through the peephole, and saw a few men climbing down the ladder from the building's roof, holding shotguns. It was terrifying. Still, she knew the neighborhood was changing, and she tried to get in on the action. She got her real estate license and started showing apartments part-time with a local firm. The job was slow at first, but suddenly there seemed to be dozens of people applying for each apartment she showed. The company she worked for told her not to accept any application unless the person's annual salary was forty times the monthly rent.

"I turned away hundreds of people," she said. "I was pulling my hair out trying to cut corners for them on applications."

She started hearing about buyouts more frequently. Her company asked her to drive an old lady around looking for apartments after she'd just been bought out of hers. The lady couldn't find anything to her liking. Then one day Heidi realized the same process was about to hit her block. She was at home alone, and she heard rustling in the hallway again. She looked at the ladder from the roof to see some men, real estate appraisers this time, climbing down.

"That was scarier than the people with shotguns," she said.

Heidi now works as a drug counselor. The money she makes isn't enough to allow her to take care of her son, pay for his college, and pay anything more than she currently pays for rent. So if the landlords eventually do figure out how to kick her out, Heidi says, she'll move to Florida. Her son can join her there after college. For now, she's just acclimating to the stress of not knowing how long she has here.

"It's nerve-racking, it's terrifying," she said. "You don't know if they're going to turn the heat off, or not make repairs. But we are getting used to it, I guess. Now it's kind of becoming a way of life."

Down two flights of stairs is apartment 1L, where Melvin Pitre lives. Melvin is forty, and he's been living here for thirty-five years. His mom threw him his fifth-birthday party in this apartment, which is now in dire need of repair. His sisters and brothers grew up and moved out, but Melvin stayed, taking care of his mother. When I met Melvin, he was sitting in his living room in a big pleather recliner in front of a small flat-screen TV. The apartment is sparsely furnished but feels lived-in. In May, when the building was being sold, Melvin's mom began battling breast cancer. She also started having heart trouble. By the time the new landlords introduced themselves to Melvin, his mom was in the ICU. One day the new landlords called to tell Melvin he no longer qualified for the apartment because it was in his mother's name; they told him he'd have to find another place, and offered to help him find one for $1,500 a month. That's three times what Melvin and his mother pay now. Melvin works in construction, but the work isn't consistent. He cannot afford $1,500 a month.

Perhaps because Melvin was paying the lowest amount of rent in the building, the new landlords tried the hardest to get him and his mother out, making excuses that the foundation of the building was in need of repair and that Melvin's living situation was dangerous. Melvin pleaded for them to at least wait until his mother got out of the hospital, but one day, with his mom back home and hooked up to a ventilator, one of the new owners came into Melvin's apartment and cornered him, yelling that Melvin did not want to make enemies out of a business that could afford powerful lawyers.

"If it would have been just me living here without my mom, I think I would have knocked him out," Melvin told me. "I was struggling not to do that because of my mom. For my mom to go through everything she's going through and then be homeless? That would have broke me." His mother passed away from heart failure shortly after the episode. And eventually Melvin went upstairs to get advice from Karen Genetta, Heidi, and the other neighbors who'd been organizing with RBSCC.

I recently met up with all of the tenants of the building. They were in Brooklyn's housing court, packed into a hallway with dozens of other Brooklyn residents in situations similar to theirs. Taped to the wall next to one courtroom was a list of about a hundred other buildings that would be involved in proceedings in court that week.

Almost every single building's owner was listed as an LLC, which meant it would be difficult to identify or trace the real owners. The Schaefer Street tenants' lawyer, Robert Cornwell from RBSCC, had sued to force the building's landlord to make repairs, and it seemed like the case was going well. While he was hammering out details with the landlord, the five tenants in the building stood in the hallway and joked about how close they'd become over the last six months of fighting. They looked like a family. Heidi picked off lint from Melvin's shirt. They argued about where they should all go on vacation together after this matter was over.

Their lawyer came out of the courtroom with good news: the landlord would make repairs. This part of the fight seemed to be over. But he warned the tenants that the landlord would likely start going after each tenant individually, attempting to sue them for non-existent back rent, pressuring them to leave, hoping the stress would break them. Despite the warning, the day felt like a victory. For now, they're safe, and each has placed a red sign in the window that in big block letters reads "No Buyouts."

- - -

New York City is in the midst of a housing crisis. New York is also, because of its liberal politics, its wealth, and its semi-strong welfare state, in possibly the best position, at least compared with other US cities, to handle a housing crisis. And unlike in other cities, where the electorate is still split on how to solve the gentrification problem (San Francisco mayor Ed Lee ran unopposed except by a few protest candidates who garnered low percentages of the vote and who were not backed by party money; mayors of other cities will not even mention the G-word), New Yorkers appear nearly united in their desire for a progressive solution. In 2013, the city's residents said as much when they elected Bill de Blasio mayor. De Blasio was supposed to be a long-shot candidate. He was polling in fourth or fifth place in the months leading up to the Democratic primary. But his campaign's message—a promise to fix the "tale of two cities" exacerbated by his immediate predecessor, Michael Bloomberg—resonated, and so he beat other, more moderate Democrats by double digits, and won the general election with nearly 75 percent of the vote.

New York, in this moment, has more of a chance of challenging gentrification than any other city in the country, yet every day rents rise and more low-income people are forced to leave. And those who don't leave face more stress daily just trying to live here. So if New York has more tools than any other place, why can't it stop gentrification?

In part, the difficulty arises from the fact that gentrification in New York has incredibly deep roots, so challenging the process there would require challenging a hundred years of the city's politics. New York was one of the earliest cities to adopt gentrification as an economic strategy. Fighting against that is like fighting the ether. But more than that, fighting gentrification here would also mean standing up to the entire philosophy of the growth machine, and to do that would require a truly radical politics. New York may be more economically progressive than most other US cities, but it, perhaps more than anywhere else, still relies on the growth of housing values for its revenue. And a progressive growth machine is still a growth machine.

In the early 1900s in New York, it started becoming clear to the city's business elite that poor people lived too close to the city's commercial center in Manhattan. There was a lot of valuable land there, but it was being occupied by crowded, dilapidated housing and factories—city inspectors had found 420,000 factory workers living below 59th Street at the time. Some of the richest men in New York got together to formulate a solution to the problem of the poor living too close to the city's center, and in 1922 they created what's now called the Regional Plan Association (RPA). It was headed by Charles Norton, an executive at First National Bank; a Long Island land baron named Robert De Forest; Frederick Delano, the uncle of FDR; and a few others. The men realized that profit could be made both by upgrading the city's center to high-end residential and commercial buildings and by speculating on land in the outer boroughs, where factories would be forced to move.

Together, the men put out a plan that essentially foretold what New York looks like today: the 1929 Regional Plan suggested that every industrial zone along both the Manhattan and Brooklyn side of the East River, as well as virtually every part of downtown Manhattan, be converted from industrial to commercial or residential. The plan explicitly recommended removing people from the Lower East Side and replacing their homes with "high class residences," as well as a highway linking the new buildings to Wall Street, where presumably the new residents of the Lower East Side would work. New York's most prominent planners and builders, including John D. Rockefeller and Robert Moses, relied heavily on the plan as they remade New York.

The Great Depression put big development plans on hold, but New York remained committed to deindustrializing and refilling itself with high-cost real estate. Deindustrialization impacted nearly every city in the United States, but New York was an exception in that it planned its industrial decline. That explains why whereas industrialization peaked in 1956 in the rest of the United States, New York's industry—mainly small manufacturing and garments—peaked ten years earlier. It also explains why New York was one of the only cities in the United States where land values *increased* as deindustrialization occurred. The planners had made way for a new kind of city, one focused on real estate, not industrial jobs, long before others caught on. Through the 1930s and '40s, New York's government continued to put pressure on the city to deindustrialize, while politicians simultaneously presented the city's industrial job loss as an inevitable consequence of cheaper labor in the South and globalization. That was a myth: during the decline of industrialization in the United States, New York actually had the cheapest labor force of any major city besides San Antonio, Texas.

The deindustrialization of New York was kicked into overdrive when an RPA-backed group called the Citizens Committee for Modern Zoning formed in the late 1950s to pressure the city to rezone. Most cities use zoning to separate industrial, commercial, and residential uses (Houston is the only major US city without zoning, but its residential neighborhoods are protected through other forms of restrictive laws), but New York uses it more extensively than perhaps anywhere in the United States. And while the city wouldn't state as much, New York mainly uses zoning to keep land values high. If factories were allowed to bloom next to Fifth Avenue, apartments on Fifth Avenue would likely be cheaper; similarly, if all of New York was zoned only for luxury housing, the luxury housing market might become oversaturated and collapse. Zoning is a way to keep the housing market in New York on a steady upward path. New York also uses zoning to privilege the wealthy, keeping areas such as the West Village and the Upper East Side zoned as low-density residential while allowing skyscrapers to be built in formerly poor areas. Bill de Blasio's plan to rezone areas of the city to add more market-rate and affordable housing rarely mentions the Village and places like it, instead relying on rezoning large sections of low-income neighborhoods such as East Harlem and East New York. So zoning regulations cause unneeded disruption for the poor, while making areas such as the Village feel rarer, more precious, and more valuable.

In the 1950s, lower Manhattan was largely still occupied by factories, especially in SoHo; that seemed unacceptable to the city's elite. "I don't know of any other area in the city where there's as good an opportunity to expand inexpensively," David Rockefeller (John D. Rockefeller's son) said. With pressure from the Citizens Committee for Modern Zoning, the city government rezoned nearly the entire city in 1961, along lines almost identical to the RPA's suggested plans. The rezoning limited manufacturing in most of downtown Manhattan, especially along its waterfront, and fit in nicely with David Rockefeller's plans to expand the financial district along the blocks hugging the East River, especially around Chase Manhattan Plaza. Rockefeller was the chief executive of Chase Manhattan bank at the time.

The rezoning caused a massive industrial flight from the city that likely wouldn't have happened without it. Between 1959 and 1989, the city lost 600,000 manufacturing jobs. Many US cities were deindustrializing at the time, but none of them as quickly as New York.

Zukin surveyed small-time manufacturers in downtown Manhattan and found that most wanted to stay put if it was economically feasible. But the rezoning meant that their buildings could be converted to lofts, which were more profitable to rent out than factories, and so most of them were booted. SoHo, as Zukin puts it, was the "creation of an investment climate" more than it was an actual neighborhood independent from the rest of downtown. Meanwhile, employment in finance, insurance, and real estate (known as the FIRE industries) increased by 25 percent, and employment in the service sector increased by 52 percent. This had the effect of adding tens of thousands of new FIRE-employed workers to the city while depressing the incomes of the middle class who had once been able to make relatively good wages in the city's factories.

It's perhaps not surprising that gutting an entire sector of employment would have adverse impacts on an economy, but when New York began looking seriously at its deteriorating employment situation in the 1970s, officials seemed befuddled that the city's economy was performing so poorly. The number of manufacturing jobs in New York City was cut in half between 1947 and 1980, and with few jobs for the middle class, and previously middle-class neighborhoods in disarray, the city nearly went bankrupt.

What New York did next would become a template for cities across the United States—it was the original test case for the "shock doctrine" strategy of redevelopment. What happened after Katrina and what's happening now in Detroit can largely be traced back to what New York did after its near bankruptcy.

On October 17, 1975, New York City owed banks nearly a half billion dollars but had just $34 million in its coffers. Mayor Abraham Beame called on President Gerald Ford to bail the city out. Ford refused. One of the most famous newspaper headlines in US history was printed by the *Daily News* the next day: "Ford to City: Drop Dead" (Ford never actually said those words, but a speech he'd given earlier made it clear he was not sympathetic to the city's financial woes). With no federal help in sight, Beame brought in Richard Ravitch, a developer and PR man, to formulate a plan. What Ravitch suggested has become commonplace today but at the time was a radical proposition: he wanted to cut city salaries, lay off city workers, and close hospitals, firehouses, and schools. He also convinced the teachers' union to bail out the city with $150 million in pension funds. Within days, thanks to the fiscal crisis caused by the purposive destruction of factory labor, Ravitch and Beame were able to bring the city down to the bare necessities of government. The change wasn't just economic but rhetorical and philosophical. Before its brush with bankruptcy, New York City represented the welfare state. Beame and Ravitch made it clear those days were over.

Today, the days when the city teetered on the brink of bankruptcy are remembered as an example of city leaders coming together to save a city from itself. Ravitch was even brought in to help Detroit with its bankruptcy in 2014. But the transition in New York was much bumpier at the time. Large protests were held all across the city. Unions got together to threaten a general strike. Garbage was thrown in the street to protest sanitation cutbacks. People occupied firehouses to draw attention to cuts, and started petitions to prevent college campuses from shutting down. The progressivism of New York did not die without a fight.

What the near-bankruptcy really was, more than a financial strategy, was a way to implement a new form of neoliberal government. In reality, New York didn't cut back on spending by much after the bankruptcy. By the early 1980s, government spending was beginning to increase every year once again. But the city began spending on different things, turning away from social programs that help the poor and toward ones that help the rich—namely, subsidizing redevelopment. The near-bankruptcy made New York the first US city to employ gentrification as governance.

Within a few years of the bankruptcy crisis, New York's elites started promoting the city as a destination for high-end businesses and tourists. In 1979, a report by the Twentieth Century Fund Task Force (another RPA-type organization with close ties to the city government) envisioned a "post-industrial" New York that would become the capital of global capital, the "principal marketplace and cultural center for the world." At the same time, the city launched a first-of-its-kind tourism campaign, which included the famous "I ♥ New York" logo still in use today. Meanwhile, as it attracted consumerist capital from across the country, the city began systematically underserving poor sections of the city. This was the start of the modern era of city-as-business. The poor in New York were becoming viewed as too unprofitable to serve, and those who were more profitable—tourists and the rich—were becoming the city's most coveted guests.

"We should not encourage people to stay where their job possibilities are daily becoming more remote," Roger Starr, the head of the city's Housing and Development Administration, said. "Stop the Puerto Ricans and the rural blacks from living in the city . . . reverse the role of the city . . . it can no longer be the place of opportunity. . . . Our urban system is based on the theory of taking the peasant and turning him into an industrial worker. Now there are no industrial jobs. Why not keep him a peasant?"

His comments angered many, and Starr resigned, but his words were nonetheless an accurate representation of city strategy at the time. Many are familiar with images of the South Bronx in the 1970s and '80s with entire blocks burning. Movies and books have been written about the landlords who lit those fires for insurance money and the gangs that flourished in the bombed-out shell of a neighborhood. Fewer people know that the phenomenon was a result not of acts by mischievous and desperate residents but of actions taken by the city itself: in the late 1960s and early 1970s, the city had targeted poor areas for intentional destruction through what New York senator Daniel Patrick Moynihan called in a letter to President Reagan "benign neglect." Essentially the city had decided it was better off without people in its poorest areas.

"Fires are in fact a 'leading indicator' of social pathology for a neighborhood," Moynihan wrote to Reagan. "They come first. Crime, and the rest follows. The psychiatric interpretation of fire-setting is complex, but it relates to the types of personalities which slums produce. . . . The time may have come when the issue of race could benefit from a period of benign neglect."

In 1976, the city cut thirty-four fire companies, relying on a study from the RAND Corporation that said the effects of shutting down those stations would be minimal, though letters from RAND employees from the time showed that at least some people knew the study was incorrect. Nearly all of the shut fire stations were in the Bronx and poor areas of Manhattan and Brooklyn. The effects were immediate and devastating. Fires destroyed entire neighborhoods.

In some neighborhoods in the South Bronx, 80 percent of the population fled between 1970 and 1980. Studies have shown that the majority of the fires during New York's decline were in areas where the city had cut fire departments. If you study the graphs of fire frequencies in New York neighborhoods where stations were closed, you can see spikes in fires right after stations are closed, and then a leveling off—a sign that nothing was left in those neighborhoods to burn. Autopsies of the crisis also show where populations were most affected: the South Bronx, East Harlem, Greenpoint, Bushwick, and the Lower East Side—all areas that today are targets for gentrification. In all, between 1972 and 1980, according to an analysis by epidemiologist Rodrick Wallace, 2 million New Yorkers were displaced from now-gentrifying neighborhoods, especially along the city's waterfront. Of those, 1.3 million, nearly all white, fled to the suburbs, and about 600,000, mostly African Americans and Latinos, were displaced to neighborhoods farther from the city's center.

With the city's poor and middle-class communities ravaged by fire and intentional neglect in the late 1970s, and the city's government on a mission to turn itself into a business-minded apparatus hostile to the needs of the poor, the ground was set for a communicable health crisis. HIV arrived at a time when the government of New York City was committed to not caring for its poor and vulnerable.

There was not a conspiracy to empty out the most gentrifiable areas through the spread of HIV, but that was nonetheless the effect: Chelsea, Harlem, the West Village, and the East Village had the highest rates of HIV in the 1980s. The deaths of tens of thousands of men, most of whom were gay, resulted in apartment vacancies in areas that were quickly becoming prime real estate. The city also began clearing out areas where LGBT people congregated—namely, the piers on the West Side Highway and Times Square. The City Council passed a health ordinance in 1985 that had the effect of shutting down gay theaters across the city.

With fires raging in the outer boroughs, safe spaces for LGBT people shuttered, and disease spreading rapidly, the city was in crisis in the 1970s and 1980s, most particularly for people of color, the poor, and LGBT New Yorkers. But the city's economy was increasingly being measured by a different marker that was unrelated to the well-being of the poor and middle class. Between 1970 and 1993 the United States lost about 1.3 million manufacturing jobs, while New York lost 480,000. In other words, while the United States lost 6.7 percent of its manufacturing jobs, New York lost 63 percent of its manufacturing jobs—its rate of industrial decline was nearly ten times that of the country as a whole. But at the same time, the FIRE industries started accounting for a larger and larger chunk of city revenue, and gentrifiers began taking a larger and larger role in New York's media narrative, so that by the time the city hit another recession in the late 1980s and early 1990s, with the AIDS crisis raging and the Bronx burning, hardly anyone outside of those most affected noticed. The recession was serious: 13.4 percent unemployment, 400,000 jobs lost in three years. But hardly a peep was heard in the media, and New York politicians seemed unfazed, because New York's economy had become, first and foremost, a real estate economy, and if real estate was doing fine, then that's all that seemed to matter.

12

Fight Back

Fighting for equitable geographies, for cities in which everyone, regardless of income, can comfortably live, is complicated. What do you fight against? The invasion of hipsters into a neighborhood? Rent increases and evictions? State and city policies? The lack of federal funds for housing? Income inequality? All of it? Pushing back against any of those things in a place such as New York means pushing back against a century of history and a deeply entrenched and wildly profitable real estate market. Since the RPA put out its first regional plan in the 1920s, New York's governance has been synonymous with a quest for higher real estate values. Today, New York's real estate is worth a combined $1 trillion. Fighting gentrification in New York feels a little like you are fighting what makes New York New York. But that also means that the old cliché about this city, "If you can make it here, you can make it anywhere," applies to the fight against gentrification. If activists can win here, at the center of global capital, it's likely their strategies will work anywhere.

- - -

Prospect Lefferts Gardens sits at the eastern edge of Prospect Park in Brooklyn. The park is Brooklyn's version of Central Park. It, like Central Park, was designed by Frederick Law Olmsted, and its curated natural beauty, like that of Central Park, has the ability to wildly inflate the real estate values of everything surrounding it. That's already happened to the neighborhoods at the north, west, and south ends of the park (Prospect Heights, Park Slope, and Windsor Terrace, respectively). Prospect Lefferts Gardens is the logical next step for developers. And the neighborhood is a good candidate for gentrification: it's filled with stately old townhouses and large prewar apartments. In 1990, Prospect Lefferts Gardens was about 80 percent black. By 2010, it was 68 percent black. The black population has likely decreased significantly since then. And that's all before a dozen luxury towers come to market, bringing thousands of new, richer, and likely white residents to the neighborhood. That's where Alicia Boyd comes in. She's a fifty-five-year-old activist, and she's singlehandedly responsible for stopping the complete gentrification of Prospect Lefferts Gardens.

I first met Boyd at a community board meeting in Brooklyn one summer. Community board meetings are usually sleepy and relatively benign affairs. The boards, made up of local residents, hold hardly any legal power in the city, but they nonetheless meet and vote on nearly everything new coming to a neighborhood, whether that be a development project, a bar, or a street redesign. I'd been to enough community board meetings as a young journalist that I expected the board to do what boards always do: talk quietly and lethargically for two hours and then disband. Within five minutes, I realized that wasn't going to happen here. For one, the board's meeting room was packed with people from the community, which I'd never seen before. I realized why: as soon as one board member spoke, Boyd rose from her chair and began screaming at the board members, saying they were conducting their meeting illegally, that they hadn't waited for public input on whatever they were voting on. The board members tried to calm Boyd down. Some were more aggressive and threatened to throw her out. But audience members began cheering for her. Several began to yell at the community board too. It became clear that this was an orchestrated disruption. Within about twenty minutes, the meeting was in such disarray that it had to be ended. Whatever was supposed to be voted on was tabled. Boyd turned around to the assembled crowd and smiled.

Boyd has become somewhat famous or notorious (depending which side you're on) for disrupting Community Board 9 meetings in Brooklyn. Every photo of her in the press is one of her screaming, finger pointed at whichever bureaucrat happens to be a few feet away from her. Politicians have painted her as unnecessarily rambunctious. Some have even called her crazy. But when I met Boyd at her townhouse on a quiet street a few blocks away from the park, she seemed like a different person. Dressed in a fuzzy pink robe and slippers and drinking a can of San Pellegrino, she was calm and engaging, and she seemed hyperaware of what she was doing. It became obvious that Boyd was far from crazy—she was just good at what she does, which is stop development from encroaching in Prospect Lefferts Gardens. The screaming was protest and performance, and possibly the only thing keeping Prospect Lefferts Gardens safe from becoming the next luxury enclave. When I saw her at community board meetings, I was seeing an actor onstage. Sitting on her plush couch in her old townhome, I got to see her in her downtime.

"Don't think my outbursts aren't calculated," she told me in her living room. "Don't think I'm not intelligent enough to know what I'm doing. The community board doesn't fear me because I yell. They fear me because when I yell they respond, and when they respond, I document, expose, and educate."

There's always a camera recording when Boyd is in the room, and when she yells, she gets people on record saying all kinds of nasty things. So far, her outbursts have led to the removal of two members of Community Board 9. But the yelling is also a stalling tactic: as long as Boyd can stop the board from asking the city for a rezoning, at least part of Prospect Lefferts Gardens will remain intact.

Mayor Bill de Blasio has attempted to rezone dozens of neighborhoods with an eye toward creating 80,000 new units of housing for low- and middle-income people. But that housing will piggyback on the construction of hundreds of thousands of new market-rate housing units. It's a strategy known as inclusionary zoning: the city lets developers build much taller buildings, as long as between 20 and 50 percent of the apartments are kept affordable (though, as we've seen, there's a lot of disagreement about what rent levels the city deems "affordable"). But even with affordable apartments, it's unclear how bringing in unprecedented levels of market-rate housing to previously affordable neighborhoods could affect current residents. One study by New York's comptroller predicted that de Blasio's planned rezoning of East New York could displace as many as 50,000 people.

After months of research and connecting the dots, Alicia Boyd realized that a neighborhood had never been rezoned without a community board first asking the Department of City Planning to do a study. So her mission now is to never let Community Board 9 hand in its request for a study. For the last year and a half, she's been successful. Nearly every community board surrounding Boyd's neighborhood is now in the process of being studied for a rezoning. Prospect Lefferts Gardens stands alone, thanks almost entirely to her.

Still, development is encroaching. On one block where tall buildings were already permitted, a twenty-three-story glass-and-concrete-fronted tower now looms over everything else in the neighborhood, casting shadows over the park. The building received a $72 million loan from the state for its construction. At least a dozen other luxury buildings are slated for the area. On Empire Boulevard, which could theoretically be rezoned if the Department of City Planning ever got around to it, warehouses sit vacant, their owners stockpiling properties to eventually sell to luxury housing developers. More and more people of color seem to be leaving the area each month. Boyd knows several friends who've moved down south. Her own daughter left New York after her rent jumped by $300 a month—she wasn't technically displaced, but she's not returning anytime soon either.

I asked Alicia why she keeps doing this, exhausting her energy and straining her vocal cords explaining to people over and over again why the city's plan, as friendly as it may seem to low-income folks, could actually be disastrous. Her answer hinted at the vastness of the work that needs to be done to combat gentrification.

"All of this country's history is a history of black resistance," she told me. "When we fight back, change happens. It's the getting us to stand up and fight back that's the issue. When do we get to a point where we stand up and say, 'I'm fired up, I can't take it no more'? I know I'm fired up. I know I can't take it no more."

- - -

The last two mayoral administrations in New York have proven the limits of our current political system's ability to deal with gentrification. Mayors Bloomberg and de Blasio don't represent opposite ends of the traditional political spectrum—they're both liberal on social issues, and both have supported higher taxes and a more expansive welfare state than most American mayors do. But they come from two different schools of thought on gentrification and housing development. Bloomberg is likely the most pro-growth, market-driven mayor the city will see for decades, and de Blasio, the first Democrat elected mayor of New York in twenty years, is likely the most liberal, pro–government intervention mayor the city will see for a long time. And both not only did little to stop gentrification, they actively promoted it.

Bloomberg, who ran as a Republican, won election against his opponent in 2001 shortly after the September 11 attacks and after spending $73 million of his own money on election materials—$98 per vote he received in the general election. His campaign message was essentially that he'd bring the private sector into public life, making government more efficient and the city more profitable. And shortly after he became mayor, he got to work courting developers and high-end companies without much regard for the ripple effects of making New York a luxury destination.

In 2003 he and the city's Economic Development Corporation held an economic summit closed to the public for a hundred of the most successful businesspeople in the city. One panel focused on attracting foreign wealth to New York. Another panel focused on the apparent need for office districts outside of New York and building New York's "first-class talent pool."

"New York City is never going to be the lowest-priced place to do business; it is just the most efficient place to do business" Bloomberg said at the summit. "If New York City is a business, it isn't Wal-Mart—it isn't trying to be the lowest-priced product in the market. It's a high-end product, maybe even a luxury product."

Two weeks later, in his State of the City address, Bloomberg laid out his rebranding of New York, saying that New York needed to compete for elites and multinational corporations with other global cities. "We must offer the best product, and sell it, forcefully," he said.

To that end, Bloomberg dispatched his economic development team to Asia and Europe to attract high-end companies to New York. On one trip, he hosted some of London's richest residents in his personal Victorian townhouse on Cadogan Square. He also created the position of chief marketing officer to help sell the city to corporations around the world.

Branding wasn't enough. While Bloomberg was more willing than most neoliberal mayors to tax the rich—in 2003, through a variety of tax increases (mostly via property tax increases), Bloomberg added another $3 billion to the city's coffers—he also spent lavishly on development, giving away $1.4 billion in subsidies to private developers in his first five years in office. And he supported giveaways to projects such as Bruce Ratner's Atlantic Yards and Related Companies' Hudson Yards.

Bloomberg refused to put protections in place for low-income New Yorkers as this new wave of capital hit. His administration did little as tens of thousands of rent-regulated apartments were deregulated, evictions spiked (there were nearly 29,000 evictions in Bloomberg's last year in office), and median rents rose by 75 percent. When New Yorkers began complaining about the increased unaffordability of their city, Bloomberg's answer was basically to get over it.

In 2014, after the mayor had been in office for twelve years (including a third term Bloomberg won after campaigning heavily to lift the two-term limit on the mayoralty and spending a record $174 per vote on campaigning in his third term), the public showed its frustration with Bloomberg's tenure by electing Bill de Blasio, largely on the strength of his promise to remedy New York's growing inequality. De Blasio pledged to usher in a new progressive era, yet his administration has become one of the most divisive in decades, possibly more so than Bloomberg's. Maybe that's because with

Bloomberg, people knew what they were getting, whereas de Blasio promised economic equality and then doubled down on many of the growth strategies Bloomberg had promoted.

To be sure, de Blasio's housing policy is more progressive: his administration set aside $36 million to help tenants facing landlord harassment, he's mandated that developers who build in rezoned areas of the city make at least 20 percent of their apartments affordable, and under his watch the city has begun building new city-sponsored affordable housing for seniors and artists. But in refusing to challenge the philosophy that corporate and residential growth is an inherent good, de Blasio has failed to stop the growth machine destroying New York's neighborhoods. Thanks to his progressive policies, the machine is now less blunt than it was in the Bloomberg years, but it is still destructive. After all, the vast majority of the new affordable housing promised by de Blasio will be built only because tens of thousands of new luxury apartments will go up in neighborhoods that are already experiencing rapidly rising rents. De Blasio is even leasing public lands to luxury developers in order to get money to fix up the public housing New York already has. The mayor says it's the only option the broke New York City Housing Authority has to maintain its dilapidated housing stock, but activists see it as yet another private encroachment on public space. Even the city's private developers have been pleasantly surprised by how pro-development the de Blasio administration is. His deputy mayor for housing and economic development, Alicia Glen, came not from a lefty think tank or nonprofit but from Goldman Sachs, where she oversaw $3 billion in investment in cities.

In 2015, I got a chance to sit down with Glen and ask her about the city's housing crisis. Our interview made it clear that she saw the need for action, but that her solution would not fundamentally challenge gentrification. De Blasio and Glen are progressives, but without challenging the fundamentals of real estate capitalism, their vision is severely limited. I asked her if she understood people's concerns about being priced out of neighborhoods that were rezoned by the administration she works for. Her answer was similar to Bloomberg's: get over it.

"The reason why so many people are pissed is that they have been conditioned to the fear of change," she told me. "I don't like it when my dry cleaner changes ownership. It pisses me off because I've known those people for years. It stresses me out. I don't like change. But change is inevitable and so how you shape the future is incredibly important as opposed to letting it wash over you. Because it's coming."

Glen said that the difference between the de Blasio and Bloomberg administrations was that growth was now coupled with new housing and infrastructure for the poor. Still, she said, growth was inevitable, and good for the city.

"We have certain tools in our municipal tool box," she said. "We can't change the entire history of capitalism and we're not Trotsky. You try to redistribute some of that growth to the people that need it."

What Glen laid out for me was an undoubtedly more progressive vision than New York had seen in decades—more low-income housing, a focus on protecting the poor from capitalism. The policies she and de Blasio propose are more progressive than virtually any others in the United States. But they're not enough. New York will still gentrify. And if one of the most progressive mayoral administrations in the United States cannot fundamentally challenge the destruction of neighborhoods and the displacement of New Yorkers, it means that something bigger, more fundamentally transformative is needed.

- - -

Municipal politics are a good start, but gentrification is a global problem that must be challenged on a global level. Mayors focused on attracting capital and jobs and focused less on providing for the poor are a logical consequence of existing in a country with little coordinated federal housing and economic policy. Capital is more mobile than ever, and if a city such as Detroit or New Orleans did not cater to the whims of banks, corporations, and ratings agencies, it would not be able to borrow money to build infrastructure. Does this excuse the city from running itself equitably? No. But there's

only so much a city can do. New York and San Francisco are in better positions—they have stable industries (finance, tech) that would
have a hard time picking up and leaving, and that's part of the reason
New York is able to get away with giving fewer tax incentives to keep
companies in its borders. But Alicia Glen is right: the city has only
a specific set of tools in its tool box. New York City cannot overturn
capitalism (and its leaders do not want to). Even small changes such
as modifying rent control would take an act by state legislators in Al-
bany, who are perpetually unfriendly to New York City–specific legislation and any laws that could be seen as anti-business. And larger
changes—say, building another round of public housing—require
more money. New York has the most robust public housing system
in the United States; it's the only major city that has not demolished
its high-rise housing projects. Yet it can hardly maintain them, much
less add to its stock. Doing that would require a New Deal–level
appropriation of federal funds.

In the United States, housing is not considered a human right,
and the ability of people to live in a given place is subject to the
whims of the market. Challenging this may sound like a radical
proposition, but it is radical only in the United States, in the same
way universal health care is a controversial concept only here. Most
other industrialized countries have realized the market will not provide for low- and middle-income people, and so their systems have
made adjustments. The United States lags behind.

There are, of course, many steps to take before the United States
adopts a fairer housing system. In a country where even things such
as a child's ability to get the food needed to survive, whether in the
form of food stamps or free school lunch, is up for constant debate
in Congress, a more rational, equitable, and compassionate housing policy may be a long way off. Getting there requires challenging
not only housing and economic policy but systemic racism as well.
It also means linking up with other movements. In the same way
that the suburbs were both an economic project *and* a race, gender,
and political project that reinforced conservative values, pro-urban,
anti-gentrification movements must recognize that what we build
and what we fund can have a disparate impact on different groups.

If we're going to challenge gentrification, we also have to untangle the web of racism and sexism that is built into housing and urban policies. How many urban planning and economics programs have courses on race and gender in cities? Harvard's planning program, one of the most esteemed in the country, does not have one, and neither do many other schools.

That does not mean gentrification is inevitable. Cities, capitalism, and inequality are human creations, and relatively recent ones at that. Still, it took an immense effort to create the unequal, environmentally destructive, and psychologically harmful ways in which we live today, and challenging that will require an equally immense effort.

Nearly sixty years ago, Jane Jacobs recognized the need for a change in how we envision cities. "Private investment shapes cities, but social ideas (and laws) shape private investment," she wrote. "First comes the image of what we want, then the machinery is adapted to turn out that image."

But Jacobs's philosophy lacked a significant racial and class analysis. There are plenty of people who already know what we want and need—better housing, better schools, better transportation, more money—but they are disenfranchised and therefore unable to achieve it. So the problem of solving gentrification is not only about economics or urban planning, but about democracy. What would cities look like if the people who lived in them, who made them function, controlled their fate?

On a weekday night one fall, I attended a planning meeting for the Brooklyn Anti-Gentrification Network, an umbrella group of about fifteen people-of-color-led activist organizations in the borough who have come together to fight tenant harassment, unequal development, and police brutality. The meeting room, a normal office in Midtown Manhattan, was packed with about a hundred people who politely discussed their strategy for fighting gentrification. For a room filled with so many people representing so many different interests and backgrounds, the conversation was remarkably level-headed and productive—a rarity among activist groups, and maybe a sign that people are fed up enough with gentrification to do away with infighting.

"Community control is our theme," Alicia Boyd told the room.

Then the activists went around the room and read their demands. Most were specific to New York: an end to tax breaks for developers, more transparency in the de Blasio administration. The group had decided it would be best to fight locally, for if they expanded to the entire city or the entire nation, they'd dilute their power. But the activists I spoke to understood this is part of a much larger fight—the process they are fighting is bigger than the individual, bigger than a new coffee shop on the corner. They understand that while their fight is local, it is connected to a global struggle to put everyday working people's decisions at the heart of community building.

A few weeks later, I heard about a protest organized by the Brooklyn Anti-Gentrification Network outside the Brooklyn Museum. Apparently an annual summit attended by some of the most powerful real estate corporations in New York was going to be held that year at the museum, one of the borough's biggest cultural institutions. The borough president, Eric Adams, and former New York governor Eliot Spitzer were scheduled to speak. The agenda included panels such as "There Goes the Neighborhood! Value Added Opportunities in an Oversaturated Market," and "Brooklyn's Finest: The Next Phase in Brooklyn's Development." The state, capital, and cultural institutions coming together to gentrify Brooklyn—the symbolism was perfect for a protest.

It was cold and windy outside the Brooklyn Museum on the day of the summit. On one side of the Brooklyn Museum is Prospect Lefferts Gardens and Flatbush—the next neighborhoods likely to be hit by a wave of gentrification, and which activists such as Alicia Boyd are trying to save. On the other sides are Prospect Heights and Crown Heights, which are already largely gentrified.

As real estate developers stepped out of their cabs and limos and walked into the museum, protesters screamed "Whose city? Our city!" over and over again. Boyd spoke about her work. So did people from the Bronx, Manhattan, Queens, and Staten Island. There were just a couple dozen protesters, holding signs and yelling chants. But the mood was upbeat. Cars stopped, drivers honked, passersby took flyers. The protesters joked around and hugged each other as they came and went. There was a feeling that despite the small size of the protest, it meant something significant. This was, after all, the sixth time this real estate summit had been held, and this was just the first protest of it. Maybe next year's protest would be bigger. It seemed like the first step to movement building. And so the protesters were energized, happy to be there in the cold, holding strong at this nexus, ready to defend what's left.

Conclusion: Toward an Un-Gentrified Future

I see my nephew growing up in New York and I wonder what he will make of it. I already feel ambivalent about my birthplace; by the time New York is all glass condos and $4 muffins, will he hate it? Or will he embrace the lifestyle he grows up in and become some new kind of New Yorker I have not seen?

His mental geography is and will be completely different from the one I hold, just as mine is completely different from the one my brother walks around with, which is completely different from my parents' mental map, which in turn is far removed from their parents' mental map of New York. We all have our own private cities within us, and how we conceive of them translates into how those cities operate. Just a few decades ago the city was viewed by many Americans as anathema to American values, as a place where the worst parts of our society—crime, poverty, decay—coalesced. To those with privilege, the city was something that could be ignored except when needed for work and play. To many older people, cities still evoke this response. My grandma still finds the idea of someone *wanting* to live in Brooklyn insane. Now, as Sarah Schulman points out, we are witnessing the first generation of young people in the United States to grow up in the suburbs and idolize the city. We are in a never-before-seen cultural and geographic moment.

If we all conceptualize the reality and possibility of the city uniquely, how can we be on the same page when it comes to building an equitable future? To the person just moving to New Orleans, all the white hipsters biking around the Bywater is not the sign of the displacement of 100,000 black people; to someone moving to Williamsburg now, the glass condos are as much a natural part of the cityscape as anything else. In this way, gentrification suppresses and displaces memory, and makes it harder to build lasting justice. This ignorance benefits the powerful—a new resident who has no memory of the old Mission District in San Francisco is much less likely to protest what others may see as its destruction when a condo comes along. So if we are committed to fighting for an ungentrified future, the first step is to build consensus about what a city should be.

Through my research on gentrification, I've learned of dozens of policy solutions to gentrification and displacement that are realistic and proven to work. The trick is convincing people that they *will* work. The following list is heavily influenced by Tom Angotti, professor of urban affairs and planning at Hunter College; Robert Fitch, the late radical journalist who wrote *The Assassination of New York*; author and critic Samuel R. Delany, who wrote the book *Times Square Red, Times Square Blue*; Brooklyn activists and educators Alicia Boyd and Imani Henry; as well as the countless activists and residents I've met in researching this book in all four cities.

Expand, protect, and make accessible public lands. In New York, 30 percent of all land is public (mostly streets and sidewalks). Half of the other 70 percent is taken up by private development, the other half by city infrastructure, institutions, and public space. The little land that's left should be land-banked—that is, taken off the market—by the city. In the 1980s, after the city's economic collapse, the city owned nearly half of the buildings in Harlem. What would have happened if, instead of selling those buildings off to private developers at bargain-basement prices, which is what the city did, it instead preserved those buildings as city property and turned them into affordable housing and community space? It's not too late to do this in some parts of New York and San Francisco, and there's an even bigger opportunity to do this in Detroit and New Orleans, where tens of thousands of parcels of land are owned by municipal governments. The current method of dealing with these properties in New Orleans and Detroit is to sell them off to the highest bidder instead of figuring out a more productive public or semi-public use for them. Land banking would not have to mean never selling the land, but it could mean adding conditions to development—for example, requiring developers to build a certain percentage of affordable housing before land is sold. And with a good land-banking program, a local government could open up the decision-making process to residents, requiring public input before a piece of land is sold off or developed. This is already happening on a small scale: all four cities in this book have small nonprofits working to collectively buy land and keep it affordable. But their work is a drop in the bucket of what's needed.

Give people an actual say in what happens in their city. New York's community boards are the closest thing any of the four cities in this book have to local democratic planning, and they have almost no power over planning decisions. The de Blasio administration is currently rezoning 15 neighborhoods, and so far nearly every single community board has rejected the administration's proposals, but those rejections had no impact on the rezonings. These boards should have real power. Because of California's unique ballot initiative system, San Francisco is the only one of the four cities profiled in this book where residents can relatively easily get a housing-related ballot initiative voted on in a citywide election. In 2015, one ballot initiative attempted to limit Airbnb rentals, and another tried to place a moratorium on development in the Mission. This is a great concept, but like nearly all elections in this country today, money wins: both ballot measures in San Francisco were defeated after multimillion-dollar ad campaigns by Airbnb and other corporations. As far as I know, there is no perfect or even relatively good system for local, democratic planning decisions in the United States, but that does not mean they are an impossibility. Community boards in New York were created after activists, including Jane

Jacobs, pressured the city to involve the community in decisions. Any new system will require an equal effort.

Heavily regulate housing. In 1942, Congress passed a law that prohibited the inflation of rents and the prices of consumer goods and made it illegal for landlords who were in search of higher rents to evict tenants. The act was meant to be temporary, to curb wartime inflation, but it became the basis of New York's rent regulations, which still keep hundreds of thousands of apartments affordable today. If the country can do it once, there's no reason it cannot do it again. Rents are rising rapidly everywhere in the United States, and not only in gentrifying cities, as banks and corporate landlords speculate on the price of land and buy up more and more apartments to eliminate competition. A national rent regulation law and/or tax on land speculation could help with this crisis.

Implement a new New Deal. Under FDR's New Deal housing program, the federal government helped build nearly $700 million in public housing across the country, the equivalent of about $12 billion today. In an age of government cutbacks, spending billions on housing may seem unrealistic, but other developed countries have proven public housing can be done well, even in hypercapitalist economies. In Hong Kong, almost half of all housing is public. New York City still manages 328 housing projects that house some 400,000 residents—impressive by US standards, and proof that public housing is still viable in this country.

End protectionism, add infrastructure. Why do Presidio Heights in San Francisco and Greenwich Village in New York look remarkably similar to how they did fifty years ago, while the Mission District and East New York are expected to bear the brunt of new development? Cities in the United States are several times less dense than their European and Asian counterparts. (New York is an exception, but its density is very uneven from neighborhood to neighborhood.) The flocks of people moving to New York undoubtedly would rather live in Manhattan than East New York, yet because the city protects much of Manhattan's residential areas with restrictive zoning but allows up-zoning in poorer areas, gentrifiers are funneled into areas that are least capable of dealing with waves of new residents. The same is true in San Francisco, where new condos are flooding the Mission and other affordable neighborhoods and the city government is allowing new, giant office buildings to be built in previously affordable neigh-borhoods. New, equitable zoning would change this. But densifying US cities would mean adding infrastructure to deal with new resi-dents, in particular more public transportation, already stretched to its breaking point in many gentrifying cities. And that would require more money in city budgets, which leads to the next point . . .

Raise taxes, raise wages, spend on the poor. In the 1950s and 1960s, the top tax rate for the richest Americans was 91 percent. Until 1981, it was 70 percent. Today it's about 40 percent, and be-cause of all the loopholes that have been added over the years, the real rate is closer to 25 percent. That means the federal government barely has enough money to spend on food stamps and road repair, much less a new New Deal–style commitment to the poor. Mean-while, with the minimum wage stagnant in many states, low- and middle-income people must spend higher portions of their income on rent. Without new taxes and a higher minimum wage, inequality is likely to continue increasing in the United States, and that means the poor will have less and less spending power and be less and less stably housed, allowing their neighborhoods to be gentrified.

- - -

Any one of these solutions would be better than what the United States currently does to house the poor—a patchwork of under-funded programs that vary from state to state, city to city, and county to county, and that are often administered through nonprofits and for-profit low-income housing organizations that are not accountable to the public to the same extent that governments are.

But achieving any of these policy solutions will require a lot of political effort. If you start to add these policies up—more regulation of land and housing, higher wages, higher taxes, federal construction of housing and infrastructure—you get something resembling socialism, and achieving that in the United States will not be an easy feat. But I believe that while there are ways to ameliorate gentrification under lightly restrained capitalism (which is what I'd call the current US economic system), there will be no solution to the crisis without true economic and racial equality.

As I wrote this book, tremendous strides were being made in that fight. The Black Lives Matter protests made police violence and continued racial oppression a daily topic in the news. Movements for queer and trans rights have recentered gender and sexuality at the forefront of social justice conversations. Even mainstream politicians are beginning to preach racial and economic justice. But housing is curiously absent from most of these conversations. The cost of housing is rising everywhere, in suburbs and in cities. The majority of the populations of San Francisco and New York fear getting priced out, yet gentrification and housing prices were hardly mentioned in the presidential debates leading up to the 2016 election (Hillary Clinton held a milquetoast forum on the issue in Oakland). While there are great national organizations, such as Right to the City, that attempt to organize tenants and connect housing issues with other social justice causes, there is no well-known national fight for tenants' rights. Compare that to London or Berlin, where gentrification is less intense than in San Francisco and New York but where protests over gentrification have been a regular occurrence over the last few years.

There seems to be a lack of consciousness about housing in this country, and that makes building an effective tenants movement hard. Perhaps our ignorance stems from suburbanization and sprawl; it's hard to build movements when people are kept far apart in separate houses on separate lots with few communal spaces except ones used for commerce—roads and malls and office parks. That suburban, individualistic mentality is now seeping into cities thanks to gentrification. With every new condo—and most now come outfitted with things like gyms and pools, day care centers, and bars in their lobby—it seems like cities become a bit more like vertical gated communities. Soon you'll be able to live in a city without experiencing it at all. Ethnographer Rachel Sherman writes in her study of upper-class hotel guests that hotel experiences are a way to reinforce class distinctions. Being doted on gives guests a sense of entitlement they do not enter the hotel with. Riffing on this study, anthropologist Julian Brash posits that a similar mentality is now affecting cities. If New York is a luxury product, how will that change its residents' sense of class and entitlement? How do you begin to form a tenants movement in a city where many residents feel like consumers of luxury products, not community members?

There's also a deeper reason that will make it hard to challenge gentrification in the United States. This country was founded on displacement—on the idea that white men have a greater right to space, and even to people's bodies, than anyone else. That's taken the form of slavery, segregation, the genocide of Native Americans, and now, to a certain extent, gentrification. As one Bushwick activist group called Mayday says in its chants and the signs it puts up around the neighborhood, gentrification is the new colonialism. This may seem like an extreme statement, but when ads for condos and *New York Times* Styles section pieces use such precise language about "frontier" neighborhoods and "pioneering" residents, it's hard not to draw parallels. Gentrification is obviously very different from colonization, but they stem from the same mentality, which tells people that one person's space is more valuable than another's. The origin story that we tell ourselves over and over again in this country—that good, brave men came and settled a foreign, dangerous, and wild land and made it civilized—is essentially a gentrification narrative, and American development has always hinged on the idea of a conquered frontier. To fight gentrification is to fight American thinking. Gentrification is in our blood.

But it doesn't have to be. First we have to decide what we want. I, for one, believe that the most interesting parts of New York are the ones that don't make people money (or at least not a lot of it): the queer scene, the activism in its streets, the random book clubs and literary events that could only happen in a city as dense as this one. But as author and activist Samuel Delany points out, living in a hypercapitalist city such as New York means that unprofitable modes of interacting are always at risk of being crushed by profitable (and therefore less interesting and radical) ones. The community space is replaced by a condo; the cheap bar where different classes can mingle is replaced by a place only the rich can afford. And so we must always be creating new institutions and new ways of interacting if we hope to challenge ourselves as individuals.

We have to find new ways of being with each other in gentrifying cities. Sarah Schulman makes that theory a bit more concrete: what happens, she asks, if a few groups of radical writers in New York got together and began thinking about how to challenge gentrification? What happens if you started a group that sought to get nonprofessional activists or writers or thinkers together? What happens if this happened ten times over? Small changes can begin to have big consequences.

I've often complained about trying to be creative or an activist in New York these days—with so much money going toward rent, how does anyone afford the time to do something rebellious? But these are precisely the moments when rebellion is most possible— when the pressure of capital causes a breaking point. I see more people angry nowadays, frustrated with New York. But instead of challenging the institutions that create the anger, most seem to complain, shut up, or leave. What happens if people started using the little space we have for radicalism not to safely critique aesthetics and individual choice, or to write yet another "goodbye to all that" essay and move to a cheaper city, but to throw our power at the institutions that make it so hard to live here? This can take the form of protesting or art, but resistance can be even simpler than that. The "street ballet" Jacobs spoke of was not a profitable act. Today, our lives are increasingly isolated and commodified, and lifestyles of consumption make those with power more money. The less community we have to satisfy our needs, the easier it is to extract capital from us. In other words, saying hi to your neighbor really can be a radical act because it's unprofitable, uncommodifiable. Is it enough? Of course not, but it's a start. The more we practice intentional and community-oriented living, the less useful we will be as consumers. Radicalism is not a matter of wishing for a revolution, but a process consisting of thousands of little actions that build toward personal and global change.

- - -

After years of living in New York and feeling depressed about its state, I finally decided to stop feeling sorry and start feeling activated. Recently I made a concerted effort to get to know my neighbors. I made sure to say hi in the halls. I emailed them when I had a question. I started offering people in the subway help with their heavy items. I filed a petition with the city to determine if the building I live in is meant to be rent-stabilized. It's unclear what the result of that will be, but it made me feel more connected to the place where I live. I began attending meetings about gentrification. These weren't just things I thought of as good deeds, but a way to help reorient myself in the city. Separately they felt insignificant, but together they helped me see myself, and my city, as connected entities that are capable of changing each other. I've begun to appreciate New York more now, and so I am more willing to fight for it. The question I still have is whether it will ever be enough. Or will the city keep changing so fast that it will not matter how many individuals attempt to put the brakes on that change or dictate how and why change happens?

In 2015, I began seeing signs of a deflation or eventual collapse: rental prices in Queens, where gentrification was predicted to spread to after Brooklyn, began decreasing. Rents in other boroughs began flattening. The consensus among real estate professionals seemed to be that there was too much luxury housing. It's not true only in New York either: Detroit is still in the midst of a building boom, but in New Orleans, things seem to be leveling off—construction rates, for example, have fallen. For the first time in five years, Silicon Valley lost more workers than it gained. The share of tech workers living in the Bay Area looking for employment outside of it increased from about 25 to 35 percent in a year, a sign that even high-income residents want to leave.

Is gentrification ending? No. But it is slowing. Cities will never go back to how they were. I highly doubt New York or San

Francisco, given their stable industries, will de-gentrify in the fore-seeable future. Detroit and New Orleans are a different story. If a few companies pull out of Detroit, the city could easily falter again; New Orleans is still extremely vulnerable to natural disaster. But I believe the process's period of hyperdrive is coming to a close, and with people now more conscious about how to grapple with its consequences, we have an opportunity to do something before the next wave of capital hits. As Sarah Schulman points out, not every moment is revolutionary. Before the hippie, antiwar, and civil rights movements of the late 1960s began to really take hold, there had been decades of foundational work laid by writers, filmmakers, poets, performers, activists, and others that helped people conceive of a different future. I believe we are in one of those foundational periods right now, on the precipice of something larger. It's time to start building.

Acknowledgments

I'd like to thank the residents and activists of New York, New Orleans, Detroit, and San Francisco I interviewed, especially Ashana Bigard, Kim Ford, Aaron Handlesman, Lauren Hood, Anabelle Bolaños, and Alicia Boyd.

I'd also like to thank the dozens of authors whose research and writing informed and inspired this book, particularly Sarah Schulman and Rebecca Solnit, whose work changed how I view my relationship to cities.

My editor at Nation Books, Katy O'Donnell, was great at every step of the way, and Alessandra Bastagli, the head of Nation Books, took a risk on me that made this book possible. Thanks to Sean Devlin, who helped me with my early research.

This book was also made possible by my family and friends who gave me the encouragement needed to go through the insane process of writing a book (turns out it's hard!) and who've argued with me over the dinner table countless times about politics, helping me refine my thinking and learn to put together a cogent argument—especially my mom, Sally, my dad, Michael, my brother, John, my sister-in-law, Christina (and hi to my nephew Julian), and my friends Zach Howe and John Walker. Also thanks to my dog, Remi, who is getting a mention only because Zach and John would say he'd feel left out otherwise. To Anne Marie Witchger and James Martin: growing up in New York would have been less crazy, less fun, and less weird without you, and you therefore deserve a lot of credit for influencing me to write a book that in many ways is a love letter to the city.

I began thinking about issues (namely, capitalism) critically because of two people: Bayard Faithfull, my eleventh-grade history teacher, and Nat Turner, another teacher in my high school. Without their communist propaganda being available to me at a young, impressionable age, I'd probably have embarked on a very different life path. Thanks for brainwashing me (in a good way). And it was Fred Bever, former news director at WFCR in Amherst, Massachusetts, who allowed me, at the age of twenty, to run around the state interviewing politicians and other high-profile people in the name of journalism, even though my palms were nearly too sweaty to grip a microphone. You taught me essentially everything I know about the profession. Thank you.

Notes

Introduction

2 **rechristened "Palazzo Chupi":** Penelope Green, "The Painter and the Pink Palazzo," *New York Times*, November 13, 2008.

2 **An average one-bedroom in the West Village:** Rent Jungle, "Rent Trend Data in New York, New York," www.rentjungle.com/average-rent-in-new-york-rent-trends, accessed September 28, 2016.

2 **In September 2014, a Texas oil heiress:** "Fortresslike Property on Greenwich St. Is One of the Most Expensive Mansions Ever Sold in Manhattan," *New York Daily News*, September 12, 2014.

2 **The only area consistently less diverse:** Arun Venugopal, "Micropolis: A Look at the Least Diverse Neighborhood in the City," WNYC, May 8, 2012.

6 **Between 2000 and 2010, the black population:** Richard Campanella, "Gentrification and Its Discontents: Notes from New Orleans," *New Geography*, March 1, 2013.

7 **Rents in these three areas have increased:** J. C. Reindl, "Rents Keep Going Up in Greater Downtown Detroit," *Detroit Free Press*, December 7, 2014.

8 **The poverty rate in the suburbs:** Metropolitan Policy Program, Brookings Institution, "Confronting Suburban Poverty in America," 2015, http://confrontingsuburbanpoverty.org.

8 **"The Hipsterfication of America":** Linton Weeks, "The Hipsterfication of America," National Public Radio, November 17, 2011.

8 **"Brooklyn: The Brand":** Stephen Metcalf, "Brooklyn: The Brand," *T: The New York Times Style Magazine*, March 17, 2013.

8 **the overuse of the word *hipster*:** Philip Corbett, "Everything Old Is Hip Again," *After Deadline* blog, *New York Times*, August 17, 2010.

8 **overzealous comparisons of everyplace to Brooklyn:** Philip Corbett, "Brooklyn, Planet Earth," *After Deadline* blog, *New York Times*, November 18, 2014.

9 **"If cultural choice and consumer preference":** Neil Smith, *The New Urban Frontier: Gentrification and the Revanchist City* (New York: Routledge, 1996), 55.

Chapter 1: Hanging On

16 **"broadened and internally whitened":** Richard Campanella, "Gentrification and Its Discontents: Notes from New Orleans," *New Geography*, March 1, 2013.

16 **"with fresh eyes and ears":** Lizzy Goodman, "Experiencing New Orleans with Fresh Eyes and Ears," *New York Times*, March 6, 2014.

16 **"In New Orleans success":** Ibid.

16 **"New Orleans is not cosmopolitan":** Ibid.

17 **New Orleans lost more than half its entire population:** "Facts for Features: Katrina Impact," Data Center, August 28, 2014, www.datacenter research.org/data-resources/katrina/facts-for-impact.

17 **by 2010, the city's white population had:** Data Center, "Who Lives in New Orleans Now?," February 2016, www.datacenterresearch.org /data-resources/who-lives-in-new-orleans-now.

17 **From what little research there is . . . Utah and New York:** Lynn Weber and Lori Peek, *Displaced: Life in the Katrina Diaspora* (Austin: University of Texas Press, 2012).

18 **"It took the storm of a lifetime":** From a press release issued by Gov. Kathleen Blanco, November 9, 2005, www.blancogovernor.com/index .cfm?md=newsroom&tmp=detail&articleID=1193.

20 **NORA was involved in funding no fewer:** "New Orleans Redevelopment Authority: Major Projects," www.noraworks.org/about/projects.

20 **It also loaned about $2 million:** Lolis Elie, "Oretha Castle Haley Boulevard Gets Help from City as It Tries to Turn the Corner," *Times-Picayune*, August 2, 2009.

20 **Finally, the city directed its anti-blight team to prioritize:** Eric Velasco, "The Battle for New Orleans," *Politico*, April 16, 2015.

20 **"I believe in leveraging the market":** Alex Woodward, "O.C. Haley Avenue: The Next Freret?" *Gambit*, April 17, 2012.

21 **over 40 percent of families live below the poverty line:** US Census Bureau, Poverty Data, 2013, http://factfinder.census.gov/bkmk/table/1.0 /en/ACS/14_5YR/S1701/8600000US70113.

23 **"Gentrification is much more":** Jason Hackworth, *The Neoliberal City: Governance, Ideology, and Development in American Urbanism* (Ithaca, NY: Cornell University Press, 2007), 120.

23 **Usually those policies come in the form:** Neil Smith, *The New Urban Frontier: Gentrification and the Revanchist City* (New York: Routledge, 1996), 37.

24 **the median area income at the 2000 census:** "Lower 9th Ward Statistical Area," Data Center, March 28, 2014, www.datacenterresearch.org/data-resources/neighborhood-data/district-8/lower-ninth-ward.

24 **one of the highest rates of African American homeownership:** Bracey Harris, "Lower Ninth Ward Residents Fight Katrina Fatigue," *New York Times*, May 27, 2014.

24 **During Katrina, the concrete barriers:** Jordan Flaherty, *Floodlines: Community and Resistance from Katrina to the Jena Six* (Chicago: Haymarket Books, 2010), 65.

24 **After the storm, residents reported hearing:** Kenneth Cooper, "'They Destroyed New Orleans,'" *AlterNet*, December 23, 2005.

25 **In 1927, the Mississippi River flooded:** Vincanne Adams, *Markets of Sorrow, Labors of Faith: New Orleans in the Wake of Katrina* (Durham, NC: Duke University Press, 2013), 43.

25 **Then in 1965, black New Orleanians experienced displacement:** Juliette Landphair, "The Forgotten People of New Orleans: Community, Vulnerability, and the Lower Ninth Ward," *Journal of American History* 94 (December 2007): 837–845.

25 **"Those who want to see this city rebuilt":** Christopher Cooper, "Old-Line Families Escape Worst of Flood and Plot the Future," *Wall Street Journal*, September 8, 2005.

26 **"The first rule of the rebuilding effort":** David Brooks, "Katrina's Silver Lining," *New York Times*, September 8, 2005.

27 **New Orleans has the highest percentage:** Paula Devlin, "The Changing Face—and Faces—of New Orleans," *Times-Picayune*, August 23, 2009.

27 **107 of the city's 128 public schools:** American Federation of Teachers, "The Track Record of the New Orleans Schools After Katrina," 2014, www.aft.org/sites/default/files/wysiwyg/no_intro.pdf.

27 **Like many in New Orleans, Bigard never received a college degree:** Approximately one-third of all New Orleans residents have a college degree, according to the US Census. That's up from 26 percent in 2000, which suggests that most of the increase came from newcomers to the city after Katrina, and not from an increase in the native-born population going to college. See Data Center, "Who Lives in New Orleans Now?"

28 **about 5,000 new nonprofit workers showed up:** Campanella, "Gentrification and Its Discontents."

28 **the Housing Authority of New Orleans was forced to revoke:** Richard Webster, "HANO Recalls 700 Section 8 Vouchers, Blames Sequester," *Times-Picayune*, March 29, 2013.

29 **River Garden . . . expire in 2017:** Richard Webster, "River Garden Residents March in Protest, Management Pushes Back," *Times-Picayune*, January 24, 2013.

Chapter 2: How Gentrification Works

31 **British sociologist Ruth Glass:** Ruth Glass et al., *London: Aspects of Change* (London: MacGibbon & Kee, 1964), introduction. Quoted in "50 Years of Gentrification: A Timeline," NextCity, 2014.

31 **"One by one, many of the working class quarters":** Ibid.

31 **"Gentrification is not 'genocide' but 'genesis'":** Everett Ortner, "Gentrification—Clarified," *The Brownstoner* 15, no. 2 (July 1984): 1.

31 **"I think one should approach the acquisition":** Ortner, quoted in Loretta Lees, Tom Slater, and Elvin Wyly, *Gentrification* (New York: Routledge, 2008), 7.

32 **"The gas-lit outside appeal of the new homes":** Quoted in Lees, Slater, and Wyly, *Gentrification*, 27.

32 **MIT urban studies professor Phillip Clay:** Phillip L. Clay, *Neighborhood Renewal: Middle-Class Resettlement and Incumbent Upgrading in American Neighborhoods* (Lexington, MA: Lexington Books, 1979).

33 **San Francisco experienced an influx of gays:** "The History of the Castro," KQED, 2009.

33 **there is evidence that the white LGBT community:** Carolyn Senn, "Gentrification, Social Capital, and the Emergence of a Lesbian Neighborhood: A Case Study of Park Slope, Brooklyn," master's thesis, Fordham University, 2013.

34 **"the reach of global capital":** Neil Smith, *The New Urban Frontier: Gentrification and the Revanchist City* (New York: Routledge, 1996), 100.

34 **a *New York Times* investigation found that 50 percent:** Julie Satow, "Pied-à-Neighborhood," *New York Times*, October 24, 2014.

35 **They came to New York to be artists, activists, authors:** For more on consumption explanations of gentrification, including a discussion of sociologist Daniel Bell and economist Richard Florida, see Lees, Slater, and Wyly, *Gentrification*, ch. 3; for more on production explanations, see ch. 2.

36 **"As part of the experience of postwar suburbanization":** Smith, *New Urban Frontier*, xxiii–xiv.

36 **"taming of the wild, wild West":** Neil Smith, "Home on the Range, Urban-Style," *New York Times*, August 12, 1985.

36 **"Here you'll find a group of like-minded settlers":** Katarina Hybenova, "How Is Life at Bushwick's Most Controversial New Building, Colony 1209?" *Bushwick Daily*, June 26, 2014.

38 **"Having produced a scarcity of capital":** Smith, *New Urban Frontier*, 23.

39 **By funding the construction of roads outside cities:** John Hansan, "WPA: The Works Progress Administration," Social Welfare History Project, Virginia Commonwealth University, 2013, socialwelfare.library.vcu.edu/eras/great-depression/wpa-the-works-progress-administration.

39 **Between 1977 and 1984, there were 130 such conversions:** Lees, Slater, and Wyly, *Gentrification*, 29.

40 **"gentrification is a back-to-the-city movement":** Smith, *New Urban Frontier*, 70.

41 **"Though the majority of residents may never contemplate":** Quoted in Jason Hackworth, *The Neoliberal City: Governance, Ideology, and Development in American Urbanism* (Ithaca, NY: Cornell University Press, 2007), 15.

41 **"They are the ones that pay a lot of the taxes":** Michael Howard Saul, "Mayor Bloomberg Wants Every Billionaire on Earth to Live in New York City," *Wall Street Journal*, September 20, 2013.

42 **Reagan cut all nonmilitary spending:** Veronique de Rugy, "President Reagan, Champion Budget-Cutter," American Enterprise Institute, June 9, 2004.

42 **That's exactly what happened to Detroit:** Reuters, "Detroit Credit Rating Downgraded Again, S&P Cuts General Obligation Debt Further into Junk Status," *Huffington Post*, July 19, 2013.

42 **The result, to paraphrase planning and geography professor Jason Hackworth:** Hackworth, *The Neoliberal City*, 39.

42 **At one point ads promoting "Life in Cbus":** Rian Bosse, "How Cities Are Trying to Attract Millennials," Donald W. Reynolds National Center for Business Journalism, April 13, 2015; Teresa Wiltz, "America's Declining Cities Try to Attract Millennials," *Governing*, April 3, 2015.

43 **Through its tax credit programs:** "Citywide Highlights," City of New Orleans website, www.nola.gov/mayor/priorities, accessed September 4, 2016.

43 **It sold off properties (many abandoned since Katrina):** Robert McClendon, "Where Will Working Poor Live in Future New Orleans, if Gentrification Continues?" *Times-Picayune*, July 30, 2015.

43 **It began marketing residential neighborhoods:** Lauren Laborde, "Go-NOLA TV: Discover New Orleans' Bywater," hosted by C. J. Hunt, GoNOLA website, September 8, 2014.

43 **"Hurricane Katrina was an awful event":** Eric Velasco, "The Battle for New Orleans," *Politico*, April 16, 2015.

Chapter 3: Destroy to Rebuild

46 **of the 1.36 million applications for assistance filed with FEMA:** "From the Graphics Archive: Mapping Katrina and Its Aftermath," *New York Times*, August 25, 2015.

46 **A year later, there were at least 111,000:** Maria Godoy, "Tracking the Katrina Diaspora: A Tricky Task," National Public Radio, August 2006.

46 **"FEMA was scrambling to get people anywhere they could":** Peter Moskowitz, "How One of Katrina's Feel-Good Stories Turned Bad," *Buzz-Feed*, August 22, 2015.

46 **Home prices in Bywater . . . doubled post-Katrina:** Richard Campanella, "Gentrification and Its Discontents: Notes from New Orleans," *New Geography*, March 1, 2013.

48 **one black New Orleanian named Henry Glover:** Elahe Izadi, "Post-Katrina Police Shooting Death Reclassified as a Homicide," *Washington Post*, April 1, 2015.

48 **Police also shot and killed two unarmed people:** Associated Press, "New Orleans Police Officers Jailed over Katrina Shootings Get New Trial," *The Guardian*, September 17, 2013.

48 **"These are some of the 40,000 extra troops":** "Military Due to Move in to New Orleans," CNN.com, September 2, 2005.

49 **Before Katrina, the New Orleans public school system:** Naomi Klein, *The Shock Doctrine: The Rise of Disaster Capitalism* (New York: Picador, 2007), 6.

50 **"This is a tragedy":** Milton Friedman, "The Promise of Vouchers," *Wall Street Journal*, December 5, 2005.

50 **Research from Tulane University:** Adrienne Dixson, "Whose Choice? A Critical Race Perspective on Charter Schools," in *The Neoliberal Deluge: Hurricane Katrina, Late Capitalism, and the Remaking of New Orleans*, ed. Cedric Johnson (Minneapolis: University of Minnesota Press, 2011), 135.

50 **Activists called the takeover an educational land grab:** "The Educational Land Grab," editorial, *Rethinking Schools* 1, no. 21 (Fall 2006).

50 **Some data suggest the RSD is indeed successful:** Alan Greenblatt, "New Orleans District Moves to an All-Charter System," National Public Radio, May 30, 2014.

50 **only about 6 percent of high school seniors in the RSD:** Mercedes Schneider, "New Orleans RSD: Far from Meeting Louisiana Four-Year College Admission Requirements," *Huffington Post*, February 9, 2015.

50 **A 2013 survey found that while 53 percent:** "K–12 Public Education through the Public's Eye: Voters' Perception of Public Education," Cowen Institute for Public Education Initiatives, April 2013.

51 **And New Orleans's system of school choice requires parents:** Mercedes Schneider, "New Orleans Parental Choice and the Walton-Funded OneApp," *deutsch29* blog, July 5, 2013.

51 **"It is about breaking unions":** "The Educational Land Grab."

51 **Those who were hired back were stripped:** United Teachers of New Orleans, Louisiana Federation of Teachers, and American Federation of Teachers, "No Experience Necessary: How the New Orleans School Takeover Experiment Devalues Experienced Teachers," June 2007, 22.

51 **During the 2004–2005 school year, only 9.7 percent:** Ibid., 29.

52 **Between 1990 and 2008, 220,000 units of public housing:** Edward Goetz, *New Deal Ruins: Race, Economic Justice, and Public Housing Policy* (Ithaca, NY: Cornell University Press, 2013), 70–72.

53 **"The storm destroyed a great deal":** Matthias Gebauer, "Will the Big Easy Become White, Rich and Republican?" *Der Spiegel*, September 20, 2005.

53 **"There's just been a lot of pampering":** Jordan Flaherty, *Floodlines: Community and Resistance from Katrina to the Jena Six* (Chicago: Haymarket Books, 2010), 186.

53 **One state representative went as far as to say:** Charles Babington, "Some GOP Legislators Hit Jarring Notes in Addressing Katrina," *Washington Post*, September 10, 2005.

53 **"We finally cleaned up public housing in New Orleans":** Flaherty, *Floodlines*, 186.

53 **the City Council finally voted to knock down:** Adam Nossiter and Leslie Eaton, "New Orleans Council Votes for Demolition of Housing," *New York Times*, December 21, 2007.

53 **that means 12,381 people:** Flaherty, *Floodlines*, 187.

54 **Instead, management groups run by nonprofits and private companies:** Richard Webster, "River Garden Residents March in Protest, Management Pushes Back," *Times-Picayune*, January 24, 2013.

54 **Road Home, Louisiana's main program:** Vincanne Adams, *Markets of Sorrow, Labors of Faith: New Orleans in the Wake of Katrina* (Durham, NC: Duke University Press, 2013), 35.

54 **And in 2011, a court found that Road Home:** Jordan Flaherty, "Settlement Reached in 'Road Home' Racial Discrimination Lawsuit," Bridge the Gulf Project, July 11, 2011.

55 **New Orleans was the second-least-affordable housing market:** Greg LaRose, "New Orleans Ranked Second Worst Housing Market for Renters," *Times-Picayune*, January 15, 2016.

56 **"We must understand that self-destruction of diversity":** Jane Jacobs, *The Death and Life of Great American Cities* (New York: Vintage, 1992; originally published 1961), 251.

58 **The proportion of vacant buildings in the Freret neighborhood:** Freret Neighborhood Center, "Freret Street Neighborhood Center Property Survey," July 2010.

58 **Home values have more than doubled:** US Census Bureau, Poverty Data, 2010. Prepared by Social Explorer.

58 **between 2000 and 2013, in Freret's most gentrified census tract:** US Census Bureau, Ethnicity Data, 2010. Prepared by Social Explorer.

60 **the state designated Freret a cultural district:** Monica Hernandez, "Cultural District Slated for University Area," WWL-TV, July 7, 2012.

60 **Thanks to that zoning overlay:** Robert Morris, "How Many More Bars Should be on Freret Street?" *Uptown Messenger*, May 9, 2012.

62 **The state gives away 21 cents per dollar:** Louise Story, "The United States of Subsidies," *New York Times*, December 3, 2012.

62 **In Louisiana, there's a ten-year tax exemption:** Greater New Orleans Inc. Regional Economic Development, "Incentive Finder," http://gnoinc.org/incentives/incentive-finder.

62 **In 2011, the state gave $214 million:** Story, "The United States of Subsidies."

62 **The same year, it approved tax incentives:** Lee Zurik, "$11 Billion Later, Louisiana's Incentives Fail to Deliver," Fox 8 (WVUE), New Orleans, February 5, 2015.

63 **In 2013 alone, the state gave away $251 million:** Gordon Russell, "Giving Away Louisiana: Film Tax Incentives," *The Advocate*, December 2, 2014.

63 **New Orleans's median income of $36,964:** US Census Bureau, Quick-Facts, per capita income in past 12 months (in 2014 dollars), 2010–2014, for New Orleans city, www.census.gov/quickfacts.

66 **"The American people don't understand":** *PBS NewsHour,* "FEMA's Mike Brown," September 1, 2005.

66 **According to Ishiwata, phrases like these:** Eric Ishiwata, "'We Are Seeing People We Didn't Know Exist': Katrina and the Neoliberal Erasure of Race," in *The Neoliberal Deluge: Hurricane Katrina, Late Capitalism, and the Remaking of New Orleans,* ed. Cedric Johnson (Minneapolis: University of Minnesota Press, 2011).

67 **"I don't know. That doesn't make sense to me":** Charles Babington, "Hastert Tries Damage Control After Remarks Hit a Nerve," *Washington Post,* September 3, 2005.

67 **The biggest study of their whereabouts:** Narayan Sastry and Christine Peterson, "The Displaced New Orleans Residents Survey Questionnaire," RAND Corporation, 2010, www.rand.org/labor/projects/dnors.html.

67 **The city has been "resurrected":** Jason Berry, "Eight Years After Hurricane Katrina, New Orleans Has Been Resurrected," *Daily Beast,* August 29, 2013.

67 **Its growth is an "economic miracle":** Adam Kushner, "How New Orleans Pulled Off an Economic Miracle," *National Journal,* April 7, 2013.

68 **People are experiencing New Orleans through fresh eyes:** Lizzy Goodman, "Experiencing New Orleans with Fresh Eyes and Ears," *New York Times,* March 6, 2014.

68 **People are moving to Detroit to change it:** Britany Robinson, "Detroit: It's Not a Blank Slate," *Mashable,* March 1, 2015.

68 **They're spotting areas of Brooklyn:** Michelle Higgins, "New York's Next Hot Neighborhoods," *New York Times,* February 26, 2016.

68 **They're finding San Francisco's next hot markets:** Anna Marie Erwert, "Oakland Poised to be the Bay Area's Hottest Market in 2016," *San Francisco Chronicle,* January 20, 2016.

68 **They're discovering renewal in the ruins:** Melena Ryzik, "Detroit's Renewal, Slow-Cooked," *New York Times,* October 19, 2010.

68 **Neighborhoods are being revitalized:** DiAngelea Millar, "7 Streets in New Orleans Working to Revitalize Neighborhoods Are Part of UNO Student's Research," *Times-Picayune,* August 19, 2012.

68 **Entire economies are being turned around:** Keith Laing, "Duggan Touts Detroit 'Turnaround' in D.C.," *Detroit News,* April 5, 2016.

68 **"Private investment shapes cities":** Jacobs, *Death and Life,* 313.

Chapter 4: The New Detroit

74 **Since then, at least fifteen development projects:** David Muller, "A Closer Look at Dan Gilbert's Plans for Capitol Park in Downtown Detroit," MLive, April 2, 2013.

74 **he now owns at least eighty buildings downtown:** J. C. Reindl, "Dan Gilbert's Bedrock Buys 3 More Buildings Downtown," *Detroit Free Press*, January 20, 2016.

75 **"Do well by doing good":** CBS News, "Developer Buying Real Estate in a Downtrodden Detroit Says He Is 'Doing Well by Doing Good' in an Effort to Revitalize the City—*60 Minutes*," press release, October 11, 2013; see also Dan Gilbert interview with Bob Simon, "Detroit," *60 Minutes*, CBS News, October 13, 2013.

75 **He's hailed by business leaders, city officials:** Tim Alberta, "Is Dan Gilbert Detroit's New Superhero?" *National Journal*, February 27, 2014.

76 **"suspend[ed] democracy":** Quinn Klinefelter, "From Water Cutoffs to an Art Scare, Detroit Has a Tumultuous Year," *All Things Considered*, National Public Radio, December 15, 2014.

76 **the per capita income is about $15,000:** US Census Bureau, American FactFinder, "Selected Economic Characteristics: 2010–2014 American Community Survey 5-Year Estimates," 2014 data for Detroit city, Michigan, http://factfinder.census.gov/bkmk/table/1.0/en/ACS/14_5 YR/DP03/1600000US2622000.

76 **Broder & Sachse received a ten-year tax abatement:** Diane Bukowski, "Tax Abatement 'Deal with Devil' in Downtown Griswold Tenants' Eviction Has Gone to Hell," *Voice of Detroit*, January 27, 2014.

76 **"I would bet you that of the 100 people":** J. C. Reindl, "Rents Keep Going Up in Greater Downtown," *Detroit Free Press*, December 7, 2014.

78 **"the re-imagining of Detroit":** "Creative Cities Summit Announcement of Keynote Speaker," press release, October 14, 2008, PR Newswire.

78 **"Already you can see the renewal":** Detroit Regional Chamber, "The State of Detroit," December 4, 2012.

78 **Detroit . . . lost 25 percent of its population:** John Wisely and Todd Spangler, "Motor City Population Declines 25 Percent," *USA Today*, March 24, 2011.

79 **a full third of Detroiters say they plan on leaving:** Kresge Foundation, "Detroit Future City: Detroit Strategic Framework Plan," December 2012.

79 **almost no US city more broke than Detroit:** Karen Bouffard, "Census Bureau: Detroit Is Poorest Big City in U.S.," *Detroit News*, September 17, 2015.

79 **According to Florida, this class of people accounted for 24 percent:** Richard Florida, *Rise of the Creative Class Revisited* (New York: Basic Books, 2012), 45.

80 **How exactly this would be done remains a mystery:** Lisa Baugh, "Five Ways the Freelance Economy Fails the Poor and the Middle Class," *Salon*, June 5, 2015.

80 **Millennials . . . are on a never-ending "quest for experience":** Florida, *Rise of the Creative Class*, 134, 135–136, 245.

80 **technology, talent, and tolerance:** For a good summary of Florida's "technology, talent, and tolerance" approach to economic development, see Hazel Borys, "Richard Florida on Technology, Talent, and Tolerance," *Place Makers*, November 18, 2013.

81 **The original edition sold 300,000 copies:** Andres Viglucci, "Miami Now Winter Home to 'Creative-Class' Thinker Richard Florida," *Miami Herald*, August 19, 2012.

81 **The Congress for New Urbanism held its 2016 conference:** 24th Annual Congress for the New Urbanism, June 8–11, 2016, Detroit, Michigan, www.cnu.org/cnu24/schedule.

82 **"One problematic consequence [of the rise of the creative class]":** Florida, *Rise of the Creative Class*, 193, 227.

82 **"We need to be clear that ultimately, we can't stop the decline":** Richard Florida, "How the Crash Will Reshape America," *The Atlantic*, March 2009.

83 **"Bring on more gentrification":** Steve Neavling, "'Bring on More Gentrification' Declares Detroit's Economic Development Czar," *Motor City Muckraker*, May 16, 2013.

83 **In 2010, the city's mayor, Dave Bing, proposed:** Edward Glaeser, "Shrinking Detroit Back to Greatness," *New York Times*, *Economix* blog, March 16, 2010.

84 **"a gleam of renewal in struggling Detroit":** Julie Alvin, "A Gleam of Renewal in Struggling Detroit," *New York Times*, June 17, 2014.

84 **Research by Wayne State University grad student Alex B. Hill:** Alex B. Hill, "Detroit: Black Problems: White Solutions," October 16, 2014, http://alexbhill.org/2014/10/16/detroit-black-problems-white-solutions.

85 **"How much good can a restaurant do?":** Melena Ryzik, "Detroit's Renewal, Slow-Cooked," *New York Times*, October 19, 2010.

88 **That provides Mosey and Midtown Inc. with a budget of about $10 million:** IRS Form 990 for University Cultural Center Association, DBA Midtown Detroit Inc., for 2014, located through foundationcenter .org.

Chapter 5: The 7.2

93 **In fact, one-half of all people who attempted to enter that program:** Patrick Sheehan, "Revitalization by Gentrification," *Jacobin*, May 11, 2015.

93 **Meanwhile, the 7.2 is booming:** Kate Abbey-Lambertz, "These Are the American Cities with the Most Abandoned Houses," *Huffington Post*, February 13, 2016; "7.2 Sq. Mi.: A Report on Greater Downtown Detroit," 2013, http://detroitsevenpointtwo.com/resources/7.2SQ_MI _Book_FINAL_LoRes.pdf.

94 **the state gave Gilbert a $50 million tax break:** Amy Lane, "Quicken Loans' Move Tops List of State Tax Incentives Approved by Mega Board," *Crain's Detroit Business*, July 21, 2009.

94 **"I'm excited that somebody successful is acquiring":** John Gallagher, "Gilbert Buys One Detroit Center, Persuades Ally to Move," *Detroit Free Press*, March 31, 2015.

94 **he's built an entire security force:** Nancy Kaffer, "Who's Watching the Detroit Watchmen?" *Detroit Free Press*, March 21, 2015.

94 **Wayne State, Detroit's main university, has taken security:** Stacy Cowley, "How Wayne State Police Helped Breathe Life Into a Blighted Detroit Strip," *New York Times*, February 25, 2015.

94 **the M-1's $179.4 million cost:** "M-1 Rail Funding Breakdown," October 2014, http://m-1rail.com/complex-funding-puts-m-1-rail-right-track.

95 **between 2000 and 2010, the white population:** "Detroit Metro Profile," Metropolitan Opportunity Unit, Ford Foundation, November 2012, https://datadrivendetroit.org/files/NWRKS/Detroit%20Profile%20 Final%20Nov2012.pdf.

96 **"Nobody wants to inject race":** Nolan Finley, "Where Are the Black People?" *Detroit News*, December 15, 2014.

96 **convinced President Barack Obama to spend $300 million:** Alex Halperin, "How Motor City Came Back from the Brink . . . and Left Most Detroiters Behind," *Mother Jones*, July 6, 2015.

97 **But an investigation by the *Detroit News*:** Joel Kurth, "Gilbert, Quicken Loans Entwined in Detroit Blight," *Detroit News*, July 1, 2015.

97 **The project will cost the city of Detroit $261.5 million:** Bill Shea, "Detroit Taxpayers to Fund 60 Percent of Red Wings Arena, Plan Shows," *Crain's Detroit Business*, July 25, 2013.

97 **Ilitch will get to keep all of the revenues:** Joe Guillen, "Ilitches to Get All Revenues from New Publicly Financed Red Wings Arena," *Detroit Free Press*, March 2, 2014.

97 **The state says it will make up the difference:** Bill Bradley, "Red Wings Stadium Upset!: Why Taxpayers Are Losing—Again—in Detroit," *Next City*, March 3, 2014.

97 **The city also awarded Marathon Petroleum $175 million:** Joe Guillen, "$175M Tax Break for Marathon Refinery Buys Detroiters Only 15 Jobs," *Detroit Free Press*, March 14, 2014.

97 **the mayor's office sold 140 acres of public land:** John Gallagher, "Council OKs Sale of 1,500 Lots for Urban Farming Project," *Detroit Free Press*, December 11, 2012.

97 **Michigan gives away 30 cents of every government dollar:** Louise Story, "The United States of Subsidies," *New York Times*, December 3, 2012.

98 **A bill introduced in the state's legislature would ban:** Ryan Felton, "House Bill Would Ban Detroit from Enacting Community Benefits Agreement Ordinance," *Detroit Metro Times*, December 4, 2014.

99 **"a Katrina without water":** Ben Duell Fraser, "A Hurricane Without Water: A Foreclosure Crisis Looms," *Deadline Detroit*, January 21, 2015.

99 **Detroit's median income is about $25,000. . . . It has a poverty rate:** US Census, American FactFinder, "Individuals Below Poverty Level," Detroit city, Michigan (data from 2010–2014 American Community Survey 5-Year Estimates); Bernadette D. Proctor, Jessica L. Semega, and Melissa A. Kollar, "Income and Poverty in the United States: 2015," US Census Bureau report no. P60-256, September 13, 2016; US Census, American FactFinder, median household income for Detroit city, Michigan (data from 2010–2014 American Community Survey 5-Year Estimates).

99 **Its unemployment rate is nearly 25 percent:** "Unemployment Rates for the 50 Largest Cities," Bureau of Labor Statistics, April 15, 2016.

99 **Detroit charges some of the highest household water rates:** Environmental Protection Agency, "Water on Tap," December 2009.

99 **Experts from the United Nations called the move:** United Nations News, "In Detroit, City-Backed Water Shut-offs 'Contrary to Human Rights,' Say UN Experts," October 20, 2014.

99 **Sixty-eight percent of all mortgages to Detroiters:** Christine MacDonald and Joel Kurth, "Foreclosures Fuel Detroit Blight, Cost City $500 Million," *Detroit News*, June 3, 2015.

99 **It's not unheard of for residents to be paying $3,000 or $4,000:** Christine MacDonald and Joel Kurth, "Detroit Braces for a Flood of Tax Foreclosures," *Detroit News*, July 1, 2015.

100 **Detroit's per capita income is less than $15,000:** US Census Bureau, American FactFinder, "Selected Economic Characteristics: 2010–2014 American Community Survey 5-Year Estimates," 2014 data for Detroit city, Michigan, http://factfinder.census.gov/bkmk/table/1.0 /en/ACS/14_5YR/DP03/1600000US2622000.

101 **Cobo was a one-man concentrator:** Thomas Sugrue, *The Origins of the Urban Crisis: Race and Inequality in Postwar Detroit* (Princeton, NJ: Princeton University Press, 1996), 82, 84–86, 159.

102 **Detroit lost 237,000 people:** Kate Linebaugh, "Detroit's Population Crashes," *Wall Street Journal*, March 23, 2011.

103 **That's the situation Kenny Brinkley and Sandi Combs are in:** Some of Sandi Combs and Kenny Brinkley's story was told in a piece I wrote for Al Jazeera America: "Detroit Homeowners Face New Wave of Foreclosures," February 21, 2015.

104 **Study after study document the stress and depression:** One study showed that evictions alone cause material hardships to increase by 20 percent: Matthew Desmond, "Eviction's Fallout: Housing, Hardship, and Health," *Social Forces* 94, no. 1 (2015): 295–324.

Chapter 6: How the Slate Got Blank

106 **One 2014 study from the University of Chicago Booth School:** Veronica Guerrieri, Daniel Hartley, and Erik Hurst, "Endogenous Gentrification and Housing Price Dynamics," National Bureau of Economic Research Working Paper No. 16237, July 2010.

107 **Massey and Denton measure the racial dissimilarity:** Douglas Massey and Nancy Denton, *American Apartheid: Segregation and the Making of the Underclass* (Cambridge, MA: Harvard University Press, 1993), 20–21.

107 **by 2010 the index had dropped just below 60:** John Logan and Brian Stults, "The Persistence of Segregation in the Metropolis: New Findings from the 2010 Census," US2010 Project, March 24, 2011.

108 **The economic boom created by World War II:** This paragraph and the next draw on Sugrue, *The Origins of the Urban Crisis*, 29.

108 **Most of the signs simply read "Whites Only":** Ibid., 247.

108 **Housing-based violence continued and even increased through the 1960s:** Ibid., 233.

109 **There were subtler but still effective ways:** This paragraph draws on ibid., 44.

109 **realtors should "never be instrumental in introducing":** Elizabeth Huttman, *Urban Housing Segregation of Minorities in Western Europe and the United States* (Durham, NC: Duke University Press, 1991), 246.

109 **Orville Hubbard:** Sugrue, *The Origins of the Urban Crisis*, 193.

110 **Mayor Albert Cobo:** Ibid., 100.

110 **"I am confident that the sentiment for home ownership":** Kenneth Jackson, *Crabgrass Frontier: The Suburbanization of the United States* (New York: Oxford University Press, 1985), 193–194.

112 **In 1933, construction began on 93,000 new homes:** Ira Katznelson, *When Affirmative Action Was White* (New York: W. W. Norton, 2005), 115–116.

113 **In St. Louis, Missouri, for example, zoning laws:** Richard Rothstein, "The Making of Ferguson: Public Policies at the Root of Its Troubles," Economic Policy Institute, October 15, 2014.

114 **In a 1939 memo about Washington, DC:** Jackson, *Crabgrass Frontier*, 213.

114 **Yet the FHA did not change its policies for years:** My summarized history of the FHA and HOLC comes mostly from Sugrue, *The Origins of the Urban Crisis*, and Jackson, *Crabgrass Frontier*.

115 **Between 1946 and 1956, GM, Chrysler, and Ford:** Jackson, *The Origins of the Urban Crisis*, 128, 140.

115 **"handy device for razing the slums":** Ibid., 47–48.

115 **Cobo called urban renewal the "price of progress":** Patrick Sheehan, "Revitalization by Gentrification," *Jacobin*, May 11, 2015.

115 **New York University sociologist Patrick Sharkey:** Patrick Sharkey, *Stuck in Place: Urban Neighborhoods and the End of Progress Toward Racial Equality* (Chicago: University of Chicago Press, 2013), 3.

115 **While white children . . . can expect to earn on average $74,000:** Ibid., 4–5. Figures are adjusted dollars.

115 **Half of middle-income black kids fall *down* the economic ladder:** Ibid., 114.

116 **"When white families advance in economic status":** Ibid., 115.

116 **When Jamie Dimon, the head of JPMorgan Chase, announced:** Rick Cohen, "Looking for Saviors in Bankrupt Detroit," Nonprofit Quarterly, August 28, 2014.

116 **Dan Gilbert has been called a superhero:** Tim Alberta, "Is Dan Gilbert Detroit's New Superhero?" *National Journal*, February 27, 2014.

117 **Lauren Hood grew up in Detroit:** I wrote a version of Hood's story in "How Two Billionaires Are Remaking Detroit in Their Flawed Image," *Gawker*, April 29, 2015.

Chapter 7: The Gentrified City

126 **the black population of San Francisco is down to 5.8 percent:** Amy Alexander, "Whither Black San Francisco," *SF Weekly*, February 25, 2015.

126 **The Hispanic population of the Mission:** "Policy Analysis Report," City and County of San Francisco Board of Supervisors, October 27, 2015.

126 **The city will be majority white by 2040:** "An Equity Profile of the San Francisco Bay Area Region," PolicyLink, April 21, 2015.

127 **the median rent for a two-bedroom apartment:** Tracy Elsen, "The Median Rent for an SF Two-Bedroom Hits $5,000 a Month," Curbed .com, October 9, 2015.

130 **as San Francisco–based writer and activist Rebecca Solnit points out:** Rebecca Solnit and Susan Schwartzenberg, *Hollow City: The Siege of San Francisco and the Crisis of American Urbanism* (New York: Verso Books, 2002), 96–97.

130 **A report from Board of Supervisors member David Campos:** "San Francisco's Eviction Crisis 2015," San Francisco Anti-Displacement Coalition, 2015.

131 **The nonprofit San Francisco Tenants Union estimates:** Ibid.

131 **the number of Latino households fell by 1,400:** "Development Without Displacement: Resisting Gentrification in the Bay Area," Causa Justa/Just Cause, 2014.

133 **4 percent of one-bedrooms in the neighborhood cost below $2,500:** Emmanuel Hapsis, "Map: San Francisco Rent Prices Most Expensive in the Nation," KQED, November 3, 2015.

133 **back in the 1950s and 1960s artists had to work:** Solnit and Schwartzenberg, *Hollow City,* 105.

133 **Ed Lee, the current mayor of the city, has been accused:** Max Cherney, "'Shrimp Boy' Lawyer Claims Judge Shielded San Francisco Mayor in Corruption Probe," *San Francisco Public Press,* January 26, 2016.

133 **Three people who have done fund-raising for Lee:** John Shutt and Rebecca Bowe, "Three Former Fundraisers for Mayor Ed Lee Charged with Bribery, Money Laundering," KQED, January 22, 2016.

134 **A ballot measure that would have limited Airbnb rentals:** Davey Alba, "Prop F Has Failed. But the Battle for SF's Soul Will Go On," *Wired,* November 4, 2015.

134 **A proposed 1.5 percent tax on tech companies:** Joshua Sabatini, "SF's Tech Tax Fails to Make November Ballot," San Francisco Examiner, August 1, 2016.

135 **San Francisco's SROs have been a backbone:** "History of SRO Residential Hotels in San Francisco," Central City SRO Collaborative, accessed September 2016.

136 **A video taken of the incident went viral:** MissionCreekVideo, "Mission Playground Is Not For Sale," YouTube, uploaded September 25, 2014, https://youtu.be/awPVYiDcupE.

136 **"the gentrification of the mind":** Sarah Schulman, *The Gentrification of the Mind: Witness to a Lost Imagination* (Berkeley: University of California Press, 2012).

Chapter 8: Growth Machine

137 **President Ronald Reagan cut taxes on the rich:** Edwin Feulner, "Reagan's Tax-Cutting Legacy," The Heritage Foundation, July 14, 2015.

138 **a $10 billion budget surplus by 2017:** "California to Have $10 Billion Budget Surplus by 2017, Analyst Says," CBS News, November 20, 2013.

138 **In *Urban Fortunes*, their foundational work:** John Logan and Harvey Molotch, *Urban Fortunes: The Political Economy of Place* (Berkeley: University of California Press, 2007), xv.

138 **Molotch and Logan point out that in the heyday of urban renewal:** Ibid., 130–132.

139 **"The crux of poor people's urban problem":** Ibid., 112.

140 **"The expansion of the big modern cities":** Friedrich Engels, "The Housing Question," 1872.

141 **Luxemburg saw grand architecture, monuments, parks:** David Harvey, *Social Justice and the City* (Athens: University of Georgia Press, 1973), 142–143.

141 **David Harvey's claim that we're being pushed:** Ibid., 190.

141 **"Redevelopment is like an oil spill":** Solnit and Schwartzenberg, *Hollow City*, 100.

142 **In Hong Kong, for example:** Jake Blumgart, "Four Public Housing Lessons the U.S. Could Learn from the Rest of the World," *Next City*, August 26, 2014.

142 **In Sweden, local governments:** Logan and Molotch, *Urban Fortunes*, 148.

142 **In Berlin, which is gentrifying:** Ruby Russell, "Berlin Becomes First German City to Make Rent Cap a Reality," *The Guardian*, June 1, 2015.

143 **There are only 6,000 units of public housing:** "Public Housing, HUD, Section 8," Housing Rights Committee of San Francisco, www.hrcsf.org/SubHousing/subhsngindex.html.

143 **We lose 10,000 units of subsidized rental housing:** "The State of the Nation's Housing 2013," Joint Center for Housing Studies, Harvard University, 2013.

145 **Section 8 also doesn't challenge the fundamental problem:** "Voucher Payment Standards and Utility Standards," New York City Housing Authority, accessed September 2016.

145 **the city now plans to lease parking lots and grasslands:** Cindy Rodriguez, "Public Housing Invites Private Developers," WNYC, June 28, 2016.

Chapter 9: The New Geography of Inequality

148 **On the Bay Bridge, which connects:** Michael Cabanatuan, "Bay Area's Worst Commute Is Westbound I-80," *San Francisco Chronicle*, December 17, 2015.

150 **"The well-off have many ways of assuaging needs":** Jane Jacobs, *The Death and Life of Great American Cities* (New York: Vintage, 1992; originally published 1961), 70–71.

151 **In eastern Contra Costa County:** Elizabeth Kneebone and Alan Berube, *Confronting Suburban Poverty in America* (Harrisonburg, VA: R. R. Donnelley, 2013), 2.

151 **in the suburbs it increased at twice the rate:** Ibid., 17.

151 **Fifty-five percent of poor people in metropolitan areas:** Ibid., 17–19.

151 **The percentage of poor black people in urban centers:** Matthew Soursourian, "Suburbanization of Poverty in the Bay Area," Community Development Research Brief, Federal Reserve Bank of San Francisco, January 2012.

151 **Just over 50 percent of first-generation immigrants:** Kneebone and Berube, *Confronting Suburban Poverty*, 33.

152 **only 4 percent of jobs are reachable:** Ibid., 60.

152 **"BART was built to transport far fewer people":** Kale Williams, "BART Gets Candid in Twitter Exchange with Angry Riders," *San Francisco Chronicle*, March 17, 2016.

152 **low-income students in Antioch and Pittsburg:** Kneebone and Berube, *Confronting Suburban Poverty*, 68.

152 **Nonprofits in the suburbs operate:** Scott Allard and Benjamin Roth, "Strained Suburbs: The Social Service Challenges of Rising Suburban Poverty," Brookings Institution, October 7, 2010; Bernadette Hanlon, *Once the American Dream* (Philadelphia: Temple University Press, 2010), 133.

153 **"It's like people are living in colonies":** Bernice Yeung, "Neglected for Decades, Unincorporated Communities Lack Basic Public Services," California Watch, April 6, 2012.

153 **Engels had warned that mass homeownership:** Jackson, *Crabgrass Frontier*, 51.

154 **they "therefore cannot afford to strike":** Ibid., 51.

154 **"No man who owns his house and lot":** Maurice Isserman and Michael Kazin, *America Divided: The Civil War of the 1960s* (New York: Oxford University Press, 2003), 12.

154 **"a breeding ground for communists":** Dolores Hayden, *Building Suburbia: Green Fields and Urban Growth* (New York: Vintage Books, 2004), 130–131.

154 **Take Robert Moses:** Robert Caro, *The Power Broker: Robert Moses and the Fall of New York* (New York: Random House, 1974), 952.

155 **The suburbs became a way to reestablish conservative values:** David Harvey, "The Right to the City," *New Left Review* 53 (September–October 2008).

155 **The suburbanization of the United States pushed whites:** Schulman, *Gentrification of the Mind*, 24–25.

156 **Some ads were placed by homebuilders:** Hayden, *Building Suburbia*, 97.

156 **"The person sitting in the living room window":** Ibid., 148.

157 **These material goods—the toaster and the television:** Ibid., 148.

157 **Hollywood got in on the propaganda too:** Ibid., 149–151.

157 **In the 1950s, one-third of all private housing was financed:** Sharkey, *Stuck in Place*, 59.

157 **the magnitude of the subsidy depressed the market:** Ibid., 60.

158 **These tax breaks end up costing the federal government:** Jackson, *Crabgrass Frontier*, 294.

158 **Ninety percent of it was funded by the federal government:** Ibid., 249.

158 **one study found that drivers pay only half the real cost:** Angie Schmitt, "Drivers Cover Just 41 Percent of U.S. Road Spending," *Streetsblog USA*, January 23, 2013.

158 **Americans subsidize the suburbs to the tune of $100 billion:** Jackson, *Crabgrass Frontier*, 155.

159 **the National Association of Realtors is the second-biggest lobbying group:** "Top Spenders," Center for Responsive Politics, 2016.

Chapter 10: An Elegy

168 **Westbeth, the first federally subsidized artists' colony:** Anemona Hartocollis, "An Enclave of Artists, Reluctant to Leave," *New York Times*, November 21, 2011.

168 **New York governor Andrew Cuomo . . . brokered a deal:** Charles Bagli, *Other People's Money* (New York: Penguin Group, 2013), 141.

169 **There were originally 70,000 rental apartments available:** Ronda Kaysen, "Divided by a Windfall: Affordable Housing in New York Sparks Debate," *New York Times*, November 14, 2014.

170 **57 percent of apartments are vacant:** Julie Satow, "Pied-à-Neighborhood: Pieds-à-Terre Owners Dominate Some New York Buildings," *New York Times*, October 24, 2014.

170 **Absentee homeownership has grown by 70 percent:** Sam Roberts, "Homes Dark and Lifeless, Kept by Out-of-Towners," *New York Times*, July 6, 2011.

170 **Because of New York's tax code, a $100 million apartment:** Kriston Capps, "Why Billionaires Don't Pay Property Taxes in New York," CityLab, May 11, 2015.

170 **"I am afraid people who do not [know the neighborhood now]":** Jane Jacobs, *The Death and Life of Great American Cities* (New York: Vintage, 1992; originally published 1961), 54.

170 **extraordinary amounts of money, forethought, and policy:** Ibid., 7.

171 **"We're constantly trying to attract a specific demographic":** Sharon Zukin, *Naked City: The Death and Life of Authentic Urban Places* (Oxford: Oxford University Press, 2011).

172 **New York University, which has been involved:** John Surico, "De Blasio, '84, Eyes NYU 2013," *Gotham Gazette*, May 12, 2014.

172 **In her study of lofts in SoHo in the 1980s:** Sharon Zukin, *Loft Living: Culture and Capital in Urban Change* (Baltimore: Johns Hopkins University Press, 1982), 36.

173 **some 33,000 workers and small-business owners were displaced:** Robert Fitch, *The Assassination of New York* (New York: Verso Books, 1993).

173 **the city uses the entire New York City region as its base:** "Income Eligibility," New York City Housing Development Corporation, accessed September 2016.

173 **The city is also on the hook for $650 million:** Juan Gonzalez, "Unfinished West Side Commercial Development Costs Taxpayers $650 Million," New York *Daily News*, November 19, 2014.

174 **State land in downtown Brooklyn was given away:** Norman Oder, "The Culture of Cheating: Forest City's Inside Track with the MTA," *Atlantic Yards/Pacific Park Report* (blog), September 18, 2012.

174 **The city and state subsidized more than $2 billion of the deal:** Rich Calder, "Your Net Loss," *New York Post*, April 14, 2008.

174 **The city's own Independent Budget Office found:** "The Proposed Arena at Atlantic Yards: An Analysis of City Fiscal Gains and Losses," Fiscal Brief, New York Independent Budget Office, September 2009.

174 **"Brooklyn is 1000 percent":** Norman Oder, "Brooklyn BP Markowitz's Atlantic Yards Falsehood," *Huffington Post*, March 7, 2011.

174 **The Hispanic population in the East Village recently fell:** Ian Duncan, "Local Hispanic Population Declines," *Local East Village*, April 8, 2011.

175 **the city's white population is now rising faster in Manhattan:** Sam Roberts, "Census Estimates Show Another Increase in New York City's Non-Hispanic White Population," *New York Times*, June 30, 2014.

175 **Tompkins Square Park:** Smith, *New Urban Frontier*, 3–6.

175 **there are 120,000 black men who would live in New York City:** Justin Wolfers, David Leonhardt, and Kevin Quealy, "1.5 Million Black Men," *New York Times*, April 20, 2015.

175 **leaving their communities destabilized and more easily infilled:** Josmar Trujillo, "Militarized Policing, Gentrifying City: Doubting NYPD Reforms," *City Limits*, June 3, 2014.

177 **gentrifiers "look in the mirror and think it's a window":** Schulman, *Gentrification of the Mind*, 28.

177 **"There is something inherently stupid about gentrified thinking":** Ibid., 51.

178 **in 2005, the city rezoned 170 blocks of Williamsburg and Greenpoint:** Zukin, *Loft Living*, 59.

179 **more than 40 percent of the city was rezoned:** Andrea Bernstein, "Rezoning Williamsburg," WNYC, April 26, 2005.

179 **"The Bloomberg administration was kind enough to rezone":** Aaron Miguel Cantú, "Anti-Gentrification Protesters vs. Brooklyn Real Estate Summit," *Gothamist*, June 17, 2015.

179 **parts of Brooklyn have become more expensive:** Michelle Higgins, "Priced Out of Brooklyn? Try Manhattan," *New York Times*, May 8, 2015.

179 **the borough has become the least affordable housing market:** Drake Baer, "Brooklyn Is Officially the Most Unaffordable Housing Market in America," *Business Insider*, January 30, 2015.

180 **"You don't want Brooklyn to become so diluted":** David Colon, "Irony Smothered with a Pillow as Forest City Ratner CEO Frets About Brooklyn Losing Its Edge," *Brokelyn*, May 21, 2015.

Chapter 11: New York Is Not Meant for People

181 **Baruch College and New York 1 . . . conducted a survey:** Bobby Cuza, "City Poll: New Yorkers Worried About Being Priced Out of Their Homes," NY1.com, February 24, 2016.

182 **the average rent for a one-bedroom in Bushwick:** "Brooklyn Rental Market Report," MNS.com, February 2016.

188 **won the general election with nearly 75 percent of the vote:** "Election Results," *New York Times*, November 6, 2013.

188 **In the early 1900s in New York:** This paragraph is based on Sharon Zukin, *Loft Living: Culture and Capital in Urban Change* (Baltimore: Johns Hopkins University Press, 1982), 38.

188 **the 1929 Regional Plan suggested:** Fitch, *Assassination.*

189 **The plan explicitly recommended removing people:** Neil Smith, *The New Urban Frontier: Gentrification and the Revanchist City* (New York: Routledge, 1996), 21.

189 **That explains why whereas industrialization peaked in 1956:** Zukin, *Loft Living*, 24.

189 **It also explains why New York was one of the only cities:** Fitch, *Assassination.*

189 **New York actually had the cheapest labor force of any major city:** Deborah Wallace and Rodrick Wallace, *A Plague on Your Houses: How New York Was Burned Down and National Public Health Crumbled* (New York: Verso Books, 1998), 12.

189 **an RPA-backed group called the Citizens Committee for Modern Zoning:** John Logan and Harvey Molotch, *Urban Fortunes: The Political Economy of Place* (Berkeley: University of California Press, 2007), 156.

190 **So zoning regulations cause unneeded disruption for the poor:** Zukin, *Loft Living*, 22–23.

190 **"I don't know of any other area in the city":** Ibid., 44.

190 **With pressure from the Citizens Committee for Modern Zoning, the city government rezoned:** Fitch, *Assassination.*

190 **Between 1959 and 1989, the city lost 600,000 manufacturing jobs:** Wallace and Wallace, *Plague*, 12.

190 **Zukin surveyed small-time manufacturers in downtown Manhattan:** Zukin, *Loft Living*, 27, 42.

190 **SoHo, as Zukin puts it, was the "creation of an investment climate":** Ibid., 16.

191 **Meanwhile, employment in finance, insurance, and real estate:** Suleiman Osman, *The Invention of Brownstone Brooklyn* (New York: Oxford University Press, 2011).

191 **officials seemed befuddled that the city's economy:** Zukin, *Loft Living*, 28–29.

191 **The number of manufacturing jobs in New York City was cut in half:** "New York City's Decline in Manufacturing Gained Momentum in 1980," *New York Times*, March 22, 1981.

191 **On October 17, 1975, New York City owed banks:** Jeff Nussbaum, "The Night New York Saved Itself from Bankruptcy," *New Yorker*, October 16, 2015.

191 **"Ford to City: Drop Dead":** Sam Roberts, "Infamous 'Drop Dead' Was Never Said by Ford," *New York Times*, December 28, 2006.

192 **Ravitch was even brought in to help Detroit:** Matthew Dolan, "Detroit Looks to Re-engineer How City Government Works," *Wall Street Journal*, November 10, 2014.

192 **Large protests were held all across the city:** Kim Phillips-Fein, "The Legacy of the 1970s Fiscal Crisis," *The Nation*, April 16, 2013.

192 **In 1979, a report by the Twentieth Century Fund Task Force:** Zukin, *Loft Living*, 26.

193 **"Fires are in fact a 'leading indicator'":** Wallace and Wallace, *Plague*, 22.

193 **In 1976, the city cut thirty-four fire companies:** Ibid., 36.

193 **Nearly all of the shut fire stations:** Massey and Denton, *American Apartheid*, 159.

194 **In some neighborhoods in the South Bronx:** Wallace and Wallace, *Plague*, 22.

194 **Studies have shown that the majority of the fires:** Ibid., 67.

194 **Autopsies of the crisis also show:** Ibid., 71.

194 **In all, between 1972 and 1980:** Ibid., 18.

194 **HIV arrived at a time:** Ibid., xvii.

194 **The deaths of tens of thousands of men, most of whom were gay:** Sarah Schulman, *The Gentrification of the Mind: Witness to a Lost Imagination* (Berkeley: University of California Press, 2012), 23.

194 **The city also began clearing out areas where LGBT people congregated:** Samuel Delany, *Times Square Red, Times Square Blue* (New York: New York University Press, 1999), 15.

195 **The recession was serious: 13.4 percent unemployment:** Ibid.

Chapter 12: Fight Back

197 **Today, New York's real estate is worth a combined $1 trillion:** Javier David, "NYC Total Property Value Surges over $1 Trillion, Setting a Record," CNBC, January 16, 2016.

198 **In 1990, Prospect Lefferts Gardens was about 80 percent black:** New York City Population Data, 2010, www.nyc.gov/html/dcp/pdf/census/census2010/t_pl_p2_cd.pdf.

200 **One study by New York's comptroller predicted:** Scott Stringer, Comptroller's Office, City of New York, "Mandatory Inclusionary Housing and the East New York Rezoning," December 2, 2015.

200 **The building received a $72 million loan from the state:** Aaron Miguel Cantú, "Progressive Gentrification: One Community's Struggle Against Affordable Housing," *Truthout*, February 5, 2015.

201 **$98 per vote he received in the general election:** David Chalian and Rogene Fisher, "Costly Campaigns," ABC News, November 8, 2005.

201 **"New York City is never going to be the lowest-priced place":** Julian Brash, *Bloomberg's New York: Class and Governance in the Luxury City* (Athens: University of Georgia Press, 2011), 111.

202 **"We must offer the best product":** Michael Bloomberg, "Mayor Michael Bloomberg's 2003 State of the City Address," *Gotham Gazette*, January 23, 2003.

202 **Bloomberg added another $3 billion to the city's coffers:** E. J. McMahon, "Pricing the Luxury Product: New York City Taxes Under Mayor Bloomberg," *Empire Center*, November 30, 2005.

202 **And he supported giveaways to projects:** John Logan and Harvey Molotch, *Urban Fortunes: The Political Economy of Place* (Berkeley: University of California Press, 2007), xiv.

202 **evictions spiked:** Nathan Tempey, "NYC Evictions Are at Their Lowest in a Decade," *Gothamist*, March 1, 2016.

202 **median rents rose by 75 percent:** Scott Stringer, Comptroller's Office, City of New York, "The Growing Gap: New York City's Housing Affordability Challenge," April 2014.

202 **Bloomberg's answer was basically to get over it:** Chris Smith, "In Conversation: Michael Bloomberg," *New York Magazine*, September 7, 2013.

203 **de Blasio's housing policy:** Konrad Putzier, "Real Estate's Love-Hate Relationship with de Blasio," *The Real Deal*, February 1, 2016.

203 **Alicia Glen:** "Deputy Mayor for Housing and Economic Development," Official Website of the City of New York, www1.nyc.gov/office-of-the-mayor/alicia-glen.page.

204 **"We have certain tools in our municipal tool box":** Parts of this interview appear in Peter Moskowitz, "Can New York Save Itself from Out-of-Control Rents?" *Vice*, November 8, 2015.

206 **How many urban planning and economics programs have courses:** Brentin Mock, "There Are No Urban Design Courses on Race and Justice, So We Made Our Own Syllabus," CityLab, May 14, 2015.

206 **"First comes the image of what we want":** Jane Jacobs, *The Death and Life of Great American Cities* (New York: Vintage, 1992; originally published 1961), 313.

Conclusion: Toward an Un-Gentrified Future

210 **In New York, 30 percent of all land is public:** Tom Angotti, *New York for Sale: Community Planning Confronts Global Real Estate* (Boston: Massachusetts Institute of Technology Press, 2008).

211 **those rejections had no impact on the rezonings:** Michael Grynbaum and Mireya Navarro, "Mayor de Blasio Seeks to Rebuild Momentum for Affordable Housing Plan," *New York Times*, December 10, 2015.

212 **In 1942, Congress passed a law that prohibited the inflation of rents:** "Emergency Price Control Act," *Gale Encyclopedia of U.S. Economic History,* 1999.

212 **Rents are rising rapidly everywhere in the United States:** Leslie Shaffer, "Rents Rise to 'Crazy' Levels: Zillow," CNBC, August 16, 2015.

212 **Under FDR's New Deal housing program:** "FDR and Housing Legislation," Franklin D. Roosevelt Presidential Library and Museum, accessed September 2016.

212 **In Hong Kong, almost half of all housing is public:** Michelle Yun, "Hong Kong Can't Build Public Homes Fast Enough as Demand Soars," Bloomberg News, February 5, 2015.

212 **New York City still manages 328 housing projects:** "About NYCHA," New York City Housing Authority, accessed September 2016.

212 **Cities in the United States are several times less dense:** Wendell Cox, "World Urban Areas Population and Density: A 2012 Update," *New Geography,* May 3, 2012.

213 **In the 1950s and 1960s, the top tax rate:** "U.S. Federal Individual Income Tax Rates History, 1962–2013," Tax Foundation, October 17, 2013.

215 **anthropologist Julian Brash posits:** Julian Brash, *Bloomberg's New York: Class and Governance in the Luxury City* (Athens: University of Georgia Press, 2011), 128.

215 **As one Bushwick activist group called Mayday says:** Rebecca Fishbein, "Bushwick Woman Fights Gentrification with Christmas Lights: 'Your Luxury Is Our Displacement,'" *Gothamist,* December 29, 2015.

215 **But as author and activist Samuel Delany points out:** Ibid., 111.

217 **rental prices in Queens . . . began decreasing:** Lauren Clark, "One Borough's Rental Prices Are Actually Decreasing," *New York Business Journal,* July 10, 2015.

217 **Rents in other boroughs began flattening:** Amy Plitt, "New York City Rents May Finally Let Up in Their Terrifying Ascent," Curbed.com, March 10, 2016.

217 **in New Orleans, things seem to be leveling off:** Jennifer Larino, "New Orleans–Area Construction Contracts Drop in May," *Times-Picayune,* June 27, 2014.

217 **Silicon Valley lost more workers than it gained:** Georgia Wells, "Silicon Valley Residents Leave for Greener Grass, Cheaper Housing," *Wall Street Journal,* March 3, 2016.

217 **The share of tech workers living in the Bay Area:** Ashley Rodriguez, "Tech Workers Are Increasingly Looking to Leave Silicon Valley," *Quartz,* February 29, 2016.

Index

photo © Emily Pober Higgins

Peter Moskowitz is a freelance journalist who has covered a wide variety of issues, from environmental disasters to the vestiges of racist urban planning. A former staff writer at *Al Jazeera America*, he has written for the *Guardian*, the *New York Times*, the *New Republic*, *Wired*, *Slate*, *Buzz-Feed*, and many others. He is a graduate of Hampshire College and the CUNY Graduate School of Journalism. He currently lives in New York City.

The Nation Institute

NATION
BOOKS

Founded in 2000, **Nation Books** has become a leading voice in American independent publishing. The imprint's mission is to tell stories that inform and empower just as they inspire or entertain readers. We publish award-winning and bestselling journalists, thought leaders, whistleblowers, and truthtellers, and we are also committed to seeking out a new generation of emerging writers, particularly voices from underrepresented communities and writers from diverse backgrounds. As a publisher with a focused list, we work closely with all our authors to ensure that their books have broad and lasting impact. With each of our books we aim to constructively affect and amplify cultural and political discourse and to engender positive social change.

Nation Books is a project of The Nation Institute, a nonprofit media center established to extend the reach of democratic ideals and strengthen the independent press. The Nation Institute is home to a dynamic range of programs: the award-winning Investigative Fund, which supports groundbreaking investigative journalism; the widely read and syndicated website TomDispatch; journalism fellowships that support and cultivate over twenty-five emerging and high-profile reporters each year; and the Victor S. Navasky Internship Program.

For more information on Nation Books and The Nation Institute, please visit:

www.nationbooks.org
www.nationinstitute.org
www.facebook.com/nationbooks.ny
Twitter: @nationbooks